D0223108

Essential
Shakespeare

San Diego Christian College
Library
Santee, CA

RELATED TITLES

Doing Shakespeare, Revised Edition, Simon Palfrey
Shakespeare and Contemporary Theory, Neema Parvini
Shakespeare Thinking, Philip Davis

822.33
D
B583e

Essential Shakespeare

The Arden Guide to Text and Interpretation

Pamela Bickley and Jenny Stevens

B L O O M S B U R Y

LONDON • NEW DELHI • NEW YORK • SYDNEY

Bloomsbury Arden Shakespeare

An imprint of Bloomsbury Publishing Plc

50 Bedford Square	1385 Broadway
London	New York
WC1B 3DP	NY 10018
UK	USA

www.bloomsbury.com

Bloomsbury is a registered trade mark of Bloomsbury Publishing PLC

First published 2013
Reprinted 2013, 2014

© Pamela Bickley and Jenny Stevens, 2013

Pamela Bickley and Jenny Stevens have asserted their right under the Copyright,
Designs and Patents Act, 1988, to be identified as Author of this work.

All rights reserved. No part of this publication may be reproduced or transmitted
in any form or by any means, electronic or mechanical, including photocopying,
recording, or any information storage or retrieval system, without prior
permission in writing from the publishers.

No responsibility for loss caused to any individual or organization acting on
or refraining from action as a result of the material in this publication can
be accepted by Bloomsbury or the author.

British Library Cataloguing-in-Publication Data
A catalogue record for this book is available from the British Library.

ISBN: HB: 978–1–4725–2027–2
PB: 978–1–4081–5873–9
ePDF: 978–1–4725–3584–9
ePUB: 978–1–4081–7066–3

Library of Congress Cataloging-in-Publication Data
Bickley, Pamela, author.
Essential Shakespeare: the Arden guide to text and interpretation/by
Pamela Bickley and Jenny Stevens.
pages cm
Includes bibliographical references and index.
ISBN 978-1-4081-5873-9 (pbk.) – ISBN 978-1-4725-2027-2 (hardback) – ISBN
978-1-4725-3584-9 (ebook (epdf)) – ISBN 978-1-4081-7066-3 (ebook (epub))
1. Shakespeare, William, 1564–1616–Criticism and interpretation. 2.
Shakespeare, William, 1564–1616–Dramatic production. 3. Shakespeare,
William, 1564–1616–Film adaptations. I. Stevens, Jennifer, 1957- author. II.
Title. III. Title: Arden guide to text and interpretation.
PR2976.B446 2013
822.3'3–dc23
2013018351

Typeset by Fakenham Prepress Solutions, Fakenham, Norfolk NR21 8NN
Printed and bound in Great Britain

CONTENTS

HOW TO USE
THIS BOOK

The purpose of this book is to introduce students new to undergraduate Shakespeare study to fourteen of the most commonly studied plays. Significant areas of recent critical debate are introduced, explained and put into practice, and the contexts in which the plays were written and performed are explored. Worked examples of close analysis demonstrate different ways of approaching both text and performance.

Each chapter is arranged through four discrete sections:

- critical theory and practice
- early modern contexts
- close reading
- performance and production

These sections can be read horizontally across the book, giving a comprehensive overview of each of these aspects of Shakespeare studies. At the same time, individual chapters provide a thought-provoking way in to the play itself.

The Further Thinking section at the foot of each chapter offers suggestions for making connections across texts and for trying out some of the critical approaches discussed. Each chapter concludes with 'Afterlives': brief references to some of the re-inventions of the plays as entirely new works of art.

Introduction

Interpreting Shakespeare

One of the challenges involved in moving from pre-university to undergraduate study is shifting away from an intense focus on a relatively narrow range of prose, poetry and drama texts to a more expansive study of topic areas, not necessarily organized by work or author. This broadening out includes becoming familiar with a variety of critical perspectives and their terminologies. First encounters with contemporary criticism can be disorientating, akin to arriving in an unknown country. Its language can be formidably technical and its conceptual underpinnings can seem rather 'foreign', derived as they sometimes are from knowledge areas such as the natural and human sciences. However, getting to grips with the ideas and idiom of modern criticism and with the increasingly interdisciplinary nature of literary study is an important part of undergraduate learning. Each chapter of this book offers a brief introduction to one critical approach at work in current Shakespeare studies, followed by a practical example. Some critical practices have been selected for their undisputed influence on Shakespearean scholarship, while others have been included to represent new and emerging fields of interpretation.

The organization of the book means that the fourteen critical approaches demonstrated appear as discrete academic fields. The truth is, though, that what are often presented as separate schools of thought, regularly cross their own perceived borders, branching out to form new and highly stimulating modes of interpretation. Academic readings of Shakespeare can also be highly combative (indeed, critical discourse is sometimes described in terms of wars, battles and conflict). Yet whether friendly or hostile, critical approaches are constantly in dialogue with each other, ensuring that literary scholarship never grows complacent or falls behind the times.

Each chapter opens with what is no more than a snapshot of a particular reading approach and a demonstration of how it might be applied to the Shakespeare text. Taken in their entirety, these sections offer an overview of critical practice – a starting point from which readers can negotiate their way through competing viewpoints to form their own responses. Given the status of Shakespeare today, the body of secondary writings about the plays is vast and contains within it a complex and fascinating history of interpretive reading. While this book focuses primarily on a range of current critical methods and writings, it also takes into account formative opinions from the mid-seventeenth century onwards, thus developing an awareness of how views of the works have changed as societies have changed and underlining the impor-tance of situating critical writings in the political, social and historical contexts in which they were produced. As you build up and refine your knowledge of criticism now and over time, so you will be increasingly able to map, situate and contex-tualize the shifts of interpretation which have driven, and continue to drive, Shakespearean scholarship.

Locating Shakespeare

Shakespeare lived at a highly exciting but unstable and dangerous period of history now usually termed early modern, although it is also referred to as the Renaissance or the Reformation. This book introduces a range of cultural contexts: some specifically theatrical such as Shakespeare's sources, traditions of revenge tragedy, boy players; others tackling significant issues of the times – kingship, religion, sexuality, the family. Shakespeare's plays were written and performed during the Protestant Reformation: Henry VIII's break with Roman Catholicism and Papal authority. The religious changes begun before Shakespeare's birth had profound effects for the whole of his lifetime, not least because of the violent deaths suffered by those who refused to renounce their Catholic beliefs or, in the reign of Mary, those who could not in conscience, return to Rome. It was a turbulent time; highly conscious of theological debate, in part because of the new availability of biblical text in translation. Religious belief was taken for granted and modern attitudes of pluralism, indifference or complete rejection would have been unimaginable. Many in Shakespeare's audience must have wrestled, like Hamlet, with 'thoughts beyond the reaches of [their] souls.'

The Renaissance is a concept connoting vigorous rejuvenation. The re-birth it implies is the rediscovery of classical (particularly Greek) texts, chiefly literary and philosophical, and the influence of classical models on the aesthetic world of literature, architecture and painting. William Golding's 1567 translation of Ovid's *Metamorphoses* is an excellent example of a classical text Shakespeare knew well and drew on frequently. Innovations in methods of production and dissemination made books such as these newly affordable and accessible, communicating ideas beyond national borders.

Early modern, by definition, sounds progressive, as if anticipating or becoming a modern age. It is certainly a period associated with the expansion of geographical and scientific knowledge. In *Twelfth Night* Maria refers to 'the new map with the augmentation of the Indies'; clearly there was widespread awareness that the world was expanding and changing. Scientific enquiry was increasingly investigative and analytical; Rembrandt's painting of an anatomy lesson shows how medical knowledge was advancing through empirical method. But it would be misleading to characterize the early seventeenth century as ushering in a bright new age of social progress. The limitations of early modern as a term include its Eurocentrism and its limitations in terms of class, race and gender. It was often an oppressive and punitive period. London, a thriving urban world of publishing, commerce and theatre was also subject to periodic devastating plagues. Nonetheless, the late sixteenth- and early seventeenth-century world is distinctive and Shakespeare is intrinsically involved in it: his poetry and plays demonstrate his involvement with significant events and ideas of his age. His theatre is part of the commodity culture of the time, disseminating ideas as well as entertaining every class of London's world.

Reading Shakespeare

Reading Shakespeare independently can seem a daunting task: for every line of text there can sometimes be half a page of explanatory information. The student unfamiliar with etymology – the derivations and changing meanings of words – might feel that the excitement of the drama does not correspond with a form of analysis more akin to reading the dictionary. Equally, the close reading of texts appears to require a specialized technical vocabulary and an ability to analyze metric form. This, too, might seem a world away from the passionate or murderous emotions of the plays. Above all, perhaps, unravelling Shakespeare's figurative language can provoke the inevitable question, 'Did Shakespeare really intend all this?' The answer to which is that language operates on the ear and the imagination in a number of ways. Shakespeare creates situations where language can have straightforward brutal clarity: Richard III, doubting Lord Hastings' loyalty, exclaims 'Chop off his head!' In *Measure for Measure*, Angelo produces the ultimate bullying line of the sexual abuser, 'Who will believe thee?' At other times, though, Shakespeare draws on figurative language, using metaphor in complex ways. This is more difficult conceptually for the modern reader who might believe that 'real' feeling should sound spontaneous and unaffected. Indeed, it might, as when Lear, emerging from sleep and madness, asks Cordelia, 'Be your tears wet?' Language can also communicate complex depths of inner reflectiveness, though, and the virtuosic brilliance of, say, Hamlet's or Macbeth's soliloquies defies simple explication. The plays exist in their unique web of words and engaging with the extraordinary range of effects achieved is exciting and rewarding.

This book introduces the reader to some key concepts of Shakespeare's use of language and clarifies some of the technical aspects of analysing Shakespeare's blank verse and prose. Shakespeare's own education included the formal study of grammar and rhetoric and although this need not be replicated, it is useful to know something of the stylistic devices that would then have been familiar. Characters such as Iago (in *Othello*) or Feste (in *Twelfth Night*) exploit language for specific purposes and do so in a highly conscious way. The performative nature of language is an important aspect of plays such as *Richard II* where linguistic formality is central to the drama. The specialized approaches offered by linguistic analysis are discussed with reference to *Much Ado* where questions of language and gender continue to be challenging. Shakespeare's audiences went to the theatre to 'hear' the play: their perception of metaphoric language was sophisticated. It would be wrong to see this as an abstract process, however. Words are often referred to in highly physical ways: Malcolm, for example, speaks of Macbeth as the tyrant whose 'sole name blisters our tongues'. Renaissance writers delighted in verbal play and the endless creative possibilities of language: artistry is to be enjoyed and appreciated. To unpack Shakespeare's language is to discover meaning and nuance as well as beauty and sensuousness.

Performing Shakespeare

Not so very long ago, text and performance were treated as separate entities in the study of Shakespeare, with the former almost invariably being privileged over the latter. At pre-university level, screen or stage performances tended to be associated with classroom 'down time' or recreational excursions; while at undergraduate level, they were often deemed to be outside the discipline of literary studies altogether. While this hierarchical placing of script over performance is not yet entirely a thing of the past, even the briefest glance at Introductions to the most current editions of Shakespeare's works reveals that a consideration of film, television and stage production is now an integral part of Shakespearean scholarship. Surveying what is sometimes referred to as the 'afterlife' of Shakespeare's dramas raises some important questions about their cultural status and influence. Is there such a thing as the 'true' Shakespeare? Do Shakespeare's plays contain immutable truths that can be transplanted from one age to another? Do we rework them because they continue to engage us, or simply as a means of making a prescribed author more palatable? How far can we extend, transpose, translate and update the texts before they become something entirely different?

This book looks in detail at a range of stage, film and television productions. The theatre examples selected represent work that, for a variety of reasons, has startled – even shocked – original audiences and, if not always finding favour with the professional critics, has received serious scholarly attention. Shakespeare on screen is a little more generously represented than staged Shakespeare, its greater accessibility and durability lending more opportunity for close analysis. Moreover, it could be argued that film and television versions, aided by the ever-increasing sophistication of new technologies, have supplanted the stage in bringing Shakespeare's work both to the general public and to the student. While it took until the late 1980s for screen Shakespeare to became an established academic field – and perhaps even longer to dispel the attitude that cinema and television productions did not properly belong to the domain of 'high culture' – it now plays a crucial role in literary studies both at pre-degree and undergraduate level. Two performance examples included with the intention of widening the scope of the section are a mid-seventeenth-century splicing and rewriting of two of Shakespeare's plays and an operatic adaptation commissioned in the present century. The first of these takes the reader back to pre-Bardolatrous times to consider how one early-Restoration dramatist sought to recreate Shakespeare's work in what was a radically new theatrical climate; the second focuses attention on what might be termed 'transformative' Shakespeare: the reimagining of a play through a different art form (opera in this instance).

That Shakespeare is one of the world's most international authors was brilliantly demonstrated by the 2012 'Globe to Globe' season mounted by London's Globe Theatre. Featuring thirty-seven prestigious theatre companies, each working in their native language, this ambitious project attracted some of the most multinational and multilingual audiences in the Globe's history. Though the performance examples covered in this book are an admittedly more modest representation of Shakespeare as a global phenomenon, limited as they are to Europe and North America, they nonetheless encourage debate about some pertinent issues: the relationship between the arts and politics, the 'sanctity' and ownership of the literary text and why belief in Shakespeare's plays as carriers of 'universal truths' still persists.

1

A Midsummer Night's Dream: Transformations, illusions, festivity

*D*ream was once seen as the ideal play for young children; light-hearted, with an unthreatening fairy world in the background. Investigating the potentially subversive qualities of comedy introduces some probing questions, however. The de-stabilizing nature of erotic love is central to *Dream*, deriving, in part, from Ovid's *Metamorphoses*. This chapter

- introduces Bakhtin's concept of the carnivalesque
- explores Shakespeare's use of Ovid
- examines rhyme, rhythm and metre in Shakespeare's blank verse
- discusses Peter Brook's 1970 production of the play

Bakhtin and the carnivalesque

What, exactly, is 'carnivalesque' in Shakespeare's comedies and to what extent is it a helpful concept for exploring the dramatic effects of *A Midsummer Night's Dream*? Further, how far does the writing of the Russian critic Bakhtin clarify thinking about the nature and function of misrule? Anarchic festive play, possibly involving delusion or madness, has been identified as an intrinsic part of Shakespeare's comedies (see, for example, François Laroque, *Shakespeare's Festive World*, 1991). *Twelfth Night* is often seen as the classic carnivalesque comedy: Olivia's court houses the licenced Fool, Feste, and her uncle, Sir Toby Belch, whose apparent purpose in life is the pursuit of pleasure accompanied by quantities of 'cakes and ale'. Sir Toby is a self-appointed Lord of Misrule, where misrule is the active encouragement of comic confusion, farce and mockery. Comic laughter might be joyous and light-hearted or darkly subversive. The carnival spirit is one of excess, associated with holiday indulgence and licence: feasting, entertainment, bawdiness, ludicrous disguise, anything, in short, which is the opposite of the workaday world of hierarchy, prohibitions, privation and constraint. In late medieval England there were abundant opportunities for festive enjoyment. There were celebrations associated with the liturgical feasts of the Catholic Church as well as older traditions, relating to nature and the cycle of the seasons. A number of these festivities survived the Reformation and lingered into the early modern age. Puritanism may have attempted to outlaw them completely but Pepys in the 1660s writes about twelfth night festivities involving the whole household 'which they continue till morning, not coming to bed at all.' Comedy as a joyous release from the tedium and constrictions of everyday life is a simple enough concept; the more difficult question is how far carnival functions merely as an interlude tolerated – even encouraged – by authority, after which the participants meekly return to their everyday duties. Or might carnival be innately dissident, its very chaos offering a possibility of revolution?

Mikhail Bakhtin (1895–1975) is a compelling theorist of these ideas and questions. Writing during a repressive Stalinist period when laughter could be subversive and dangerous, Bakhtin explores the writing of Rabelais (a French Renaissance humanist) to formulate his own theory of populist laughter:

Let us say a few initial words about the complex nature of carnival laughter. It is, first of all, a festive laughter. Therefore it is not an individual reaction to some isolated 'comic' event. Carnival laughter is the laughter of all the people. Second, it is universal in scope; it is directed at all and everyone, including the carnival's participants. The entire world is seen in its droll aspect, in its gay relativity. Third, this laughter is ambivalent: it is gay, triumphant, and at the same time mocking, deriding. It asserts and denies, it buries and revives. Such is the laughter of carnival.

(*Rabelais and his World*, translated 1984, 11–12)

So the defining characteristics of the carnivalesque are threefold: a spirit of temporary licence; the populist, topsy-turvy inversion of normal hierarchies; the predominance of physical bodily humour. Bakhtin's *Rabelais and His World* was first translated in 1968 and subsequently influenced critical analysis of the varying moods of comedy. Shakespeare's bawdy, Shakespeare's Fools and Shakespeare's 'Festive Comedy' were already areas of fruitful discussion and academic enquiry, but Bakhtin raises new questions, proposing a theory of carnival which operates as a mode of understanding the complex world(s) of Shakespearean comedy.

How might this model of thought offer an enlightening reading of *A Midsummer Night's Dream*? Shakespeare's world of enchantment, moonlight, fairies and artless artisans has been traditionally enjoyed as a happy world of innocent bucolic frolics. Should the play be seen as benignly carnivalesque, a 'holiday humour' with a happy ending? In the latter half of the twentieth century, commentators and directors have perceived darker overtones in the text. The troubling questions of authority and the anarchic subversiveness of the erotic are areas of discourse which lend themselves to Bakhtinian analysis. The shape and structure of the play would seem to be inherently carnivalesque. At the outset, a wedding ceremony is anticipated with an accompanying fortnight of feasting and entertainment which will involve all classes of society. Beyond the Athenian court and Theseus' authority, there is an alternative realm ruled by Oberon, 'King of Shadows'. Here, fairy misrule operates: magic and mischief can reign unchallenged. Puck exists to promote carnivalesque mirth:

> The wisest aunt, telling the saddest tale,
> Sometime for three-foot stool mistaketh me;
> Then slip I from her bum, down topples she,
> And 'tailor' cries, and falls into a cough;
> And then the whole quire hold their hips and loffe
> And waxen in their mirth, and neeze, and swear
> A merrier hour was never wasted there.

> (2.1.51–7)

But beneath the play's different spheres there is dissent, a challenge to authority, and potential for disaster. *Dream* combines four distinct levels of dramatic action: Theseus and Hippolyta, Titania and Oberon, the young lovers, and the Pyramus and Thisbe story as enacted by Bottom and his companions. The subtle complexity created by these interwoven threads corresponds with Bakhtin's concept of **polyphonic** voices.

Theseus and Hippolyta are the mature and experienced lovers whose marriage will be celebrated 'with pomp, with triumph, and with revelling.' Yet, as Theseus observes,

> I woo'd thee with my sword,
> And won thy love doing thee injuries

> (1.1.16–17)

Erotic love is, then, paradoxical and destabilizing from the opening lines of the play. How can romance be associated with the violent overthrow of Hippolyta and her Amazonian warriors? Furthermore, the bridal couple appear to have their own 'back story' entangling them with the fairy rulers: Titania speaks scornfully of 'the bouncing Amazon/Your buskin'd mistress and your warrior love' (2.1.70–1). And Oberon turns the tables on her by alluding to Titania's previous entanglement with Theseus:

> Didst thou not lead him through the glimmering night
> From Perigouna, whom he ravished;
> And make him him with fair Aegles break his faith,
> With Ariadne and Antiopa?

> (2.1.77–80)

Violence, rape and infidelity seem to characterize both mortal and supernatural worlds. The youthful lovers repeat this pattern; Helena, in particular, expressing the painful realization that love might be both uncontrollable and undeserved:

> Things base and vile, holding no quantity,
> Love can transpose to form and dignity.

> (1.1.232–3)

All four younger lovers believe themselves to be full of passion and conviction, but are subject to reversals and contradictions as the night wears on. Both men change their affections and both women deny the mutual friendship of their girlhood. The intervention of Oberon and Puck is partly to blame, but the love potion only intensifies a fickleness we have already seen. What emerges as profoundly destabilizing is the capriciousness of sexual desire, lacking in reason, control – even choice. This is at its most extreme in the encounter between Titania and Bottom: the mid-centre of the play and its nocturnal events. Does Shakespeare suggest simple merriment here or, at the heart of the play, a challenge? Titania's 'enchantment' is certainly not brought about by benevolence or in a spirit of fun. Oberon wants revenge for her flouting of his authority; she will not yield up her changeling boy to him and so he resolves to 'torment [her] for this injury' (2.1.147). His stated intention is that she should pursue with 'the soul of love' any random creature – 'some vile thing' (2.2.33). And he lists the beasts of nightmare for his exalted partner to 'dote on in extremity'. To the editor of Arden 2 it is 'of course [Titania] who is principally at fault' (cvi); she has 'got her priorities wrong' and 'her obstinacy has to be overcome' (cviii). For Diane Purkiss, on the other hand, this display of Oberon's power reveals late sixteenth-century fears of female dominance:

> It is about the taming of a fairy queen, and hence about subduing the very dark anxieties generated for masculinity by a female ruler.
>
> (*At the Bottom of the Garden*, 2003, 180)

What follows? Critics tend to distance themselves from the idea of a sexualized Titania, despite the Ovidian implications:

> They are going off to bed, but there is nothing torrid about it. The forest might have been a place of unbridled eroticism, but it is not.
>
> (Alexander Leggatt, *Shakespeare's Comedy of Love*, 1974, 111)

There are, perhaps, two points to observe here: it is not just late twentieth-century, post-censorship readers and directors who see Bottom and Titania as fully sexual. Fuseli, the great eighteenth-century painter of the Gothic, depicts an uncompromisingly sexual duo; further, the Ovidian source material can only imply sexual congress, however improbable or ironical. The usual pattern is for the god – commanding and powerful – to assume the form of a beast in order to satiate his lust for a vulnerable mortal maiden. Shakespeare brilliantly undermines this: 'sweet bully Bottom' with his ass's head is amiable but not godlike; Titania is no shrinking maid. As she leads her lover away, she refers to flowers weeping to lament 'some enforced chastity'. Consensual physical love is obviously her intention. In the topsy-turvy world of the midsummer night, theirs is the only consummated love and, as such, is 'the climax of the polyphonic interplay' (Barber, *Shakespeare's Festive Comedy*, 1963, 154). To bring a Bakhtinian reading to this scene is to confirm its sexual intention: for Bottom to be King for a night is exactly the comic usurpation of authority popular with carnivalesque revelry. Animal masks (or suggestive body parts) were a familiar feature of carnival; the ass traditionally has phallic associations. Titania emphasizes Bottom's kingly status when she crowns Bottom's 'hairy temples' with 'coronet of fresh and fragrant flowers' (4.1.51) – a challenge to Oberon's authority to which he takes exception. Bottom, in his turn, acts as a lord, commanding the attendant fairies in parodic imitation of courtly manner. Jan Kott emphasizes the transgressive nature of sexual desire, uniting Freudian and Bakhtinian perspectives:

> The slender, tender and lyrical Titania longs for animal love. Puck and Oberon call the transformed Bottom a monster. The frail and sweet Titania drags the monster to bed, almost by force. This is the lover she wanted and dreamed of; only she never wanted to admit it, even to herself. Sleep frees her from her inhibitions. The monstrous ass is being raped by the poetic Titania, while she keeps on chattering about flowers.
>
> (*Shakespeare our Contemporary*, 1983, 183)

But is the theatre world genuinely disruptive, even when evidently transgressive? Much depends on how the play's restoration is defined. Is there a return to the normative? Beneath the holiday magic there is in fact a fundamental questioning of the masculine authority that has asserted itself in typically patriarchal and martial terms. Egeus, at the beginning of the play, proclaims that he would prefer his daughter to die rather than marry the object of her own choice and Theseus will enforce this:

To you your father should be as a god:
      [...]
To whom you are but as a form in wax
By him imprinted, and within his power
To leave the figure, or disfigure it.

                                        (1.1.47–51)

But when the lovers wake at dawn, Egeus is simply over-ruled; in theory by the judgement of Theseus, but in reality by the fact that Demetrius no longer wants to marry Hermia. Theseus is later contradicted by Hippolyta when she sees that far more has happened to the lovers than Theseus can comprehend, 'something of great constancy; / But howsoever, strange and admirable' (5.1.26–7). Theseus can never know what the audience see – that his ringing conclusion to events at the end of the play does not express finality because he is followed by Puck bearing a broom. The authority of the daytime world is less secure than it believes and the authority of the shadowy world of night similarly challenged: Oberon can cruelly deceive Titania but perhaps at the expense of the most comic cuckoldry – his love has betrayed him for an ass.

The Pyramus and Thisbe interlude plays a significant part in the tradition of carnivalesque buffoonery, both for the comedy of the mechanicals and for the complex relations between the play-within-the-play and the onstage audience. Here, the 'hempen homespuns' take over the stage and the ruling classes are secondary to the action. The plurality of perspectives resembles Bakhtin's defining of polyphonic voices where differing voices express their own mental worlds rather than conform to one single centre of authority. The key player is undoubtedly Bottom – again, the lover and hero. As Annabel Patterson suggests,

As visual pun and emblem, Bottom stands at the fulcrum of Shakespeare's analysis of the festive impulse in human social structures ... [Bottom's] vision ... is a revaluation of those 'unpresentable' members of society normally mocked as fools and burdened like asses, whose energies the social system relies on.

(*Shakespeare and the Popular Voice*, 1989, 67, 69)

Shakespeare, typically, invites the larger audience to see far more than a parodying of epic or romantic style. The virtues of 'gentle' courtly behaviour are demonstrated entirely by the mechanicals; Hippolyta and the younger lovers are openly derisive and Theseus is tolerant simply because he believes that everything connected with imagination is pointless. Peter Quince's company, on the other hand, has gone to some pains to avoid alarming the tender sensibilities of the female courtiers. Their script betrays them, however, with unintentioned but comic obscenities:

My cherry lips have often kiss'd thy stones,
Thy stones with lime and hair knit up in thee.

(5.1.188–9)

But perhaps the mocking participation of the now-happy lovers is a result of their experiences of the night. They need to endorse normative values and re-possess their cultural superiority in order to return to their hierarchized world. Unlike Bottom, they have not experienced transcendence in the wood. Their language on waking is fumbling and incoherent where Shakespeare makes Bottom's waking monologue spiritual and mystical. The Pyramus and Thisbe play addresses their anxieties and simultaneously mocks their cultural certainties; classical high art becomes at once accessible and potentially farcical. Tragic possibility is redeemed by laughter:

Laughter purifies from dogmatism, from the intolerant and the petrified; it liberates from fanaticism and pedantry, from fear and intimidation, from didacticism, naïveté and

illusion ... Laughter does not permit seriousness to atrophy
... It restores this ambivalent wholeness.

(Bakhtin, 123)

Shakespeare's sources: Ovid

In all the world there is not that that standeth at a stay.
Things ebb and flow, and every shape is made to pass
    away.
The time itself continually is fleeting like a brook,
For neither brook nor lightsome time can tarry still.

(*Metamorphoses* Book XV, 197–200)

As Catherine Belsey has wisely observed, source-hunting
is hardly part of a play's appeal to an audience (see *Why
Shakespeare*, 2007, x). Yet, source-hunting has long been
part of the Shakespeare scholar's repertoire of approaches to
the text. With the Roman or History plays this would seem
inevitable: editors investigate major sources such as Holinshed
or Plutarch in order to determine how far Shakespeare
can be seen to have an 'angle'. On the microcosmic level,
individual lines can sometimes be seen to echo current English
translations of the Bible, or well-known classical writers such
as Ovid. Shakespeare and his contemporary audience would
pick up key biblical and religious echoes effortlessly; would
naturally be acquainted with popular tales and legends of
the day, as well as being alert to any subversive political
reference. Grammar school education was based around the
learning by rote of texts in classical Latin. Titania's name
only appears as such in Ovid's original text so it tends to
be assumed that Shakespeare had some recollection of the
original. Arden editor Harold Brooks identifies a dozen
possible sources within the complex fabric of the text and
Bullough's classic study gives extracts from ten, plus one

analogue (see *Narrative and Dramatic Sources of Shakespeare,* 1957–75). Acquaintance with all of these might enable some access to the rich complexity of Shakespeare's imagination, as if scholarly research could conjure up a mental map of reference and allusion.

Ovid's *Metamorphoses* has long been recognized as a significant source: both the Latin text and Golding's translation of 1565/7. Why was it popular? Classical texts supply an inexhaustible treasure-trove of stories conveyed with artistry and feeling. They intrigue and attract partly because they are free from any didactic Christian intention. They evoke a world of capricious and often cruel deities and passionate, often doomed, mortals. Of course, the paganism of some of the writing did prove unacceptable to religious authorities: Ovid's *Ars Amatoria* and *Amores* are not simply stories, but useful advice to would-be lovers; Marlowe's translation of the latter was burnt by the Archbishop of Canterbury for inciting promiscuity. Greek texts were denounced for homosexuality. But Ovid's *Metamorphoses* was widely influential, inspiring great Renaissance paintings as well as literature. It is a text fictionalising desire and pursuit – with some bizarre conquests. Love is an absolute and inescapable force which can be immediate and disastrous. Stark and often brutal passions reign, with revenge and cruelty frequently overwhelming hapless mortals; this is a world ruled by intrusive and jealous gods. Beyond this is the overarching concept of metamorphosis itself – change, transformation, mutability. This might signify, variously, man's descent into brutality, ascent towards immortality or absorption into nature. It was easier for Renaissance humanist writers to approve *Metamorphoses* as the central theme could be readily adapted to moral reflections: the god who gratifies his desire disguised as a bull is, of course, symbolic of the bestial nature of untrammelled lust. And the mutability of worldly affairs contrasts with God's immutable sphere.

So, in what ways does it enhance knowledge or understanding of *A Midsummer Night's Dream* to know something of this classical writer? As well as suggesting more than one of the fictional strands of the play, Ovid could be said to infuse the language, particularly where patterns of imagery are expressive of central thematic motifs. Theseus makes a number of appearances in *Metamorphoses*, the tragic tale of Pyramus and Thisbe is drawn directly from Ovid's account, and Shakespeare offers a brilliantly comic version of transformation in Bottom. The irrationality of love is pursued to the furthest degree in the play and, more subtly, Shakespeare makes connections between passion and nature. In *Metamorphoses* transmutation seems always possible, characters dissolving into the natural world they inhabit or becoming bestial. In *Twelfth Night* Orsino refers to himself as Actaeon, the hunter who is turned into a stag and agonisingly destroyed by his own hounds, while retaining all his human perception of his fate. Actaeon is suffering punishment from Diana after seeing the goddess bathing naked. What Orsino's allusion suggests, therefore, is that the chaste Olivia is deliberately punishing him, causing him fierce physical and emotional torment – the analogy also suggesting that he thinks he is not at fault. When the nymph Syrinx is pursued by Pan, conversely, she appeals to her fellow spirits of the river to transform her so that when Pan attempts to grab her, he finds himself clutching a handful of reeds. Yet Pan is enchanted by the subtle music of the reeds and creates a musical instrument from them to preserve something of Syrinx's sweetness. Ovid's universe is endlessly shape-shifting; it lends itself to theatrical illusion as well as to the idea that love changes and transforms individuals. In *Dream* Shakespeare creates a world similarly instinct with such sympathy between nature and the gods and mortals that inhabit it. The quarrel between Oberon and Titania has caused, 'as in revenge', discord and disaster, a failure of the harvest and a lack of 'winter cheer'. As the fairy gods squabble over possession of the 'changeling boy', they seem very like Ovid's meddlesome and capricious gods. The disordered seasons further resemble the chaos caused by Ceres when she seeks her lost daughter, Proserpine. Oberon's punishment of his queen, as well as the enchantment of Demetrius, is realized through 'love-in-idleness', a flower stained by the blood of Pyramus. Oberon's description would alert the knowledgeable: 'Before milk-white, now purple with love's wound' (2.1.167). Shakespeare is faithful to Ovid's story of the star-crossed lovers: forbidden by their parents they whisper through the chink in the adjoining wall, elope by night, planning to meet in the forest where Thisbe is frightened by the lion which mauls her veil. Pyramus is described by Ovid as bleeding profusely over the fruits of the mulberry tree – changed forever by the gods from snowy white to purple-black in mourning for the lovers.

Shakespeare introduces 'The most lamentable comedy and most cruel death of Pyramus and Thisbe' in the second scene of the play with Quince's distribution of parts and Bottom's attempt to volunteer for every role. Helena has already anticipated Bottom's 'translation' as well as articulating her own despair and bitterness: she, too, would like to be transformed:

> Were the world mine, Demetrius being bated,
> The rest I'd give to be to you translated.

> (1.1.190–1)

She understands that she reverses the usual Ovidian pattern when she styles herself as a monster and 'ugly as a bear'; her choice of reference signals her awareness of her departure from mythological norms of love and pursuit:

> Run when you will; the story shall be chang'd:
> Apollo flies, and Daphne holds the chase;
> The dove pursues the griffin, the mild hind
> Makes speed to catch the tiger ...

> (2.1.230–3)

In Act 1, the audience have encountered Theseus and Hippolyta, the forbidden love of Lysander and Hermia, and the failure of love between Helena and Demetrius:

[He] won her soul: and she, sweet lady, dotes,
Devoutly dotes, dotes in idolatry,
Upon this spotted and inconstant man.

(1.1.108–10)

So, before the appearance of Titania and Oberon with their
own quarrel, love has been firmly established as unstable.
Shakespeare's dramatic juxtapositions are also significant
here: inviting comparison or implying inherent ironies. It is
characteristic of Shakespeare, though, to pursue the motif to
its ultimate manifestation – and then beyond. Bottom with the
ass's head might lack the grandeur of Jupiter, although Titania
greets him as an angel; equally, she is no innocent Syrinx or
Daphne fleeing from his embraces. Their union is a benign
version of Ovid's diverse couplings: sexual but not savage.
And Bottom is left entranced:

> I have had a most rare vision. I have had a dream, past the
> wit of man to say what dream it was. Man is but an ass if
> he go about to expound this dream. … The eye of man hath
> not heard, the ear of man hath not seen, man's hand is not
> able to taste, his tongue to conceive, nor his heart to report
> what my dream was.

(4.1.203–6, 209–12)

He has experienced transformation, even transcendence, and
the audience sympathize with his otherworldly experience
in a way that Theseus cannot. But Shakespeare is making
a witty joke at his expense, for all his authority and final
triumphalism. He dismisses all the events of the night – 'I
never may believe/These antique fables, nor these fairy toys'
(5.1.2–3) – but Theseus, too, is part of Ovid's 'antique fable'.
As Barber observes, '[Shakespeare's] game was not so much
to lift things gracefully from Ovid as it was to make up fresh
things in Ovid's manner' (Barber, 122).

A Midsummer Night's Dream: Rhyme, rhythm and metre

Experiencing Shakespeare's language in the theatre is, of course, fundamentally different from the activity of close textual analysis. The impact of the play, though, comes from the unique effect of its metre and rhythms. Actors and directors spend a considerable amount of time in rehearsal working on the precise stresses and emphases required by the verse in order to achieve a natural but powerful dramatic effect. It is worth remembering that Pepys invariably referred to 'hearing' a play as though the principal effect is aural, not visual. Any analysis of Shakespeare's language focuses on two areas: imagery and versification. Patterns of figurative language operate imaginatively, triggering echoes and analogies in the listener's mind. This subtle and intricate process is conveyed through the rhythm of the verse and this fusion creates the unique sound of the play.

It is helpful to distinguish clearly between rhyme, rhythm and metre. The most straightforward device is rhyme: in *A Midsummer Night's Dream* Shakespeare uses rhyming couplets more frequently than in any other play, sometimes to create the dreamlike atmosphere of magic and mystery that is at the heart of the play, at other times to create a strongly emphatic effect. The latter part of the opening scene is entirely in rhyming couplets (and occasionally **quatrains**) and introduces some of the play's key motifs:

> Before the time I did Lysander see,
> Seem'd Athens as a paradise to me.
> O then what graces in my love do dwell,
> That he hath turn'd a heaven into a hell!

> (1.1.204–7)

Here Hermia expresses astonishment that love has entirely altered her familiar world, while the unhappy Helena despises herself for an infatuation for a man whose devotions are fickle:

> Things base and vile, holding no quantity,
> Love can transpose to form and dignity:
> Love looks not with the eyes, but with the mind,
> And therefore is wing'd Cupid painted blind ...

$$(1.1.232–5)$$

The closed form of the couplet creates both expectation and certainty; the listener anticipates the rhyming word that must inevitably follow. The statements seem unarguable because syntax and rhythm are enclosed within the couplet – precisely the reason why Shakespeare chooses to conclude a scene (or a sonnet) with a resounding couplet. In the examples quoted above, each couplet articulates a single discrete idea; furthermore, the rhyming words themselves – sight/blindness for example – underline a recurrent metaphor. Oberon's rhyming couplets function differently; in the following lines, the couplets are far more flexible because of the **enjambement** that connects ideas across the blank verse line. What he describes here is the fairy king's enchanted pagan world of freedom, love, nature: an extraordinary evocation of changing colours, light, air, and sea.

> But we are spirits of another sort:
> I with the Morning's love have oft made sport;
> And like a forester the groves may tread
> Even till the eastern gate, all fiery-red,
> Opening on Neptune with fair blessed beams,
> Turns into yellow gold his salt green streams.

$$(3.2.388–93)$$

Rhythm and metre are linked but they are not identical. Shakespeare's plays tend to move between prose and verse where the verse is, for the most part, unrhymed **iambic pentameter**.

Commentators often observe that the Shakespearean line is one of ten syllables but the number of five strong stresses (rather like the beats in a bar of music) is more important, creating the distinctive Shakespearean sound. Rhythm varies according to meaning and emphasis. (The distinction is clearly seen in Hamlet's 'To **be** or **not** to **be: that** is the **question**': five strong stresses but the accented syllables are not alternating; indeed if a determined effort is made to accentuate each alternative syllable, the result sounds nonsensical.) The **iamb** is the metric 'foot' of English verse; a weak stress followed by a stronger one:

The **fāiry lānd** buys **nōt** the **chīld** of **mē.**

Titania's determination is established clearly through the metre and the insistent rhythm of the line. A particularly emphatic effect is achieved with the **spondee** where two stressed syllables occur together: the **'big-bell**ied with the wanton wind' is an excellent example where the combination of the spondee, the **alliteration,** and the **transferred epithet** of 'wanton wind' play their part together. An inverted iamb or **trochaic** metre begins with the stronger syllable:

Mūsĭc hō! Mūsĭc sūch ăs chārmĕth slēep.

Here, Titania, waking from her 'visions' conjures music as a magic that will resolve the plight of the four lovers as well as symbolize her new harmony with Oberon; the trochaic metre establishes difference. Essentially, Shakespeare's metre is generally stable whereas the rhythm can be variable, and this creates the subtle musical effects that the ear discerns. In *Dream*, Shakespeare is particularly inventive in his metrical effects. He creates an immediately striking effect at the opening of Act 2 and the exchanges between Puck and one of Titania's fairy retinue:

Over hill, over dale,
  Thorough bush, thorough briar,

Over park, over pale,
  Thorough flood, thorough fire,
I do wander everywhere,
Swifter than the moon's sphere;
And I serve the Fairy Queen,
To dew her orbs upon the green.

(2.1.2–9)

This **tetrameter** (four strong stresses) is repeated in the various fairy charms which operate throughout the action; it has an incantatory effect which Shakespeare uses again for the witches in *Macbeth*. Here it tends to be benign, as it is when Oberon concludes the drama with his fairy blessing:

Now, until the break of day,
Through this house each fairy stray.
To the best bride-bed will we,
Which by us shall blessed be;
And the issue there create
Ever shall be fortunate.

(5.1.387–92)

The language of the Pyramus and Thisbe interlude complicates matters further. Their 'very tragical mirth' rhymes throughout, either in rhyming couplets or with alternate lines rhyming; the prologue and initial speeches are in a homespun form of blank verse, its artlessness drawing attention to the ornate language elsewhere in the play:

O grim-look'd night! O night with hue so black!
O night, which ever art when day is not!
O night, O night, alack, alack, alack,
  I fear my Thisbe's promise is forgot!

(5.1.168–71)

The lovers' tragic discoveries vary between **dimeter** and **trimeter** (two or three strong stresses) which might be viewed as Shakespeare's playful amusement with verse-forms. Thisbe's grief and loss is comic because her brief exclamations are woefully incongruous:

> *These lily lips,*
> *This cherry nose,*
> *These yellow cowslip cheeks,*
> *Are gone, are gone!*

(5.1.317–20)

A Midsummer Night's Dream is often described as the most lyrical of all the plays and its variety of metric effects supplies the necessary structural framework: not consciously perceived but essential to the unique magic of the play.

Peter Brook's *Dream* (1970)

'Shakespeare doesn't belong to the past. If his material is valid, it is valid now.'

(Peter Brook, The Shifting Point, 1987, 95)

A Midsummer Night's Dream has retained a consistent popularity with producers and directors and there are a number of studies which focus specifically on the performance history of the play, on stage and on screen. It may seem that performance study belongs to 'Drama' as an academic discipline, rather than 'English' but the analysis of specific directorial choices and emphases can clarify aspects of the play, returning the focus of attention back to the text and its possibilities. There are memorable productions which might be seen as forging new directions and challenging traditional views of a play. Equally, a play may appear in a particular light at certain historical moments. Certainly, to see any play as a constant for all audiences across time would be misleading. Each new audience finds new meanings.

Individual productions are, of course, products of their time and cultural moment; even the seemingly consistent language of the text can be subject to change. Modern directors make cuts according to their perception of how much Elizabethan language the audience will accept or enjoy, just as Victorian directors scrutinized the plays for possible overtones of indecency. Hollywood's most recent adaptation of the play (Michael Hoffmann, 1999) features a gramophone and intercuts the text with operatic arias.

A Midsummer Night's Dream has, until relatively recently, been associated with its own myth of performance. It was supposed to have been written for an aristocratic wedding, graciously attended by Queen Elizabeth I. A total of thirteen possible wedding ceremonies have been proposed. This would inevitably influence interpretation of the play. Would the royal presence and courtly context confer decorum on the revelry and chaos of the night? Certainly it would uphold the authority of the ruling elite and the status of marriage. Yet Elizabeth's aura of Virgin Queen would heighten the references to Diana and chastity. The wedding theory has now been discredited as a desire to see the play in a certain, celebratory, light as if Shakespeare himself is promoting a 'Merrie England' complete with Gloriana, fairies, and Bottom the weaver.

The 'landmark' twentieth-century production, severing decisively any connection with the nineteenth century's 'gauzy Pre-Raphaelite fairies', is always seen as Peter Brook's 1970 version. Jan Kott's writing is clearly influential, demonstrating the interaction between academic critic and theatre director. Brook saw the need to discard the reverential attitude towards Shakespeare as cultural icon. He desired to rediscover the magic of theatre and spectacle, disavowing both the notion of 'realist' drama and the formal perfection of art:

Shakespeare's plays are not slices of life, nor are they poems, nor are they beautiful pieces of ornate writing.

(*The Shifting Point*, 206)

Visually, Brook's *Dream* would have seemed startling: critics who liked or disliked the production are unanimous that set and staging were strikingly, even bizarrely, different from anything previously encountered. Sally Jacobs's set, a three-sided white box, can be seen in photographs of the production:

It resembled a stark white squash court, with two small stage doors in the rear wall, and ladders on the downstage edges leading to railed catwalks, or galleries above the walls ... A hammock made of scarlet ostrich feathers was Titania's bower, and trapezes were flown down for the fairies to swing on as occasion demanded. The entire set was brilliantly lit.

(quoted Jay Halio, *Shakespeare in Performance: A Midsummer Night's Dream*, 1994, 49–50)

Victorian productions were famous for creating entire forests on stage; both woodland paintings and real trees were commonplace. Brook made no attempt to imitate fake woodland, and coils of wire suspended on fishing rods were the only concession to the notion of physical impediment. His intention was to 'provide a white daylight magic' where every nuance of movement and sound would be vividly displayed. All the characters were onstage throughout and the stage managers, lighting operators and drummers were also visible presences. This revolutionary technique makes two points: first, forcing a re-think of the world of theatrical illusion; second, suggesting that the supernatural world is ever-present and interacting with the human world, whether benignly or not. John Kane, who played Puck, later recalled the fairy world as essentially malevolent, 'exud[ing] a primitive savagery that infected everyone' (Roger Warren,

A Midsummer Night's Dream Text and Performance, 1983, 56). Puck and other characters commanded the stage on stilts. Costumes were chosen to resemble the world of the circus, baggy and colourful with the mechanicals in neutral everyday street clothes. Brook was not the first director to use the same actors for Hippolyta/Titania and Theseus/Oberon but the revolutionary nature of the production made the doubling particularly notable. It would have been inconceivable in this context to see the fairies played by young children or prettified by costume and Brook turns again to the language of circus to find an appropriate analogy:

> Today we have no symbols that can conjure up fairyland and magic for a modern audience. On the other hand there are a number of actions that a performer can execute that are quite breathtaking. So we went to the art of the circus and the acrobat because they both made purely theatrical statements. We've worked through a language of acrobatics to find a new approach to magic that we know cannot be reached by nineteenth century conventions.

> (interview in *The Daily Telegraph*, 14 September 1970)

The influence of Jan Kott would have been most evident in the relations between Titania and Bottom making their carnivalesque 'love scene' a riotous climax to the first half of the play. Bottom was hoisted triumphantly on the shoulders of the vigorously masculine fairies and a clenched fist and muscular arm appeared between Bottom's legs, in parody of a monstrous erection – to Titania's evident admiration. Oberon swung across the stage on a trapeze, the rest of the cast threw streamers and paper plates like confetti and the unmistakable music of Mendelssohn's Wedding March (then a familiar cliché of wedding ceremonies) accompanied the lovers to Titania's bower where loud and frenzied orgasm was achieved. For many of the earliest critics of the production, the *Dream* had become a fearful nightmare.

Further thinking

➤ Consider the implications of the carnivalesque in a play from a different genre (for example, is the pastoralism of *The Winter's Tale* carnivalesque?) Might Bakhtin's ideas shed an interesting light on *Measure for Measure*?

➤ Analysing Shakespeare's metre can reveal a great deal about characterization as well as mood and atmosphere. A close analysis of Theseus's speech at the opening of Act 5 shows how Shakespeare creates effects of certainty and authority. Alternatively, try comparing the trimeter of *Dream* with the witches' incantations in *Macbeth*.

➤ For many theatre critics, Peter Brook's challenging production of the play continues to be influential. Choose one of the many film versions/adaptations of *Dream*: how would you define the director's perspective?

Afterlives ...

One of the most fascinating versions of the play is Frederick Ashton's ballet, *The Dream* (1964). This is a fifty-minute, one-act work set to Mendelssohn's incidental music. Ashton omits Theseus and Hippolyta completely and the entire ballet is set in the moonlit world of the forest. Comparing the playscript with dance opens up entirely different perspectives.

2

Much Ado About Nothing: Exploring language and gender

Gender debates were especially prominent around the time that Shakespeare was writing. Controversial literature dealing with male and female physiologies, behaviours and roles circulated in the form of pamphlets and 'conduct-books', with the theatre providing a more dynamic medium for these issues to be explored. *Much Ado About Nothing* is a provocative treatment of the sexual politics of the early modern period, aspects of which still ring true with today's audiences.

This chapter

- employs some of the tools of sociolinguistics to analyze the language used by male and female characters in the play
- evaluates how far female talk was directed and constrained by societal expectations
- analyzes how a modern reworking of *Much Ado* for a television audience presents the 'merry war' between the sexes and what this updating suggests about the transhistorical potential of Shakespeare

Linguistics and the literary text

Linguistics as a formal discipline devoted to the scientific study of language was established in the early twentieth century. Before then, language scholarship was mainly focused on its historical development (philology), elements of which are still discernible in some British university English courses (the study of Anglo-Saxon, for example). Core elements of linguistics include phonetics (the study of speech sounds), morphology (the study of word formation), semantics (the study of how meaning is formed) and pragmatics (the study of language in practice). One specialized branch of pragmatics is sociolinguistics, which examines how language shapes and is shaped by its contexts. It might, for example, look at how certain speech modes serve to assert and enforce power relations, or analyze inter-generational conversations. As an area of linguistics that brings important perspectives to bear on issues of gender, it has obvious connections to feminist critical practice, and can lend some valuable insights into a text such as *Much Ado*.

The starting point of what we now call linguistics is usually thought to be Ferdinand de Saussure's *Course in General Linguistics* (1916). Saussure's definition of language as a system of signs, with no fixed meaning, came to underpin some of the most influential critical-theoretical approaches of the last quarter of the twentieth century: structuralism and post-structuralism. That is not to say, however, that the relationship between linguistics and literary criticism has always been an easy one. Beginning in the 1960s, some linguistic practitioners sought to dismantle what they saw as the unnecessary separation of language and literature studies. In *The Languages of Literature* (1971), Roger Fowler, a prominent linguist in the second half of the twentieth century, wrote about how 'there was a regular Berlin Wall down the middle of English studies' (2). Fowler argued that defining literary effects in a text through reference to what he deems the 'objective structures of language' (*Linguistic Criticism*, 1986, 1) could only strengthen the discipline by moving it away from the kind of value-laden criticism Terry Eagleton memorably described as 'gush about sunsets' (*Literary Theory: An Introduction*, 1983, 124). On the other side of the wall, literary specialists questioned the fitness of linguistics to express what they saw as the inherently subjective nature of forms such as lyric poetry. While debates about the relationship between language and literature study continue, the past twenty years or so has seen a steady convergence of the two. Today's university English courses often feature both literary and linguistic elements and, as a consequence, many students are possessed of a hybrid critical vocabulary: a mixture of the technical terms they learnt at school, the conceptual language of critical theory, and the specialized terminologies of linguistics.

Since the mid–1970s, sociolinguistic research into language and gender has flourished. Questions have been asked about how far prevailing patriarchal structures are both evident in, and held in place by, discourse, with attempts being made to define differences between male and female speech and to challenge the androcentric assumption that the former should be regarded as normative. Such interrogations are, of course, of their time, given impetus by second-wave feminism and the radical socio-economic and cultural changes it encouraged. Yet that is not to say that their analytical methods can have no meaningful connection with Shakespeare's society and the works produced within it. As the feminist linguist, Deborah Cameron, points out: 'Ideas about how women and men use language, and how they ought ideally to use it, have been a recurring theme in discourse about language produced by many societies in many historical periods' ('Gender and Language Ideologies' in *Language and Gender: A Reader*, Jennifer Coates and Pia Pichler (eds), 2011, 584).

'Female talk and marital suitability'

'A silent wife is a gift of the Lord' (*Ecclesiasticus* 26.14)

Of all Shakespeare's comedies, *Much Ado* concentrates most fully on the relationship between female talk and marital suitability. A prime requirement of the Renaissance wife was that she should obey and serve her spouse, imperatives enshrined in the marriage service (Book of Common Prayer, 1559), as well as being vital to the husband's reputation in what was a generally homosocial climate. A talkative wife was a highly disturbing prospect for the early modern man. On the one hand, it threatened the domination of the scolding wife over the 'hen-pecked' husband, leaving the man exposed to ridicule in a society where he was expected to 'naturally' govern and hold sway. On the other hand, a wife's looseness of tongue suggested sexual incontinence, raising the spectre of cuckoldry. Not for nothing does Leonato warn Beatrice that her constant back-chat will scare off any potential suitors (2.1.16–17). The canonical texts of the day, not least the Holy Bible, were frequently invoked to endorse the association of talkativeness with female disobedience. The account of Eve and the serpent in the book of Genesis vividly demonstrated the consequences of the female proclivity for unguarded talk and provided St Paul with the ideal example to support his decree that no woman should 'teach or … have authority over men', but should 'keep silent' (I Timothy 2.12–13).

Across Europe, the stereotype of the loquacious woman was also fixed in proverbial expressions, providing an interesting example of cross-cultural agreement. Classified today as 'folklinguistics', such expressions captured beliefs that played a significant part in perpetuating sexist attitudes to women and talk. One Danish proverb expressed how 'the North Sea will sooner be found wanting in water than a woman be at a loss for a word', a sentiment also found in the English saying: 'A woman's tongue wags like a lamb's tail'. *Much Ado* takes the proverbial female tongue as one of its central tropes. Benedick tells Beatrice that he wished his horse were as fast as her tongue, later referring to her in conversation with Don Pedro as 'my Lady Tongue!' (2.1.252). Not only does this traditional **synecdoche** reduce the female to a bodily part – and a small one at that – it also hones in on what men commonly feared as a potential weapon to be used against them. As Lisa Jardine points out in her influential study *Still Harping on Daughters* (1983) 'the woman with a sharp tongue breaks the social order ... Discordant, disruptive, unruly, she threatens to sabotage the domestic harmony which depends upon her general submissiveness' (106). Elizabethan audiences would no doubt have identified Beatrice as one such sharp-tongued woman.

If a woman's tongue is both a substitute weapon and, by traditional association, a substitute for her phallic 'lack', so the male tongue could be seen as a kind of replacement for the uniquely masculine activities of war. The opening of *Much Ado* brings in an atmosphere not only of victorious celebration, but also of the relief, even euphoria, which comes from returning from battle unscathed. Safe from the threat of opposing armies, the men can indulge in a purely verbal form of warfare, with only their *amour propre* at risk of being wounded. Yet just as martial combat has its rules, so too does the linguistic competition of Messina's golden youth. One of the primary interdictions is the resistance of feminine influences. Though being relieved of his 'rougher task' (1.1.280) means that Claudio can allow himself the pleasure of being swayed by 'soft and delicate desires' (1.1.284), it also puts him at risk of losing his masculine ability to 'speak plain and to the purpose' (2.3.18). Benedick, of course, never misses an opportunity to state his resistance to feminizing emotions; yet by engaging with Beatrice in the cut-and-thrust of linguistic sparring, he allows her into what should be an exclusively male club.

The couple's shared enjoyment of agonistic discourse is often seen to make them ideal companions. However, this romantic, even sentimentalised, vision of Beatrice and Benedick as a charming, if eccentric, example of a companionate marriage has been contested by a number of literary critics who view the couple as being coerced into marriage by social and cultural pressures (see, for example, Stephen Greenblatt's introduction to *Much Ado* in *The Norton Shakespeare*, 1997). Putting such arguments aside, if the more conventionally romantic reading is adopted, it would seem that Shakespeare is offering his audiences a glimpse into a future where a couple could find affinities with each other in areas which had formerly been designated 'men only' or 'women only'. That comedy had the capacity to portray such harmonious gender relations was a view held by the Victorian writer George Meredith. In a piece entitled *An Essay on Comedy and the Uses of the Comic Spirit*, first published in 1877, he argues that:

> The Comic poet dares to show us men and women coming to this mutual likeness; he is for saying that when they draw together in social life their minds grow liker; just as the philosopher discerns the similarity of boy and girl, until the girl is marched away to the nursery.

> (30)

In the concluding phrase of the extract, Meredith underscores the realities of the world outside the theatre, thus insisting on drama as an art that can offer audiences tantalizing scenarios which, though recognizable in their surface realism, nonetheless belong to the stuff of the ideal imagination.

Whether we regard the marriage of Beatrice and Benedick as the union of two ideally suited people, or an essentially patriarchal match made to look like one made in heaven, Claudio and Hero undoubtedly stand as the norm against which they are to be measured. The brides-in-waiting are set in stark counterpoint: the silent, decorous maid and the talkative 'shrew' of contemporary antifeminism. From a Renaissance perspective at least, Hero ticks all the 'ideal woman' boxes and would continue to do so for some time to come. Consider this definition of the perfect 'maid' in a popular late seventeenth-century work *The Illustrious History of Women* (1686) by John Shirley:

> She delights not in much discourse ... her words are few ... amongst strangers she rarely speaks ... at the repetition of any wanton discourse she blushes and turns away ... her obedience to her parents is wonderful.

Shakespeare's Hero embodies all such expectations. In adhering strictly to the demands of her social milieu, her obedience is, indeed, 'wonderful', in contradistinction to her cousin, Beatrice. Yet the play does not mete out rewards and punishments for the cousins in any straightforward way. If anything, Hero's silence, while supposedly an outward sign of her conformity, seems to rouse the kind of male fear and suspicion borne out of misogyny. While her whispering in Claudio's ear after his proposal of marriage appears suitably shy and modest, it is also a moment when something is kept back from the predominantly male company. Far from being uncomplicatedly decorous, then, silence becomes synonymous with secrecy and female inscrutability. As one critic, Carol Cook, suggests, Hero, the silent woman, proves to be the '"nothing" that generates so much ado' (' "The Sign and Semblance of Her Honor": Reading Gender Difference in *Much Ado About Nothing*' in *Shakespeare and Gender: A History*, Deborah E. Barker and Ivo Kamps (eds), 1995, 85).

What then of Hero's verbal opposite? Are the words uttered by Beatrice in public, however audacious, ultimately less dangerous than those whispered privately? Certainly, Beatrice's linguistic braggadocio seems to be tolerated, even encouraged, by the men in her society, its impact moderated by familiarity, perhaps. Moreover, though Beatrice seems to be breaching female decorum by joining in the badinage of men, in doing so she is also accepting their terms, playing by their rules. Looked at this way, she becomes 'one of the lads', battling for a dominance which resides in masculinity, one that everyone knows she can never actually achieve – though it is fun seeing her try. Far from the proto-feminist some critics have made her out to be, there is a convincing case to be made for her being just as much in thrall to a patriarchal system as her cousin. Jardine identifies the crux of the matter as residing in Beatrice's most memorable line 'Kill Claudio' (4.1.288):

> At this moment she recognizes the tongue as the symbol of impotence and inaction, of the threat which will never become a deed. When Beatrice ... [is] enclosed in matrimony ... the sharpness of her tongue which has marred their courtship is domesticated.
>
> (*Still Harping on Daughters*, 113)

According to Jardine, then, what in the mouth of a man would be a performative statement becomes in the mouth of a female just a collection of sounds.

Leonato's handing over his niece to her husband-to-be, safe in the knowledge that a wedding will soon 'stop [her] mouth' (5.4.97), seems to put linguistic control back in the male arena. It could be argued, though, that the teasing glimpse the play offers us into what it might be like if women spoke like men, unleashes some disturbing challenges for Shakespeare's society – and even for our own. Beatrice's ludic language not only goes against the feminine ideal, it also strikes at the established status of men as the coiners and controllers of words. By displaying an ability to 'fright[...] the word out of his right sense' (5.2.52–3) Beatrice demonstrates that, far from being slavish adherents to the male word, women could be key agents in opening up the polysemic potential of language and making it their own. Though the systematic fixing of grammar, spelling and vocabulary would not become a principal endeavour until the eighteenth century, the wind was already set in that direction. Women engaged in changing, manipulating or supplementing the established linguistic order would have been an unsettling prospect in a society where the female was supposed to be the defined, not the definer.

Analysing the play's opening scene: Two different approaches

Conversational analysis

In sociolinguistics, conversational analysis sets out to analyze how language operates in social interaction, most usually in 'real life' situations. Stage dialogue can never perfectly represent actual speech and it must be said that, unless the writer were blessed with the creative gifts of a Harold Pinter, any attempt to create a drama modelled on a 'live' example of spoken language (perhaps by basing it on a transcript) would most likely end up unwatchable. Everyday speech is too full of hesitations, repetitions and overlapping for it to hold the attention of a theatre audience for very long. The successful dramatist creates the *effect* of conversation: a feat which is only accomplished with a good deal of skill.

Read 1.1.1–90 and think about:

- who speaks the most lines
- what types of questions are asked and by whom
- how new topics are introduced into the conversation
- who plays most energetically with words

The belief that women talk more than men has been around for some time, though recent linguistic investigation has shown it to be unfounded: while women tend to talk a lot in single-sex situations, they talk considerably less than men in mixed company, especially in public situations. Totting up the number of lines spoken by male and female characters in Shakespeare's plays certainly confirms that men get the lion's share, though audience perceptions often run counter to the evidence: Juliet and Cleopatra might give the impression of speaking more than their partners, but the opposite is actually the case. In fact, there are only four plays in which women have the longest roles: Helena in *All's Well that Ends Well*, Portia in *The Merchant of Venice*, Rosalind in *As You Like It* and Imogen in *Cymbeline* and, of these, only Helena makes it through the whole play without dressing up and acting as a man.

In the given extract, Beatrice has the most lines of the four actors on stage by some considerable margin, despite only beginning to speak about a third of the way through; the Messenger has the next highest number, more than Leonato, the character with the highest status. Of course, the apportioning of lines in a play is driven by dramaturgical concerns and it is clear that in allowing a woman and a messenger to hold the floor, Shakespeare is also encouraging his first audiences to sit up and take notice. Speaking more than others in a conversation, as Beatrice does here, is not in itself a sign of power or value. Some of Shakespeare's most vocal characters can also be rather foolish (think of Polonius in *Hamlet* or Bottom in *A Midsummer Night's Dream*); nor is silence necessarily a sign of weakness. Attention must be paid to the immediate context of the dialogue – its twists and turns, its management of topic and its interactivity – before any conclusions about power dynamics can be drawn.

The situation which opens *Much Ado* is one of male celebration: the triumphal return of war heroes. It is a relatively public scene, the Messenger being from outside the family circle, bringing in joyful news that he might well expect to be received with pleasure, even gratitude. What he could not have foreseen is that his good tidings would be interrogated by a woman. Beatrice breaks into the scene with a question: 'I pray you, is Signor Mountanto returned from the wars or no?' According to the findings of conversational analysis, direct questions such as this are more characteristic of men than women. Female questioning is more likely to feature tag questions ('Isn't it?' 'Won't we?'), offered as a means of avoiding awkward silences or confrontation. Beatrice's direct interrogative here and later in the extract (look at lines 40–1, 51–2, 67, 76) effectively derails the Messenger, cutting into the stately flourishes of male talk. In so doing, she violates the accepted rules of turn-taking, switching the topic of conversation from the newly honoured Claudio to Benedick. Indeed, this sudden interjection of Beatrice's could be read as the first indication of her strong feelings for Benedick; she may go on to speak rudely about him, but her abrupt interruption of the formal male discourse suggests an eagerness to know whether or not he has come through the battle unscathed.

Beatrice runs rings round the Messenger with her linguistic game-playing. She exploits the semantic elasticity of words, wrenching the Messenger's heroic language out of its stylized shape and undermining his fixed ideas about soldierly virtue. The soldier 'stuffed with all honourable virtues' is transformed within a line into a 'stuffed man': an overfed sensualist who is unlikely to squeeze himself into a suit of armour, let alone fight the enemy. When the Messenger tries to cut off this spirited attack, he fails miserably:

MESSENGER: I see, lady, the gentleman is not in your books.
BEATRICE: No; an he were, I would burn my study.

Beatrice seizes the metaphor of the Messenger's sober idiomatic phrase, literalizing it in a way that draws attention to her bookishness – another example of how she aligns herself with a predominantly male world.

As the Messenger struggles to cope with Beatrice's flouting of female decorum, both Hero and Leonato attempt what sociolinguists term 'face-saving'. Hero's only line of the extract 'translates' Beatrice's sexually suggestive 'Signor Mountanto' into the more respectful 'Signor Benedick of Padua', while

Leonato urges the Messenger not to 'mistake' his niece. Both interventions amount to apologizing for Beatrice's behaviour. At the same time, in assuring the other male on stage – albeit one of much less standing – that the niece for whom he is responsible is firmly under his patriarchal control, Leonato saves his own face as head of the household. The face-saving at work in this scene, then, is as much to do with protecting the male power structure as it is about saving an outspoken female from making a fool of herself in public.

Sociolinguistic studies suggest that men talk more than women in public spaces, compete with other men in conversation (whereas women are much more likely to cooperate), use vulgar language more frequently in mixed company than women do, and are more likely to ask direct questions and control the topic of conversation. Featuring men who are largely cooperative and an indefatigably competitive woman who derails the male topic of heroism through direct questions and interventions, the opening of *Much Ado* seems to go against all such norms of discourse.

'Posh prose': Shakespeare's use of euphuism

Prose in Shakespeare's plays is often said to be the language of the socially inferior, the clown or the madman, with verse being reserved for characters of high status and for scenes of solemnity and import. Clearly, such generalizations overlook the subtle and complex effects which the movement between the two dramatic modes of speech can create. The shift from one to the other can, for example, signal tensions in a relationship or effect a change in tone between one scene and another. With the exception of *The Merry Wives of Windsor*, *Much Ado* has the highest proportion of prose of any Shakespeare play (just over 70 per cent), with verse tending to be employed for the more sombre and troubling scenes of the Hero and Claudio plot. The flexibility and speed of prose allows for the creation of the play's spontaneous witty dialogue and, being more akin to 'ordinary' speech than verse, helps establish the relatively realistic setting of Messina. That is not to say, however, that prose is the binary inferior of verse: lacking in rhythm, elevated diction and complex imagery.

One of the characteristics of the prose in *Much Ado* is its use of **euphuism**: highly wrought rhetorical language. The term derives from the eponymous hero of the highly influential prose romance by John Lyly entitled *Euphues*. Published in two parts in 1578 and 1580, the work is written in a style rich in antithesis, alliteration and various other rhetorical devices. Euphuistic prose can prove quite challenging to read and, indeed, to listen to; this is perhaps why Shakespeare goes some way to naturalizing its stiff and formalized artifice. As the influential Victorian critic, Edward Dowden, observed in *Shakespeare as a Comic Dramatist*:

> Shakespeare must have perceived the lack of human interest in Lyly's plays ... the mechanical artificiality and monotonous balance of certain elements in Euphuistic prose. What was sprightly and ingenious in Lyly's dialogue he preserved; but of Euphuism in the strict sense we find nothing in Shakespeare's plays.
>
> (in *Representative English Comedies*, ed. C. M. Gayley, 1903, 646)

While there might be some toning down of Lyly's style in *Much Ado*, it is clear that Shakespeare is interested in exploring the power that verbal adroitness can wield. In the linguistically self-conscious world of Messina words provide a vital means of male bonding.

⁇ *Look again at the first ninety lines of the play and think about:*

- which lines employ the most elaborate linguistic strategies
- which character seems most intent on maintaining formal rhetoric
- how Beatrice responds to such verbal elaborateness

Given the association of euphuism with high social standing, it is perhaps surprising that it is the Messenger who most insists on rhetorical talk, though perhaps not so surprising that he takes full advantage of the festive nature of his news to show off his verbal accomplishments (a carrier of ill tidings would no doubt keep his language pithy). Beatrice remains silent on stage for some considerable time, listening to the Messenger's words and to her uncle's responses to them. Leonato eventually joins in the linguistic competition (25–7), perhaps taking mercy on the Messenger; after all, euphuistic language is an invitation to the addressee to join in and not to take up that invitation carries a form of rebuff. To deprive the Messenger of his chance to impress his superiors would be plain churlish on such a happy occasion.

Yet while Leonato receives the Messenger's rhetoric graciously (if a little tongue-in-cheek), Beatrice cannot resist the temptation of livening it up a little. For the first twenty-eight lines of the play the Messenger is allowed free rein to display his best euphuistic jewels. He uses **antithesis** (words or ideas set up in contrast to each other, usually in balanced constructions) to describe the victorious Claudio 'doing in the figure of a **lamb** the feats of a **lion**', and **polyptoton** (the repetition of a word with the same root in a different form) to emphasize that in doing so he '**better bettered** expectations'. Beatrice's first line (a direct question) interrupts just at the moment when the rhetorical game seems to be taking off. Leonato has just responded to the messenger with his own example of polyptoton ('A **kind** overflow of **kindness**'), following it with a line so replete with rhetorical devices it wins hands down: 'How much better is it to **weep** at **joy** than to **joy** at **weeping**!'; here, in just fourteen words, Leonato packs in a muscular example of **antimetabole** (words in an initial clause repeated in reverse grammatical order in a succeeding clause), nominalizes 'weep' to become 'weeping' (polyptoton again), and revises the Messenger's use of **ploce** (the repetition of a word in the same line or clause) in line 20 by nimbly shifting the noun 'joy' to act as a verb in its repeated form (the Messenger only manages a simple repetition of the word).

Such linguistic density may well be fun for those taking part (though we sense that, for different reasons, neither Leonato nor the Messenger is having a particularly enjoyable time of it), but there is a limit to how dramatically engaging it is for an audience. Beatrice's intervention introduces life and energy to the scene, as she cuts through rhetorical patterns and unsettles semantics, leaving the Messenger somewhat nonplussed. On the surface, his addressing Beatrice as 'lady' no fewer than five times in the space of forty lines might appear no more than a formality; however, if we look at the examples of the address more closely, we realize that they perform a significant dramatic function. The more the word 'lady' is repeated, the more the speaker seems to struggle with keeping word and meaning together. Beatrice might have all the appearance of a lady, but her behaviour would seem to indicate otherwise. If by repeating the term the Messenger hopes to remind Beatrice of her proper place, he is to be disappointed. Perhaps alert to his emphatic use of 'lady', she takes the title at line 50 and, by the mere addition of the indefinite article, disengages it from her own person.

While Beatrice proves herself more than capable of linguistic cleverness and euphuistic competition, her preference for a more direct and down-to-earth idiom is made clear. She cuts through the elaborate language of the scene with talk of bird-bolts, hat blocks and 'musty victual', upsetting the balanced cadences of rhetorical phrasing with a prose which is at once dynamic and spontaneous. The linguistic contrasts set up here are strongly felt by the audience, which cannot help but be relieved that the rather static and exclusive rhetorical male discourse put on display in this opening scene is challenged and disrupted by the more entertaining verbal agility of a woman.

Shakespeare Retold (2005)

Very much in the spirit of the new millennium, the BBC commissioned modern re-workings of four Shakespeare plays: *Much Ado*, *Macbeth*, *The Taming of the Shrew* and *A Midsummer Night's Dream*. *Much Ado* was selected to launch the series, no doubt because of its being popularly regarded as a prototypical romcom: a genre guaranteed to attract a suitably large audience for its prime-time evening slot.

⁇ *Watch the* Shakespeare Retold *version of* Much Ado *and think about the following questions:*

- Which elements of the play seem to have been the easiest or the most difficult to adapt?
- The setting for the television retelling was originally a department store. Why do you think this was changed to a television studio?
- Which lines from the play have been retained and why?
- Has the modern version managed to capture the spirit of the original script (if such a thing can be defined)?

The decision of screenwriter David Nicholls to leave all but a few lines of the play on the cutting-room floor was no doubt based on the premise that a mainstream television audience would be unlikely to sit through three hours or so of Elizabethan English. Purists are bound to consider such drastic editing a travesty; Shakespeare's language is, after all, generally considered the most remarkable aspect of his work. Nonetheless, Nicholls composes a modern idiom which succeeds in capturing and sustaining the rhythms and spirit of Shakespeare's comic language. As anchors for a regional news programme, this twenty-first-century Beatrice and Benedick rely on their facility with words to succeed in their jobs, although we also see them make full use of their verbal skills off-air. 'Bad hair day?' asks Benedick, seconds before the cameras start rolling, only to be put down with Beatrice's lightening retort 'Bad face day?' Shakespearean bawdy also translates with a good degree of ease as Beatrice revels in wisecracks such as 'You really do put the "w" into "anchor man"'. Even the soliloquy, often thought to grate with an audience accustomed to realistic drama, is more than adequately served by the televisual technique of the voiceover.

Yet while David Nicholls demonstrates that Shakespeare's language can be updated in a manner which preserves at least some of its vigour, the historical specificity of the play proves more of a barrier. The centuries of feminist thought and action which post-date the play make it difficult to retain the transgressive nature of Shakespeare's Beatrice. The sassy language and feisty behaviour of the modern-day heroine provide little cause for comment in a world where sex before marriage and salacious talk constitute acceptable female behaviour. Equally difficult to represent is the misogyny of Messinian society. While no one would declare misogynistic attitudes to be a thing of the past, there is now a generally established view that they are not socially acceptable. So, when the misogynistic posturing that marks out Shakespeare's Benedick as typically male is transplanted to a character 400 years hence, it marks him out as a sexist dinosaur who has failed to adapt to the 'new man' role forged in the last two decades of the twentieth century. The modern Benedick's womanizing habits, outdated facial hair, and desire to feature a local beauty competition as a major news item make him appear foolish and out-of-step with the age (which is not the case in the original). And where Shakespeare's Benedick spends much of his time sharing cuckold jokes with his male companions, his filmic twin spends more time sweet-talking women than joshing with members of his own sex. What this updating quite emphatically demonstrates is that in today's equivalent of Shakespeare's society, with the exception of hen parties and toilet facilities, mixed company is the norm.

The role of Hero is equally resistant to a revision of equivalence. While a passive virgin, unfailingly obedient to her father would have been the accepted pattern of femininity in the 1600s, by twenty-first-century standards, she would be deemed at best quaint, at worst aberrant. Perhaps bearing this in mind, Nicholls gives us a Hero who is chatty and easy-going, with a sexual history typical of a young woman of her time. Her job as a television weather girl has been secured for her by her father, Leonard, the programme's producer, a detail which manages in part to retain the power structure between father and daughter which is so vital to the original. As the stereotypically young, pretty – and not overly bright – girl who reads the forecast is set alongside the fast-talking television anchor, so the contrasts drawn between the cousins in Shakespeare's drama are replicated. Transforming the masked ball of the play into a fancy dress party enables such contrasts to be visually underscored as Beatrice appears as Elizabeth I, an embodiment of power and strength, and Hero opts for Marilyn Monroe, the vulnerable sex goddess whose value depended on the approval of the male gaze.

Perhaps the most altered character in this modern adaptation is Don John. Today's television viewers would be unlikely to accept a figure of motiveless malignity, or one with a brooding resentment from being base born, so his modern equivalent is given more concrete motives to make him convincing for a post-Freudian audience. The morose cameraman, Don, has enjoyed a one-night stand with Hero and refuses to accept that the relationship between them is going no further. Immediately recognizable to television audiences as the stalker figure of numerous psychological dramas, his feelings of humiliation at her rejection are intensified when he overhears Hero tell her female friends how she slept with him more out of pity than passion. Where Don John's deception succeeds more as a result of the misogynistic mistrust which lies beneath the surface geniality of Leonato and Claudio than from the enactment of the feigned 'impediment', Don's succeeds largely thanks to the 'evidence' offered by modern technology: photographs and text messaging. In this respect, Claude seems more a victim of an elaborate hoax than a man trapped by his own antifeminist prejudices, and the viciousness of Hero's rejection in Shakespeare's play is tempered accordingly.

As the Hero-Claudio plot moves towards a resolution, so it begins to veer most noticeably from the Shakespearean plot line. With Hero recovered from a life-threatening head injury, and Claude suitably remorseful, all seems set for a double wedding. Following our sense of the usual romcom trajectory, we read Hero's declaration that she can never forgive Claude as the final hurdle before the romantic wrap-up. But we are to be disappointed. While Beatrice and her sparring partner are safely married off, Claude seems destined to be best man, but never bridegroom. By resisting the clichéd ending, the production insists that, in the twenty-first century, even conventional young women are free to turn down the eligible bachelor.

The dissonant closure of *Shakespeare Retold* succinctly captures the production's self-conscious modernity, both in terms of gender politics and aesthetic form. Yet although it is set up in contrast to the finale of its seventeenth-century counterpart – a celebratory dance that brings the major characters into harmonious synchronicity – its impact is arguably less complex and less disturbing. Don John might be excluded from the festivities but, as Benedick reminds us, he is still in Messina and, as feminist critics often point out, in a drama where a woman is transformed by the male imagination from 'the sweetest lady' to a 'rotten orange', even the happiest of endings is not without its sour notes.

Further thinking

➤ Try out the conversational analysis tools demonstrated in this chapter by reading Act 3 Scene 3 of *Antony and Cleopatra* and analysing the power dynamics at work.

➤ Look over Act 4 Scene 1 of *Much Ado* and think about the dramatic effects of the shifts between prose and verse. You could also try this out on the first meeting between Olivia and Viola in *Twelfth Night* (1.5.214–80).

➤ The *Shakespeare Retold* series was aimed at a mainstream audience. Should this be seen as a democratic gesture or an imposition of 'high culture'?

Afterlives …

William Congreve's Restoration comedy *The Way of the World* (1700) features the lovers Millamant and Mirabell, often regarded as ancestors to Beatrice and Benedick. The influence of Shakespeare is particularly keenly felt in the proposal scene in which Millamant agrees to 'dwindle into a wife' (4.1).

3

Twelfth Night: Disguises and desires

T*welfth Night* is the last of Shakespeare's romantic comedies and is an elaborate and complex variation on the theme. The play combines the carnivalesque festivity of Sir Toby's 'cakes and ale' with the rarefied world of Orsino's courtly love. Shipwrecked twins bring confusion and resolution.

This chapter examines

- Queer theory and cross-dressing in the play
- Romantic comedy as a genre
- the role of song
- The Renaissance Theatre Company's production for stage and screen

Cross-dressing and Queer theory

Queer theory is the interpretation of texts from a lesbian or gay perspective. As a relatively recent critical development stemming from sociologically or historically based gender studies, it demonstrates quite how considerably attitudes towards Shakespeare's plays have been subject to change and re-definition, both academically and in the theatre itself. Queer theory as a term sounds combative, as it is: 'Queer' as a homophobic insult makes its first appearance in the

early twentieth century and is unambiguously pejorative; the
OED cites an American source, 1931, where 'queer' equates
to 'effeminate or degenerate men or boys'. Although, in the
UK, homosexuality was decriminalized in 1967, anti-gay
prejudice intensified in the late twentieth century with the
emergence of HIV/AIDS, initially associated with gay men.
The notorious 'Section 28' (of the Local Government Act,
1988) fuelled controversy by prohibiting local authorities
from 'promoting homosexuality'. Gay rights movements then
appropriated the term Queer as an act of defiance signalling a
new campaigning mood emerging in liberal western societies;
gay men and women refused to deny or conceal their sexual
orientation and claimed equality and legal rights. Anti-gay
prejudice has abated, although in Britain and America there
are still debates over gay marriage and, to date, the ordination
of gay priests. 'Queer', then, is, first, a political statement. As a
mode of textual analysis, queer theory challenges and seeks to
destabilize assumptions of the 'normative', seeing all texts as
expressive of the conflicts of class, race, gender, and sexuality
within social structures that are ideologically coercive. In
particular, it rejects any proposition that heterosexuality is
'normal' and homosexuality is 'other'. Queer theory would
propose, first, that gender and sexuality are not identical: that
gender is a set of cultural assumptions imposed by society;
sexuality is any individual's choice of sexual expression(s).
Second, Queer theorists would oppose antitheses such as
male/female; gay/straight as oppressively narrow, arguing
that such polar opposites do not adequately encompass the
complexities of individual identity and sexuality.

But how far is this relevant to Shakespeare? In literary
terms, Queer theory has two central concerns: the first is to
question preconceived ideas of the canon, advancing those
writers who may have been marginalized or neglected; the
second is to identify gay perspectives within familiar texts,
especially where these may have been ignored or denied. A
further question might be how far the critical methods of
Queer theory can be applied to early modern texts. Here,

it must be acknowledged that modern ideas of 'gayness' simply did not exist. As Alan Bray establishes, 'To talk of an individual in this period as being or not being "a homosexual" is an anachronism and ruinously misleading' (*Homosexuality in Renaissance England*, 1995, 16). There would certainly have been religious opposition to sodomy – although it seems that this would have been defined as a range of disruptive activities, not uniquely sexual. So there was no official recognition of homosexuality – although there were, of course, gay relationships. To the educated Elizabethan, classical models sanctioned the love of a mature man for a boy. Stephen Orgel argues that English Renaissance culture did not display 'a morbid fear of homoeroticism':

> On the contrary, the love of men for other men was both a fact of life and an essential element in the operation of the patronage system.
>
> ('Shakespeare, sexuality and gender' in *The New Cambridge Companion to Shakespeare*, 2010, 227)

The theatrical position is intriguingly speculative. A number of critics argue that early modern audiences simply accept, unquestioningly, the convention of boys in female roles. Yet *Twelfth Night* is a subtle and complex play where Viola constantly draws attention to the falseness of her situation: 'I am not that I play' (1.5.179) is a statement that resonates with multiple possibilities. Key critic of this field, Susan Zimmerman, argues that Renaissance theatre enabled the release of transgressive impulses, the cross-dressing beautiful boys liberating anarchic and disturbing potential (*Erotic Politics*, 1992). Catherine Belsey also suggests that gender difference is radically challenged in the world of Shakespeare's comedies. The sexual ambiguity of the boy acting the female role but assuming male clothing as a 'disguise' could be seen as 'disrupting sexual difference', blurring all clear boundaries:

Of course, the male disguise of these female heroines allows for plenty of dramatic ironies and double meanings, and thus offers the audience the pleasures of a knowingness which depends on a knowledge of sexual difference. But it can also be read as undermining that knowledge from time to time, calling it in question by indicating that it is possible, at least in fiction, to speak from a position which is not that of a full unified, gendered subject.

('Disrupting sexual difference: meaning and gender in the comedies' in *Alternative Shakespeares,* ed. Drakakis, 1985, 180)

Modern critics have drawn attention to the multiplicity of possibilities inherent in the spectator's gaze – where **'the gaze'** is a figure of critical discourse usually connected with male appraisal or intimidation of the female. Is Shakespeare's male spectator aroused by homoerotic possibilities or the suggestion of female form in male attire? Perhaps it is the uncertainty that is exciting, an androgynous youth, neither fully male nor female. Both art and music suggest helpful analogies. The practice of using castrati for female roles in early opera performances creates similar ambiguities; the castrati being viewed as 'artificial', a beautiful voice 'upon which fantasies can be projected.' Musicologist Dorothy Keyser writes of the early seventeenth century that:

[Castrati] appear to have been perceived as blank canvases on which either sexual role could be projected, in real life as on the stage ... In a society that prized virility in its men and fertility in its women, the ambiguous figure of the castrato was endlessly fascinating.

('Cross-sexual casting in Baroque Opera: Musical and Theatrical Conventions', cited in *Queering the Pitch: The New Gay and Lesbian Musicology,* Brett, Wood, Thomas (eds), 1994, 143)

Certainly, the cult of the beautiful young male is an important part of Renaissance art. An excellent example might be Donatello's statue of *David* (1408–9, Bargello Museum, Florence) or, in English portraiture, Henry Wriothesley, third Earl of Southampton, one of the chief suspects for Shakespeare's young man of the sonnets. Indeed the sonnets do appear to fetishise youthful male beauty: Sonnet 20 is often cited in connection with *Twelfth Night* and the complications of Viola's transvestism:

> A woman's face with nature's own hand painted
> Hast thou, the master mistress of my passion;
> A woman's gentle heart but not acquainted
> With shifting change as is false woman's fashion ...

The sonnet is a witty teasing acknowledgement that the lovely young man has been endowed with 'one thing' which makes him appeal to female desire. Queer theory, then, would foreground Renaissance aesthetics with its cult of the beautiful young man as an object of desire, and would explore ways in which Shakespeare's theatre addresses same-sex desire and transvestism. Research into early modern attitudes reveals, unsurprisingly, that early seventeenth-century Puritans objected vociferously to cross-dressing in the theatre, but of course they objected to theatrical performance itself. Philip Stubbes (writing 1583–91) efficiently dismissed every form of theatre as an occasion for 'play[ing] the sodomite, or worse':

> '[Such] kissing and bussing, such clipping and culling, such winking and glancing of wanton eyes.'
>
> (Bruce R. Smith, *Twelfth Night Texts and Contexts*, 2001, 349)

The Oxford academic, John Rainoldes, cited biblical authority forbidding a man to 'put on women's raiment' and roared against the homoerotic possibilities of cross-dressing boys provoking 'sparkles of lust' and 'uncleane affections' (Smith, 276).

In *Twelfth Night* there are two specific areas of interest: the possibility of homoeroticism between Antonio and Sebastian, and the complexities caused by 'Cesario'. Viola's role is unique: in disguise she could be seen as the object of two homosexual passions, Orsino's stated fondness for the boy Cesario, and Olivia's attraction to the beardless boy, quite possibly a lesbian attraction. Within this dizzying comic virtuosity, Viola herself is consistent; unlike Portia or Rosalind, she never takes delight in her disguise – yet her false appearance is precisely what causes confusion in everyone else.

'A witchcraft drew me hither': Sebastian and Antonio

What exactly is the dramatic purpose of this relationship? Sebastian is crucial to the resolution of the drama but Antonio's role serves no function other than the hint to Viola that her brother may be alive. The language of their first brief scene is strangely elaborate for a prose scene: all Antonio's brief interjections are of love and longing:

> If you will not murder me for my love, let me be your
>   servant.
>   [...]
> Come what may, I do adore thee so.
>
> (2.1.33, 43)

Sebastian's speeches emphasize his intense emotions and his physical resemblance to a beautiful twin sister. Throughout the scene he speaks of his tears, identifying himself with female sensibility in exact opposite to Viola who, shipwrecked, speaks first of the loss of her brother, then references her father in response to the Captain's information about Illyria: 'I have heard my father name [Orsino]'. She defines herself through the male line before making herself a 'eunuch'. Sebastian, conversely, apologizes for his inability to control his feelings:

> My bosom is full of kindness, and I am yet so near the manners of my mother that upon the least occasion more mine eyes will tell tales of me.

> (2.1.36–8)

Ironically, the scene follows immediately after Olivia has heard and succumbed to Cesario's speeches of Orsino's love. She repeats to herself Cesario's 'I am a gentleman'; concluding 'I'll be sworn thou art' (1.5.282). Olivia is apparently overwhelmed by Cesario's masculinity while the male twin, conversely, weeps and sees himself as his mother. This first dramatic juxtaposition between the twins might encourage the audience to question whether Shakespeare is deliberately confusing stereotypical gender roles. Antonio defines his role as protective when he pursues Sebastian:

> I could not stay behind you. My desire,
> More sharp than filed steel, did spur me forth,
> And not all love to see you – though so much
>   [...]
> But jealousy what might befall your travel.

> (3.3.4–6, 8)

The relationship could be seen in the light of intense male friendship: Antonio claims at the end of the play that they have been together for three months 'both day and night' and should the audience be tempted to assume that such affection is one-sided, Sebastian also greets Antonio in fulsome words:

> Antonio! O my dear Antonio!
> How have the hours racked and tortured me
> Since I have lost thee?

> (5.1.214–6)

In this respect, Antonio must be seen as part of the subtly inconclusive world of the play's resolution. After Sebastian's effusive greeting, no further exchange takes place and Antonio is simply forgotten: Illyria, as he himself has observed, has proved 'rough and inhospitable'. In this play, with its virtuosic variations upon Shakespeare's own conventions of romantic comedy, it would be entirely consistent to add to the mix a longing homoerotic passion which will, in any case, be rejected in the final analysis by Sebastian's willingness to marry Olivia and embrace conventionality, property and position.

Ovid's *Metamorphoses* might be relevant in this context: in the opening scene, Shakespeare elaborates one of the most searching and Ovidian metaphors of the play – Orsino's comparison of himself with Actaeon, the hunter consumed by his own dogs. In Ovid's text, sexual passion is shifting and unstable. Orpheus, after the final loss of Eurydice, turns to 'pretty boys' and sings of Jupiter's love for the boy Ganymede. Contrastingly, there may also be a model in religious iconography: St Sebastian the Christian martyr is invariably depicted in Renaissance art as the vulnerable perfect youth, bound and naked, as he is pierced by arrows. Antonio certainly uses language which is explicitly idolatrous:

> This youth that you see here
> I snatched one half out of the jaws of death,
> Relieved him with such sanctity of love,
> And to his image, which methought did promise
> Most venerable worth, did I devotion.

> (3.4.356–60)

Critic Joseph Pequigney suggests a link with Antonio in *The Merchant of Venice;* similarly prone to melancholy, expressing overwhelming love for his friend Bassanio and suffering a similar rejection, ending the play solitary and abandoned (see Pequigney, 'The Two Antonios and same-sex love in *Twelfth Night* and *The Merchant of Venice*', ELR, 22, 1992,

201–2). In the light of Renaissance painting; Shakespeare's own writing; the popularity of Golding's Ovid, a glimpse of homoerotic passion could be seen as an inevitable part of the depiction of desire and attraction.

It is more difficult to discuss the lesbian possibilities of the play accurately. Here again, Ovid may shed helpful light: the story of Iphis and Ianthe is a tale of a youthful couple who love and are to be married – but both are girls. Iphis has been brought up as a boy to avoid a curse but loves Ianthe and longs for their wedding night. Golding's words are strikingly similar to the conundrum Sebastian presents to Olivia:

> Herself, a maiden, with a maid (right strange!) in love became.
>
> (*Metamorphoses*, 291)

'I am the man': Viola as Cesario

When Shakespeare's heroines assume a male disguise, they often do so for survival (Rosalind in *As You Like It* for example). Portia in *The Merchant of Venice* desires to gain a male advantage, successfully transforming herself into a young defence barrister. The disguise itself encourages a degree of ribald comedy and offers the heroine the ability to mock male braggadocio: Rosalind appears to relish the 'gallant curtle-axe upon my thigh/A boar-spear in my hand' and a 'swashing and a martial outside' *AYL*,1.3.114–5,7). The heroines' consciousness of difference can be a temporary liberation from petticoats and modesty; often forms part of the humour of the play and, in Portia's case, establishes her intellectual superiority over Bassanio and Antonio. Portia's disguise is never suspected; in *Twelfth Night* several characters comment on Cesario's girlishness. Orsino's description in Act 1 leads the way:

> they shall yet belie thy happy years
> That say thou art a man. Diana's lip

Is not more smooth and rubious. Thy small pipe
Is as the maiden's organ, shrill and sound,
And all is semblative a woman's part.

(1.4.30–4)

In *Much Ado* Beatrice expresses desire to be a man, whereas
Viola expresses dissatisfaction with her condition as it distances
her from Orsino. In disguise, she is a 'poor monster' and
dissembling is a 'wickedness' that tempts the resourcefulness
of Satan. Viola's case is exceptional: the jokes shared with the
audience about her lack of masculinity are always exploiting
complex ironies inherent in her situation. The scenes between
Viola and Sir Andrew are invariably played for laughs: he's a
big coward; she's a girl. But, uniquely, Viola's disguise is an
attempt to re-create a lost twin:

He named Sebastian. I my brother know
Yet living in my glass. Even such and so
In favour was my brother, and he went
Still in this fashion, colour, ornament,
For him I imitate.

(3.4.376–80)

Portia and Rosalind can enjoy, even exploit, their temporary
transvestism. It is altogether a more poignant business with
Viola. It is intriguing that she initially conceives herself as
a 'eunuch', a castrated male rather than a girl in a man's
clothes. Later, she dismisses her story as a 'blank' – she cannot
surmise what might be written on the empty pages of her
uncertain narrative. When she terms herself a 'monster' she
goes further still. On stage, she is never called 'Viola' until
re-united with her twin, and her name is then passed between
them three times in rapid succession. The epiphany implied
in the title is the confrontation of these two in the final scene
where both look upon their likeness and, in doing so, recover
their individual identities. Shakespeare moves beyond theatre

time in postponing the moment when Viola can become 'Orsino's mistress and his fancy's queen'; neither Orsino nor the audience will see her in her female identity, whereas it is quite usual for Rosalind to appear at the end of *As You Like It* attired in a handy wedding dress. In retaining Viola's disguise, Shakespeare keeps gender ambiguity at the forefront of the drama. As the couples exit at the end of the play we witness, first, Olivia and Sebastian, the conventional courtly couple, then Orsino and Cesario, the courtly Duke with young attractive male. Orsino refers to Cesario as 'the lamb that I do love' – is he in love with Cesario, or with Viola? And does it matter?

Twelfth Night and romantic comedy: Defining genre

Twelfth Night seems to conform, obligingly, to every convention of romantic comedy as Shakespeare's last, triumphant version of the genre with its 'brazen plundering of virtually all Shakespeare's previous comedies for characters, predicaments, theatrical devices and motifs.' (Kiernan Ryan, *Shakespeare's Comedies*, 2009, 235) Love is elevated throughout as the ideal state to which everyone aspires, and the play duly concludes with the promise of joint marriage ceremonies. Illyria is a place which appears remote from the sordid commercial bustle of the urban world; it offers music, festivity and 'golden time'. There is ample opportunity for laughter, whether at drunken antics or sophisticated verbal play. Obstacles are overcome and confusion yields to benign resolution. Yet, while the final effect of the drama might be joyous, the action and language of the play is, of course, more complex. As John Creaser argues, 'the subject of drama is confusion: whether evoking horror or hope, drama gives shape to the disarray and precariousness of our lives' ('Forms of confusion' in *Cambridge Companion to Shakespearean*

Comedy, 2001, 81). The familiar model of comedy featuring a period of threatened chaos which can resolve in marriage, perhaps with all the comic potential of disguise and mistaken identities is, in fact, Shakespeare's invention; he shaped existing theatrical traditions into the definitive experience of romantic comedy. Shakespeare's comedies were all written at a time of considerable debate over traditions of theatrical comedy, with new vernacular sub-genres appearing from the 1550s. Shakespeare's contemporary, playwright Ben Jonson, supplies a valuable basis for comparison:

> [Comedy] would show an Image of the times,
> And sport with human follies, not with crimes.
>
> (*Every Man in his Humour,* 1598)

Jonson's city comedies engage satirically with the urban issues of money, class and status, sex. Other playwrights such as John Lyly chose classical subjects and modelled their plots on Plautus and Terence. Theatre-goers clearly enjoyed the robustly carnivalesque as well as the elegant re-hashing of classical sources from the university wits. From the late sixteenth century, dramatists experimented with comic structures, settings and subject-matter to the extent that Renaissance comedy has been singled out for its 'myriad configurations' (Jill Levenson, 'Comedy' in *The Cambridge Companion to English Renaissance Drama,* 1994). *Twelfth Night* juxtaposes the rarefied, literary sensitivities of Orsino with the roistering activities of Sir Toby, rather as *Midsummer Night's Dream* moves between the Athenian court and Bottom's 'hempen homespuns'. Shakespeare's comic world offers a plurality of perspectives; it extends and includes and, as such, should be distinguished from the narrower vision of Jonsonian satire. Shakespeare never claims a didactic intention even where 'human follies' play their part. A pervasive anti-comic mood cannot be ignored, however: all the comedies and romances emphasize the extraordinary propensity for human affairs to go awry, sometimes from individual malice, sometimes from more random, and therefore troubling, causes.

Most commentators on the plays would concur with Lisa Hopkins that '[the] most outstanding feature of Shakespearean comedy is its pervading obsession with marriage' (Lisa Hopkins, 'Marriage as Comic Closure' in *Shakespeare's Comedies*, ed. Emma Smith, 2004, 36). In terms of both courtship and marriage, the most radical notion central to Shakespeare's mature comedies must be the prevalence of the female voice and the possibility of female choice. The aspiration towards companionate marriage; a union of emotional intimacy and equality, is a significant factor. In *Twelfth Night*, Olivia's refusal of Orsino is highly revealing in this respect. Were marriage principally a formal (or financial) arrangement for reasons of status and class, then obviously she would marry Orsino. Toby, speaking as the conservative older male, sees the Duke as 'above her degree'. Clearly it would be an advantageous match and, as her father and brother are lost to her, one which might be immediately appealing. Even Olivia concedes how immaculate Orsino is as a suitor, and in the language of her rejection there is perhaps a note of bewilderment:

Your lord does know my mind: I cannot love him.
Yet I suppose him virtuous, know him noble,
Of great estate, of fresh and stainless youth,
In voices well-divulged, free, learn'd and valiant,
And in dimension and the shape of nature
A gracious person; but yet I cannot love him.

(1.5.249–54)

She expects, in other words, to feel overwhelmed by passion. The duke is socially appropriate and she can respect his virtues, but that is not enough. Her private and subjective world operates independently from convention. And, indeed, once she is in love, she constantly articulates the pain and intensity of her feelings. Comparing herself to the tortured bear tied to the stake, she woos the reluctant Cesario and proposes marriage to Sebastian. Her voice is thus a commanding one; she expects self-determination and, above all, choice. When she brutally rejects Orsino in the final scene, she is already married yet she elects to dismiss him in such unambiguous terms that he calls her an 'uncivil lady'. She has offended against courtly codes of female reticence and courtesy. For Viola, similarly, love is stronger than the restraining etiquette of class and gender. Her protestation at the end of the play, that she loves Orsino 'More than I love these eyes. More than my life' bursts from her, despite Orsino's threats of violence. And she speaks, significantly, before Sebastian returns to the stage to rescue and confirm her identity as female twin. Neither Olivia nor Viola nor, indeed, Maria, appears as 'the silent woman' of the (male-authored) conduct books of the period. In this play, Shakespeare doesn't offer one outspoken heroine as he does in *Much Ado* or *As You Like It*, nor does he simply employ disguise as a means of transient opportunity and freedom. Viola is resilient from her first appearance; Olivia rules a household and expects to make her own choices and judgements. She even takes charge of the wedding arrangements – '[here] at my house and at my proper cost.'

Audience expectation is an absorbing question of any critique of genre: at what point in a play does an audience begin to feel a confident likelihood of a happy outcome? It is a familiar observation that *Twelfth Night*, in common with other mature comedies, opens on a world of tragic possibility with death and mourning dominating the first scenes. How does the play emerge from this initial solemnity? Rather than simply identifying Toby and his farcical excesses as contrary to tragedy, it might be more constructive to see Shakespeare's comic vision as paralleling the play's tragic possibilities. The verbal and visual complexity of the play constantly disorientates – 'Nothing that is so, is so' (4.1.8). Viola's first words, for example, express grief for her brother's loss: 'My brother he is in Elysium.' But the Captain immediately counters this with an image of hope and endurance:

> I saw your brother,
> Most provident in peril, bind himself –
> Courage and hope both teaching him the practice –
> To a strong mast that lived upon the sea,
> Where, like Arion on the dolphin's back,
> I saw him hold acquaintance with the waves
> So long as I could see.

(1.2.10–16)

Sebastian's youthful resourcefulness and determination to survive is immediately matched by Viola herself, as if she patterns herself on what the Captain has just said. She will become a version of her brother as a means of ensuring their joint survival. The combination of robust practicality fused with connotations of the magical and mythological creates a distinctive tone signalling hope and redemption. Olivia's grief differs from Viola's in that her brother is truly lost to her, but its inherent pointlessness is mocked by Feste:

> The more fool, madonna, to mourn for your brother's soul, being in heaven.

(1.5.66–7)

It is a point which Olivia concedes as she defends Feste against Malvolio's opposition. In this way we see language, plus the inventiveness of the play's women, holding out possibilities of re-invention and renewal. Audience expectation is subtly manoeuvred towards a positive outcome even from unpromising beginnings. The shipwreck and the bereavement have had a similar effect: a world turned upside down, from which there may be 'a happiness not yet attained, a brave new world wherein man's life may be fuller, his sensations more exquisite and his joys more widespread' (H. B. Charlton, cited Ryan, *Shakespeare*, 2002, 106).

Song in *Twelfth Night*

Music features in all Shakespeare's comedies and romances, ranging from bawdy Elizabethan ballads to elaborate courtly song-settings with instrumental accompaniment. In *Twelfth Night*, uniquely, music begins and ends the play, encompassing these varied forms of musical expression. Music is, of course, an entertainment in itself; creating its own mood and atmosphere. As an aspect of performance, song demands that the on-stage players become an audience; during Feste's songs speech and action are entirely halted. Music also suggests a particular social milieu or context. At the opening of *Twelfth Night*, the chamber music summoned by Orsino would be played by the household consort resident in his court, immediately establishing his status as a Renaissance aristocrat. Castiglione's *The Courtier* (1528) emphasizes the importance of understanding and appreciating music; interestingly, the debate also considers whether music might render a man 'effeminate':

> So you must not wish to deprive our courtier of music, which not only soothes the souls of men but often tames wild beasts. Indeed, the man who does not enjoy music can be sure that there is no harmony in his soul. And remember that it has such powers that once it caused a fish to let itself be ridden by a man over the tempestuous sea.

Feste's closing song, on the other hand, typifies Elizabethan minstrelsy, albeit in particularly ambiguous and elusive style. The lyrical, melancholy music of the play and the jester's ballad function as bookends to the drama, drawing attention to the studied artifice of the entire play.

The wordless music of the opening establishes the tone of Orsino's erotic yearning and discontent, a mood not dispelled until the third scene and Sir Toby's raucous festivities. Orsino alludes to conventional Renaissance theory of music in his belief that his musicians have the power to assuage his troubled spirit. Indeed, the magical force of music is implied in the next scene in the Captain's attempt to reassure Viola that her brother might live, carried to safety like 'Arion on the dolphin's back'. In Ovid's *Fasti*, Arion's songs charm a dolphin to carry him to dry land, rescuing him from death at sea. *A Midsummer Night's Dream* draws on the same idea that music can subdue the waves and command Nature:

> once I sat upon a promontory
> And heard a mermaid on a dolphin's back
> Uttering such dulcet and harmonious breath
> That the rude sea grew civil at her song.

(2.1.149–52)

Renaissance humanist belief in the power of music was widespread; Milton frequently employs musical harmony to symbolize the macrocosmic harmony of the created universe. This classical (Platonic and Pythagorean) concept became fused with Christian cosmology: Olivia's reference to the 'music of the spheres' implies divine music, audible to man before the Fall. Lorenzo articulates precisely this notion in *The Merchant of Venice*:

> There's not the smallest orb which thou behold'st
> But in his motion like an angel sings,
> Still quiring to the young ey'd cherubins;
> Such harmony is in immortal souls,
> But whilst this muddy vesture of decay
> Doth grossly close it in, we cannot hear it …

(5, 1, 60–6)

Such courtly romantic sentiment and rarefied emotion is exemplified in the song Orsino later requests Feste to perform, 'Come away, come away, death'. He elevates the song for its idyllic simplicity and innocence, harking back to a mythical 'old age'; Viola too praises it for 'giv[ing] a very echo to the seat / Where love is throned' (2.4.21–2). In Orsino's imagination love, death and music are united, revealing the extent to which he is arrested in his self-image of rejected lover:

> I am slain by a fair cruel maid.
> My shroud of white, stuck all with yew,
> O prepare it.
> My part of death no one so true
> Did share it.

(2.4.54–8)

The song is more than 'background' music; it creates the complex theatrical moment where Orsino and Viola are both isolated in contemplation of their unrequited loves and Viola comes as close as possible to communicating her concealed identity to Orsino. The music sets Orsino's court apart from other spaces in the play: there is a consistency here which is lacking in Olivia's court with its warring and discordant elements.

Intriguingly, Toby first requests from Feste a 'love song', a poignant one in Toby's case since it concludes that 'Youth's a stuff will not endure'. And this is perhaps the reason for Toby's response – 'A contagious breath', a statement which might mean that the song is affecting, or, more brutally, that Feste's breath stinks. Toby certainly rebels in challenging his fellow revellers to a very different type of music:

> But shall we make the welkin dance indeed? Shall we rouse the night-owl in a catch [...]?

(2.3.56–7)

A catch song can only be secular, populist and rowdy – precisely what Malvolio as 'a kind of Puritan' would object to, as he does:

> My masters, are you mad or what are you? Have you no wit, manners nor honesty but to gabble like tinkers at this time of night? Do ye make an alehouse out of my lady's house [...]?
>
> (2.3.85–8)

This midnight scene is the heart of the play's revelry and can readily be connected with the festivities of twelfth night itself. Fragments of five songs are included, four of which can be identified as familiar to the contemporary audience, suggesting that Shakespeare desires to encourage participation in Toby's and Feste's mockery of Malvolio (see Arden 3, 385–94 for songs and music). These songs operate on a number of levels in that:

- they are in themselves amusing and offer almost unlimited licence for bawdiness ('I shall never begin if I hold my peace' which contains suggestions of 'piece' or penis)
- they demonstrate the centrality of Feste and also his musical versatility from love ballad to street song
- they connect the play with its title in the audience's mind
- they establish a defiant counter-mood to Olivia's mourning
- they establish the opposition between Toby and Malvolio and further the rivalry between Feste and Malvolio

This scene of drunken carousing and Toby's offended sense of rank provoke the revenge against Malvolio. A revenge, furthermore, that Feste pursues through song: when he appears as himself to the incarcerated Malvolio, his snatches of song seem designed to torment. 'My lady ... loves another', with its implication that Toby's ambition has been misplaced, was a familiar song by William Cornish. And he leaves

Malvolio with a mocking farewell, 'I am gone, sir, and anon, sir' flaunting his own liberty and concluding 'Adieu goodman devil' which firmly establishes the victory of jester over Puritan.

Feste's final riddling and evocative song also exists in original form; it is a song for solo voice in a haunting minor key, perhaps the very opposite to the marriage and dance music that concludes *As You Like It* or *Much Ado*. The refrain, 'For the rain it raineth every day' has its own 'What you Will' quality: through boyhood, youth and age, the unfolding scenes of life, there will be rain. As Barber observes, it is a song 'accepting disillusion', yet it reminds us that the play itself 'is keeping out the wind and the rain' (Barber, 260).

Renaissance Theatre Company production for stage and screen (1987/8)

Branagh's Renaissance Theatre production of *Twelfth Night* appeared at the Lyric Studios, Hammersmith in December 1987, subsequently touring before being re-made as a film for Thames Television in December 1988 under the directorship of Paul Kafno. The film seems, at the beginning, to be a strikingly bleak and melancholy interpretation of the text; visually a complete contrast to the 1980 BBC traditional Elizabethan country house version. Branagh made the unusual decision to preserve the effect of the stage version, with its wintry outdoor setting, giving the film a static and frozen atmosphere. The period is impliedly late Victorian/Edwardian; the set features iron gates and broken crosses; a landscape of leafless tress is distantly suggested; the effect resembles a ruined graveyard more than a Renaissance palace. Classical statuary might suggest a Mediterranean or Greek Illyria. The stark black and white effects are repeated in the unrelieved black and grey shades of the costumes worn by the major characters. Orsino's Illyria is an elegiac, perhaps effete, world. In common with Trevor Nunn's 1996 film, the opening two scenes are reversed: storm, shipwreck and Viola's grief and loss begin the drama. Theatre critic Michael Billington reviewed this as 'a pointless reversal that completely ignores the first scene's announcement of the play's major themes' (*Directors' Shakespeare: Approaches to 'Twelfth Night'*, 1990, xvii). Orsino's speech is uttered not in the usual courtly setting but outside in the falling snow. This is clearly a waste-land Illyria; like a fairy or folk tale, Orsino is condemned to pursue forever a coldly remote Olivia. It is certainly a muted and funereal opening, more in tune with tragedy than festive comedy. Olivia disappears behind the large closed door, or behind her black veil, refusing to engage with Orsino's courtship, while Orsino identifies himself as the tormented Actaeon. Orsino's melancholy also pervades the scenes with Viola, particularly their introverted preoccupation throughout Feste's 'Come away, come away death'. Branagh himself later observed that he wanted the 'mysterious Victorian garden' to 'bring out the brooding melancholy of the play ... [the] dark undertow of rejection and loneliness and cruelty experienced by many of the characters' (*Beginning*, 1989, 198). The bleakness of the set is intensified by the characterization of Feste – far from a merry jester in this version. Anton Lesser's unkempt and frequently drunk Feste appears often withdrawn and solitary as he moves with his large carpet bag between the two households. Malvolio, exuding disapproval as the severe Puritan, seems entirely at one with the atmosphere of cheerless denial.

How, then, can this interpretation of the play accommodate its festive implications? As a Christian festival, Twelfth Night would seem to be the essence of the carnivalesque and, indeed, has often been discussed in this light. The occasion is one of feasting and merrymaking, commanded by a Lord of Misrule who ensures the necessary topsy-turvy confusion of the carnival spirit. Branagh and Kafno resolve this effectively: as if the mournfulness of Olivia's household precipitates Sir

Toby into extreme reaction; the carnivalesque is a form of rebellion against his niece's studied withdrawal. The scene of midnight revelry – here beside a glowing brazier – is a tour de force of their drunken carousing and combined determination to pursue revenge against Malvolio. When Maria appears, first, to upbraid Toby she is drawn into the party atmosphere, wooed by Toby's exaggerated singing. Malvolio, absurd in his white night-shirt and night-cap, will never be seduced by merriment and must be punished for his failure to participate.

In festive spirit, the appearance of the Christmas tree at the beginning of Act 2 signals the possibility of renewal, as well as usefully becoming the box-tree necessary for the further humiliation of Malvolio in Act 3. There is no doubt that this production suggests the victory of the carnivalesque over the puritanical: Malvolio's punishment is made brutally savage in his imprisonment in the 'dark house' and he emerges into the light of the final scene totally humiliated. His final, off-stage, cry of revenge seems impotent as he disappears out of the gate. Feste's victory over him is complete: he quotes Malvolio's earlier insults and then adds his crowning victory – 'And thus the whirligig of time brings in his revenges'. But the phrase is whispered by Lesser, as if a private feud has now been settled.

Branagh chooses to leave the homoerotic possibilities of the play ambiguous: Sebastian is certainly the epitome of sensibility here – he weeps over the loss of his sister and seems equally moved by his final reunion with Antonio. The comedy of Viola's disguise is exaggerated in the fight-scene with Sir Andrew where the terrified Viola falls screaming to the ground before Andrew has raised his sword. The comedy of the encounter is also exploited through Sir Andrew's greater height but overwhelming cowardice. In the end Branagh elects heteronormativity though, symbolizing this in the film's lighting and setting: the muted light of the opening scenes gives way to bright sunshine and the suggestion of reviving greenness. Sebastian's Act 4 soliloquy, 'This is the air, that is the glorious sun', transforms Illyria completely: brilliant sunshine has replaced the wintry opening now Olivia has secured Sebastian. Cesario can become Viola – but not, of course, within the scope of the film. Indeed, the final moments are subtle and elusive: the kiss between Orsino and Cesario still teeters on the verge of unresolved sexuality – why would Orsino address his future wife as 'Boy'? In the final frames we see the dejected and wounded Sir Andrew, an unwelcome guest now spurned by Toby; Antonio, silently released from his handcuffs simply disappears. In an original final gesture, Feste concludes his last song then he too exits through the iron gate as if departing forever.

Further thinking

> Would interpreting *Othello* or *Much Ado* in the light of Queer Theory shed an interesting light on aspects of the play(s)?

> Thinking about comedy as a genre, how far would you agree with the Romantic writer Schlegel that it is as powerful as tragedy?

> In Kafno's film version of *Twelfth Night*, Malvolio is totally humiliated. Compare other productions of the play and consider how far modern audiences tend to sympathize with Malvolio's plight at the end of the drama.

Afterlives ...

Mary Cowden Clarke's *The Girlhood of Shakespeare's Heroines* (1850–2) is an extraordinary attempt to invent prequels to fifteen of the plays. 'Olivia: The Lady of Illyria' addresses Olivia's mistrust of aggressive masculinity by hinting at incest and child abuse. Olivia desires to fall in love with a (male or female) version of her beloved brother. A wicked (Victorian) gentleman appears to have a predatory interest in young girls ...

4

Measure for Measure (and its problems …)

It was F. S. Boas in *Shakspere [sic] and his Predecessors* (1896), who first named *Measure for Measure* a 'problem play'. It was a label used at the time to describe the drama of radical European playwrights such as Henrik Ibsen, and while considered rather old-fashioned by today's critics, it is still to be replaced by a more satisfactory term. In the first instance, the categorizing of the play as problematic stemmed mainly from the difficulties encountered in assigning it a neat generic identity: its dark, often savage, undertones making it unfit for a comedy and its happy resolution (albeit a problem in itself) excluding it from the tragedies. Over the centuries, emphasis has moved from the problems *with* the play to the problems explored *by* it, with critics and audiences alike coming to agree with George Bernard Shaw's view that its author was several hundred years ahead of his time.

This chapter considers some 'problematic' areas of the play:

- the psychosexual complexities of the individual
- the relationship between religious faith and human behaviour
- the 'wrapping up' of the drama
- and how these were treated by one Restoration dramatist, William Davenant.

Reading Shakespeare psychoanalytically

In *Psychoanalysis and Shakespeare* (1964), Norman Holland remarks how 'psychoanalysis seems to have touched everyone from the carefree delinquent on the corner to the scholar in his study' (3). Leaving aside the rather outdated expression, this is an observation that still holds true. Commenting on the size of someone's ego, noting slips of the tongue (parapraxis), or recognizing the phallic imagery of car advertising, are all habits of mind that can be traced back to psychoanalytic theory. Yet if Freudianism is deeply rooted in everyday discourse and thought processes, its epistemological validity is less secure. For decades now, Freudian psychoanalysis has been taken to task for being ineffective as a practice, lacking in rigour as a scientific discipline, male-dominated in its aims and outcomes, and reductive and deterministic as a theory of the mind. Why then has it gained such a strong foothold in the modern consciousness and in literary studies in particular?

Psychoanalysis and literary criticism are often said to share certain characteristics. Both are interested in what lies beneath the surface, in the indirect expression of ideas or states of mind, in probing the significance of absence and the unstated, and in notions of selfhood. Equally, both pay close attention to words, whether found in the text of the writer or the talk of the patient under analysis. There are also historical and biographical convergences. The late nineteenth century saw the emergence of Freudianism and literary criticism as we know it today and their growing up together may well have fostered connections between them. While there is a tendency to think of the art discipline as being the main 'borrower' in the relationship, there is a strong case to be made for literary works (*Hamlet*, for example) having played an active role in the formation of the new science. Extremely well read, a great admirer of Shakespeare, and intrigued by the psychology of creativity, Freud produced a major volume on art and literature, and made frequent reference to literary texts from a range of periods in his other writings.

Reading Shakespeare psychoanalytically can be daunting. *The Standard Edition of the Complete Psychological Works of Sigmund Freud* (1953–74), translated and edited by James Strachey, runs to twenty-four volumes and includes writing produced over four decades. Acquiring even a rudimentary grasp of such a huge body of material would be an onerous preliminary task to have to complete before applying psychoanalytic ideas to a literary text; fortunately, much of the critical practice which derives from psychoanalytical concepts focuses on a relatively contained area of Freud's work. Being familiar with Freudian notions such as the unconscious (the part of the mind which is beyond our control and knowledge), repression (the mechanism by which desires and traumas are pushed from our consciousness) and sublimation (the transformation of what has been repressed into socially acceptable endeavours) provides a sturdy foundation for reading and applying psychoanalytic literary theory.

Freud's narrative of human development sees the individual self as radically split from an early stage. While initially driven by what Freud terms the 'pleasure principle' to gratify emotional and physical desires, people soon learn to bow down to the 'reality principle' as exterior forces threaten repercussions which outweigh immediate gratification. This process involves the 'id' and the 'ego': the former being the libidinous, greedy part of us and the latter the part which reins it in and makes it behave in public. Freud uses an equine analogy to explain his theory of the mind:

> The ego represents what may be called reason and common sense, in contrast to the id, which contains the passions ... in its [the ego's] relation to the id it is like a man on horseback who has to hold in check the superior strength of the horse.
>
> (The Pelican Freud Library, vol. 11, 364)

Yet while the rider can separate himself from the beast beneath him, the id and the ego remain connected, the latter developing in response to the former. The relationship between the two is made more complex by the 'super-ego', forces of external authority such as the church and the state, the roots of which Freud locates in the figure of the father. The Oedipus complex provides the most familiar paradigm of the id, the ego and the super-ego: the male child takes his mother as his first object of desire, grows to realize that the father has invincible power, fears castration (having recognized the 'absent' genitalia of the female), and finally submits to the law of the father. His desire for the mother now repressed, it will subsequently be transferred onto other females once puberty arrives.

Freud, rather like teachers of English Literature, is often accused of boiling everything down to sex and it is certainly the case that he believed sexuality to be at the core of the human. In this regard, *Measure for Measure* lends itself particularly well to a psychoanalytic approach, dominated as it is by the psychosexual lives of individuals and wider issues concerning the control of sexual behaviour in society. Over the past half century or so, critics have generated varied readings of the play's presentation of sexuality: at one extreme regarding it as refreshingly open and life-affirming and at another as overwhelmingly polluting and menacing. Arguably, the only normative sexual relationship is that between Claudio and Juliet, its fertile outcome described in imagery conspicuously at odds with the prevailing idiom of the play:

Your brother and his lover have embrac'd;
As those that feed grow full, as blossoming time
That from the seedness the bare fallow brings
To teeming foison, even so her plenteous womb
Expresseth his full tilth and husbandry.

(1.4.40–4)

Where sexuality here is defined in terms of natural beauty and fecundity, elsewhere in the play it is more commonly associated with disease, aggression and 'dark corners', the two main sites of the dramatic action – the brothel and the prison – seeming to signal a clear trajectory from desire to punishment.

It is of course true that, at the outset of the drama at least, the audience is offered an alternative to the sordidness of sexuality through the puritanism of Angelo and through Isabella's decision to commit herself to the convent. It is not long, however, before the Deputy's commitment to asceticism breaks down and he exhorts the novitiate to give herself up to 'sweet uncleanness' (2.4.54), seeming to validate Freud's belief that 'No substitutive or reactive formations and no sublimations will suffice to remove the repressed instinct's persisting tension' (The Pelican Freud Library, vol. 11, 315). Angelo's proposition to Isabella is indisputably hypocritical and base, yet his self-reflectiveness prevents him from assuming a straightforwardly villainous role and creates the impression of a complex personality open to psychoanalytic interpretation. Once alone after his first encounter with Isabella, he attempts to analyze the sexual arousal he has experienced while in her presence, wondering that 'modesty may more betray our sense/Than woman's lightness' (2.2.169–70). Freudian theory offers a number of explanations as to why what can be assumed to be Angelo's first erotic experience is stimulated by a nun-in-waiting rather than 'the strumpet/With all her double vigour, art and nature' (2.2.183–4). One such can be found in a paper entitled 'On the Universal Tendency to Debasement in the Sphere of Love' (1912) in which Freud argues that 'the psychical value of erotic needs is reduced as soon as their satisfaction becomes easy. An obstacle is required in order to heighten libido' (The Freud Pelican Library, vol. 7, 256). For Angelo, then, the obstacle of a young woman on the brink of devoting herself to a life of chastity proves a good deal more arousing than the easy availability of the prostitute.

Isabella's psychosexuality has possibly received even more critical attention than Angelo's. The focus of such attention falls most frequently on her rebuttal of the Deputy's indecent proposal:

                        were I under the terms of death,
          Th'impression of keen whips I'd wear as rubies,
          And strip myself to death as to a bed
          That longing have been sick for, ere I'd yield
          My body up to shame.

                                                    (2.4.100–4)

This speech is often cited as evidence of what F. R. Leavis
called 'the sensuality of martyrdom' ('The Greatness of
Measure for Measure', *Scrutiny*, 10, 234), an eroticism which
springs from the whips and torments of the saint-in-waiting
or the stigmatic. This link between fervent religiosity and
sexual pleasure is centuries old and accords with Freud's
contention that religion itself is based 'on the suppression,
the renunciation, of certain instinctual impulses' (The Pelican
Freud Library, vol. 13, 39). In Freudian terms, Isabella's words
betray the instinctive desires which have been sublimated into
Christian ritual. While some feminist critics have resisted a
psychoanalytic reading of the speech, preferring to see it more
in terms of Isabella's insistence on determining her own body
and bodily practices, and some new historicists have placed
it in the context of well-known lives of the saints, few deny
that the language is more evocative of heated desire than cold
chastity. Some commentators have gone so far as likening
Shakespeare's choice of words here to the writings of the
Marquis de Sade: Isabella playing the passive masochist to
Angelo's active sadist (Freud saw the contrast between the two
as a universal characteristic of human sexuality).
     Carolyn E. Brown's article 'Erotic Religious Flagellation
and Shakespeare's *Measure for Measure*' (*ELR*, 16, 1986)
marries psychoanalysis and historicism in an argument that
places Shakespeare's heroine in an unholy *ménage à trois*, in
which 'The Duke subliminally enjoys observing brutal acts,
Angelo inflicting them, Isabella receiving them' (165).

⟨?⟩ *Look over 1.4.1–15 of* **Measure for Measure** *and then read the extract from Brown's article printed below:*

Isabella herself unwittingly betrays the sexual satisfaction that she secretly derives from her life of repression. She regards severe restraints as 'privileges,' and they bring her so much satisfaction that she requests more – 'And have you nuns no farther privileges?'(1.4.1). Isabella betrays one of the danger signs that critics of flagellation noted in actual anchorites: she is beginning to enjoy her rigorous self-abnegation more than she should, and, thus subjecting herself to more than is required. Even Francisca, a fellow nun who appreciates self-denial, thinks Isabella's request gratuitous and expresses incredulity: 'Are not these large enough?' (1.4.2). Isabella fears that Francisca detects her pleasure-in-pain, and her insecurities cause her to indict herself in her own denial:

Yes, truly; I speak not as desiring more,
But rather wishing a more strict restraint
Upon the sisters stood, the votarists of Saint Clare.

(ll.3–5)

Francisca does not intimate a sexual failing in the novitiate, but Isabella's guilt makes her read a slight and prods her to justify her request. Isabella overreacts and denies that restraints satisfy her 'desires' or that she 'desires' restraints and makes a verbal slip, speaking of self-denial in conjunction with desires and revealing the perversion of her religious life ... Consciously, she thinks that her dedication to pain and self-denial attests to her spiritual purity and repudiation of worldly pleasures; subconsciously, however, she fears a perverse pleasure and guardedly tries to deny it.

(153)

⑦ *And now ...*

- Pick out terms and ideas which are clearly grounded in psychoanalytic thought.

- How convincing do you find Brown's argument that Isabella is dedicated 'to pain and self-denial'?

- Could you offer any other reading of Isabella's behaviour and speech in this scene?

Brown's analysis of the scene employs some core Freudian concepts: repression, sublimation and masochism. Isabella's eagerness to join the order of Saint Clare (known for its austerity) is seen to reveal her repressed sexuality and the kind of masochistic desire recognized in Freudianism as a concomitant of the religious disposition. The pleasure she gains from such severity is detected through linguistic slips, in Freudian terms one of the most common manifestations of unconscious forces at work.

Opening *in medias res,* the audience assumes that the women have been discussing the rules of the convent, the opening question being posed by Isabella as a means of checking that she has correctly understood its restrictions and allowances (one of the most puzzling aspects of the extract is Brown's insistence on reading 'privileges' not as signifying allowed freedoms, but 'restraint'). This is the first time Isabella appears on stage; nonetheless, from her first four lines, Brown reads signs of a highly complex, even pathological, psychology. Such a reading omits the less exciting possibility that the scene simply depicts an exchange between an overzealous 'new girl', keen to impress her superior – or even that a devotion to Christ could be genuine.

Critical methods such as Brown's are sometimes taken to task by Shakespearean scholars. In *Appropriating Shakespeare* (1993), a polemical study of late twentieth-century literary approaches, Brian Vickers outlines what he sees as the weaknesses inherent in psychoanalytic criticism:

> Literary critics ... ignore the richness of the societies depicted, the forces of history, the role of institutions and office, conflicts of love and duty, or anything else except the psycho-sexual nature of the main characters ... Psychocritics are essentially concerned with individuals, often 'analysing' them in separate character-studies, that most primitive of critical modes.
>
> (284–5)

And Vickers is by no means alone in his objections. For new historicists, such an approach is incompatible with their commitment to contextual readings: how, they ask, can a theoretical framework rooted in a late nineteenth-century scientific paradigm be imposed on an early modern work and how can what is essentially a Romantic view of individual selfhood be grafted onto fictional figures created by and for the Renaissance mind. To apply Freudian concepts to dramatic characters formed in the early seventeenth century is to assume a timeless universal humanity at odds with today's literary-critical outlook. Indeed, as Vickers points out, the very notion of 'characters' is one that has been thoroughly interrogated by critical theorists who prefer to talk of them as representatives of 'sites of struggle', agents of **polyphony**, or aesthetic effects of the text. There is, perhaps, no getting away from the fact that while patients under psychoanalysis come with a rich and complex history of experiences for the analyst to draw upon, Shakespearean characters have nothing to offer the critic beyond the script which, when performed, creates what is ultimately an *illusion* of interiority and a past life.

For all the arguments ranged against psychoanalytic criticism, it remains an active and influential discipline. Since the 1980s psychoanalytic literary studies have been transformed by the work of French psychoanalyst, Jacques Lacan. Convinced that Freud's ideas had been diluted to make them more palatable for the mainstream, Lacan set about a radical review of the original writings. One of his major conclusions was that the unconscious is structured like a language: an idea that served to bring the linguistic to the forefront of psychoanalytic theory and proved to be a profound influence on post-structuralist thought. One of today's leading literary theorists, Catherine Belsey, has drawn extensively on Lacan's ideas in her work on subjectivity and desire. In *Shakespeare in Theory and Practice* (2008), she puts forward a vision of psychoanalytic literary practice that moves it away from character to the text itself. The following extract from this study raises some thought-provoking questions with which to conclude this section:

> What if ... the Freudian account of the unconscious, modified and developed by Lacan's recognition of Saussurean linguistics, were to offer us, rather than a version of the human condition, whether eternal or histori-cally relative, an approach to the necessary condition of meaning? Then the advantage of psychoanalysis for historicists would lie not in its account of themes, or what is *meant by* early modern texts, but rather in its perception of the waywardness of textuality itself ... Its contribution would be methodological rather than explanatory, a way above all of paying attention to the workings of the texts.
>
> (16–17)

Tensions between the old and the new: *Measure for Measure* and the Bible

Measure for Measure was first performed in 1604, the same year that James I endorsed Parliament's tightening of anti-Catholic legislation. Following on from the first year of his reign, which saw him take a rather more tolerant attitude to the religious minority, this came as somewhat of a surprise, and some critics have suggested that Shakespeare's play is a dramatization of the King's *volte face*, with the sudden tightening of Vienna's laws providing a fictional parallel to the renewed persecution of recusants. This is, of course, only speculation and stands as one theory among several which find contemporary religious debates being played out in the drama. It has also been read as an anti-Catholic satire, a sub-genre which can be traced back to the medieval period. Such a reading colours, even distorts, some of the most crucial issues of the play, such as Isabella's motivations for entering the convent. Mocking conventual life was a staple of anti-Catholic satire and Lucio's first words to Isabella 'Hail virgin, if you be –' (1.4.16), combining as they do an echo of the 'Hail Mary', one of the most recited prayers in the Catholic church, with the insinuation of sexual experience, could certainly be read as such. Where Catholics followed St Paul in believing celibacy to be a higher spiritual state than marriage (I Corinthians 7.1–11), early modern Protestants regarded marriage as the superior state, not least because it is endorsed in both the Gospels and the Old Testament. Isabella's novitiate status might have been regarded by some of Shakespeare's audience, then, as anachronistic and misguided, especially when compared to the alternative: the Duke's offer of the companionate marriage favoured by most Protestants.

Anti-Catholic satire or not, *Measure for Measure* is one of the most overtly Catholic of Shakespeare's works and one which dramatizes the enduring tensions between the old and new dispensations. One of the major shifts in Tudor religious faith and practice, and one which played a crucial role in defining Reformation Christianity, centred on the Bible in English. Enabled by the technology of the printing-press, it moved the heart of faith away from the sacred images of the pre-Schism church to the Scriptures, providing an increasingly literate population with an important means of self-improvement. Where Catholicism had kept the sacred texts away from the layman, insisting they should be mediated through the priest, Protestantism placed emphasis on both collective and individual Bible-reading. But which version of the Bible would have been read? Nowadays, there is a tendency to assume that Shakespeare and his contemporaries would have read the King James translation, though attention to chronology confirms that this was not the case. Also known as the Authorized Version, it was not completed until 1611, when Shakespeare was in the final stage of his career. Prior to this, the most commonly read version would have been the Geneva Bible (though the Bishop's Bible of 1568 was the one usually read aloud in churches). Published in its complete form in 1560, this particular text had been produced by Protestants forced into exile in Geneva during Mary Tudor's reign. Its lively, direct style had great appeal for the common reader and the 'most profitable annotations upon all the hard places', announced on its frontispiece and supplied in the margins, made it ideal for independent study.

The association of Shakespeare's plays and the Bible has a long and fascinating history and much scholarly work has gone into tracing the connections between these secular and sacred texts. In *Biblical References in Shakespeare's Comedies* (1993) Naseeb Shaheen points out that, as far as *Measure for Measure* is concerned, although 'there are many lines in the play that express religious ideas, the number of biblical references is not exceptionally large' (186). Yet while the *quantity* of biblical citations is unremarkable, the same could not be said of Shakespeare's choice of a familiar New Testament phrase to stand as the work's title. Christ's warning 'Judge not, that you be not judged. For with the judgement you pronounce you will be judged, and the measure you give will be the measure you get' (Matthew 7.1–2) resonates throughout the play, serving as a lens through which to view stage action and dialogue, as well as the Duke's 'final judgement'. How the morality of the biblical text is to be interpreted and acted upon is one of the central 'problems' of the play, raising some difficult questions. How far should Scripture provide a rule book for moral behaviour? How far should state law be in line with religious teaching? How far is an ideal morality workable in the real world? The title also invites an audience to consider the relationship between the Old and New Testaments, between the laws handed down by the patriarchs and the teachings of Christ. Taken as a simple statement 'measure for measure' evokes the letter of Mosaic Law: 'you shall give life for life, eye for eye, tooth for tooth' (Exodus 21.23–4); but taken as a fragment of the Gospel verses, it stands more as a question for debate.

Some critics such as G. Wilson Knight have regarded the play's title as its guiding force. In *The Wheel of Fire* (1930) Knight insists that 'the play must be read in the light of the Gospel teaching' (82), and works through an allegorical reading in which the Duke represents the new Christian order of the Gospels defeating the old Judaic laws embodied in the Pharisaical Angelo. This reading is certainly sustainable from the first half of the play. As the most outspoken critics of Christ's teaching and actions, the Pharisees are cast in the New Testament as staunch opponents of early Christianity and came to be associated in the early modern popular consciousness with hypocrisy, self-righteousness and unyielding formalism, all traits found in the 'precise' Angelo. At various points in the play, he articulates views of criminality which seem in direct opposition to Christ's teaching. His insisting to Escalus that ''Tis one thing to be tempted [...]/Another thing to fall' (2.1.17–18) runs counter to Jesus' pronouncement that 'every one who looks at a woman lustfully has already committed adultery with her in his heart' (Matthew 5.28). In forcing home the penalties for fornication at the same time as forcing a novitiate to have sex with him, he embodies exactly the kind of hypocrite Jesus instructs: 'take the log out of your own eye' (Matthew 7.5). However, such a straightforwardly dichotomous reading of the play becomes more and more complicated, if not untenable, as the play moves towards its puzzling conclusion.

Measure for Measure's troubling final act

Structure is perhaps the least noticeable element of a drama, especially in performance, when the audience tends to be caught up in the moment. Yet though playgoers might not pay that much attention to the juxtaposition of scenes, the ironic parallels or linguistic echoes of a play, they are nonetheless affected by them. After all, unlike the play-reader who can cast the script aside at any time, the theatre audience is bound – if only for the sake of politeness – to sit through the entire work, and to feel the accretive impact of its construction. Experienced theatregoers build up a kind of dramatic intuition and can sense when happiness is about to be blasted, when the apex of chaos has been reached, and when the loose ends are ready to be tied up.

The structure of *Measure for Measure* often proves testing to such dramatic intuition. Having played the role of Isabella to great acclaim in Adrian Noble's 1983 production of the play, Juliet Stevenson remarked on how the 'two halves of the play are antithetical: the first half is all abstract debate … the second is all action. It's like a casuistic tract followed by a Whitehall farce' (*Clamorous Voices,* Carol Rutter, 1988, 28). This view of the drama's structure is frequently pointed out in critical arguments – if not always so memorably expressed. Not only has *Measure for Measure* been said to be split down the middle, it has also been seen to abound with ironic parallels, reversals and substitutions, some of them carrying disturbing implications which are never fully resolved in the final act. The play opens with the law punishing an engaged couple for consummating their marriage prematurely and ends with punishing those who have steadfastly resisted marriage with marriage itself, leaving the audience to decide whether the sacrament is to be celebrated or feared. Isabella is prevented from entering the convent by male intervention in both Act 1 and Act 5, a repetition which suggests that a self-determined chastity is as threatening to a patriarchal society as engaging in pre-marital sex. Most disturbing of all is the play's insistence on the substitution of one body (or bodily part) for another: a sister's hymen for a brother's head; Mariana's body for Isabella's; the 'head of Ragozine for Claudio's' (5.1.529).

All but the most inexperienced of theatre-goers will have pre-determined generic expectations by which to make sense of a play's finale. On the surface at least, the ending of *Measure for Measure* delivers the basic stuff of comedy: no one dies, there are multiple marriages and the villain is publicly denounced. Conspicuously lacking for the majority of audiences and critics, though, is any real sense of joy, regeneration or poetic justice. The conclusion may well have four marriages lined up, but the motivation for at least two of these is punitive; Angelo's misdemeanour might have been exposed, but his punishment seems to be exceptionally lenient; and the moral fabric of Vienna seems to have undergone little significant improvement.

For much of the play we see distressed characters in secluded or confined circumstances. It comes as a relief, then, when the final act moves the action to a public place near the city gates, a shift of location that promises more openness, both literally and metaphorically. As both victims and offenders are brought into the arena, so the stage begins to resemble a public court, and an audience might settle back to watch justice be done. What follows, however, is more likely to leave them feeling perplexed than satisfied. Though the Duke might be seen as showing a compassionate concern for the women of the play in bringing the males who have wronged them to make amends, he is equally capable of tormenting them. Forced to lie and declare herself no longer a virgin to the assembled crowd, Isabella's situation in Act 5 resembles that of a sexual offender brought before the local 'bawdy court' to be publicly shamed – a stark contrast to her first appearance in the play as 'a thing enskied and sainted' (1.4.34). Yet in this instance at least, she has the comfort of knowing the truth of her situation. Not so the truth about her brother, which is held back from her until the closing moments of the scene; moreover, he is restored to her in such a way that suggests a deal is being struck – the life of a sibling in exchange for a hand in marriage.

Those critics who view the play as a neat Christian allegory can only do so by ignoring the Duke-Christ's callous disregard for Isabella's feelings. Similarly, they must overlook the ethics of Isabella's public defence of Angelo which are by no means consistent with New Testament teaching. Isabella's plea rests on the fact that 'His act did not o'ertake his bad intent' (5.1.448), a moral stance at odds with Christ's teaching about sexual behaviour – thoughts are every bit as sinful as deeds. Rather, it is disturbingly consistent with that declared by Angelo at the start of the play: to imagine a sin is in no way as serious as committing one. Equally inconsistent on a logical, if not a theological level, is Isabella's argument that her brother deserved punishment because he had committed a sexual sin, whereas Angelo had only intended one, given that Angelo, like Claudio, has actually slept with his future wife.

In the final act of the play audience anticipation rests not only on the working out of due justice, but also on the more inscrutable characters revealing something of themselves. After four acts of duologues, eavesdropping and equivocations, bringing together all the main players to face each other in broad daylight seems to invite personal revelation. Instead, the play concludes leaving more questions than answers. How does Isabella feel about the Duke's keeping her in the dark about her brother being alive? How does Claudio feel about a sister whose last words to him before his threatened execution are ''Tis best that thou diest quickly' (3.1.149)? How do Claudio and Juliet respond to their reunion? How does Angelo feel about his fast-track wedding? The extant text offers no real clues to such questions, nor does it provide any words or gestures to indicate Isabella's response to Claudio's Lazarus-like resurrection. Perhaps most conspicuous of all the silences of the denouement is Isabella's, following the Duke's proposal of marriage. This dramatic lacuna continues to challenge stage directors. Does she gesture a refusal by turning away? Does she joylessly submit to the Duke's request and the patriarchal desiderata of the silent wife? Or is her silence to be played as a lost-for-words happiness, a speechless prologue to a lifetime of marital bliss? Directors and actors have to fill in the gap somehow and whatever decision they make will leave a lasting impression on the audience.

Each age tends to shape Isabella's response to the Duke in its own image. Feminist influences from the mid-twentieth century onwards have given rise to independent Isabellas, choosing to forsake the yoke of matrimony for the relative autonomy of the nunnery; while earlier productions preferred the more conventionally 'happy' ending, with the heroine rushing joyfully towards wifely duty and childbearing. The literal-minded option would be to put Isabella's silence down to a compositor's failure to read a few lines of assent – or refusal – on the reverse of a sheet of paper, but such a theory would not explain why Isabella falls silent eighty-four lines from the play's end. From her storming speeches at the start of the act, powered by **epizeuxis**, she concludes with a rather more subdued speech, more than likely spoken against her true feelings. The extended silence which ensues could indicate an exhausted submission, an acceptance that elective celibacy is an unattainable dream in a world were women's sexuality is there to be gainfully employed: to save the life of a brother, to test the probity of a puritan, or to meet the will of a ruler who finds himself suddenly troubled by the 'dribbling dart of love' (1.3.2).

Perhaps what stands out as most unsettling in this final act is its refusal to offer us a single character with a deep and selfless love for another. While only the most perverse of audiences could doubt that Antony is passionately in love with Cleopatra, or that Cordelia loves Lear unconditionally, they would be hard pressed to find such surety of emotion in Shakespeare's Vienna. Does Isabella love the Duke and does he love her? Does Isabella love her chastity more than her brother? Can Mariana really love a man as perverse as Angelo? Answers to these questions can never be anything more than speculative about a play in which love appears hesitant, conditional, even paltry.

Making Shakespeare 'fit': William Davenant's *The Law Against Lovers* (1662)

Making minor changes to the Shakespearean text is common practice in all theatre companies, whether to shorten performance time, to erase textual obscurities or to drive a particular interpretation. Peter Brook's highly influential 1950 production of *Measure for Measure*, for example, smoothed out some of the more troublesome elements of its final act, excising the Duke's withholding of the truth about Claudio's execution, his direct proposal of marriage, and his pardoning of Barnardine. One twentieth-century author went much further than simply making a few textual cuts. Charles Marowitz, one of Brook's American collaborators, rewrote most of the second half, so that Isabella sleeps with Angelo, turns down his subsequent proposal of marriage and is then led away to prison at the Duke's command. In Marowitz's final scene, Duke Vincentio, Escalus and Angelo – all men together – drink heavily and mock the very idea of justice, the curtain falling as the Duke pours wine over his Deputy's head.

While twentieth-century rewritings of Shakespeare by writers such as Marowitz, Bertolt Brecht and Edward Bond have tended to unsettle the theatrical status quo, those undertaken in the Restoration period aimed more at appeasing audiences than challenging them. Having suffered the closure of the theatres during the Civil War, people looked for entertainment which would delight and titivate. If the records are to be trusted, *Measure for Measure* was not performed during this period, though it did appear in a drastically altered form, thanks to the efforts of Sir William Davenant. Poet, playwright, theatre manager, and staunch royalist, Davenant's support for Charles I during the Civil War had earned him a knighthood and, with the accession of Charles II, the rights to nine of Shakespeare's plays. At a time when few new dramas were available, such a monopoly was highly desirable, though it came with strings attached, namely the responsibility to 'make them fit' for a Restoration audience by relieving them of obscure or obsolete expressions and suiting them to the theatrical conditions of the day: female performers, lavish scenery and a socially elite audience. With these considerations in mind, Davenant took *Measure for Measure* and *Much Ado* and conflated them into the comedy, *The Law Against Lovers*.

Set in Turin, Davenant's play makes Angelo the somewhat unlikely brother of *Much Ado's* Benedick, as well as Beatrice's guardian; Lucio gains a side-kick in Balthasar, and Beatrice a pert younger sister, Viola. The sexual and religious issues raised in Shakespeare's play are toned down so that, as the title suggests, the spotlight can shine on the various sets of lovers and the intrigues which bring them to final union. Davenant's Turin is an altogether less threatening place than Shakespeare's Vienna. The audience's spirits are kept buoyant through well-placed songs and dances, plenty of urbane wit, and a modish playfulness. Both casts are *re*cast in more moderate form. No low-life characters disturb this essentially aristocratic comedy, Lucio and his crew appearing more as high-spirited young courtiers, than confirmed libertines. Angelo is really not all that bad, never really intending to execute Claudio and propositioning Isabella only to test out her suitability as a wife. And Isabella is really not all that good, suggesting that Juliet take her place in Angelo's bed, reasoning that, with her virginity already lost, it would seem the most expedient course of action. The Duke is more senescent ruler than meddling manipulator or Christ-like figure and never even thought of as a potential husband for Isabella. Such changes erase all discontent and ambiguity from the final act: the Duke withdraws to a contented retirement, Beatrice and Benedick finally acknowledge their feelings for one another, and Isabella and Angelo discover that they are a match made in heaven. The distribution of justice is uncontroversial. It is the guilty Angelo and not the innocent Isabella who is made to believe – for a short time at least – that Claudio has really been executed. Shakespeare's Lucio, reshaped into a lovable rogue by Davenant, is let off scot-free and the incorrigible Barnardine of the original repents fully before he is pardoned, ensuring that the dramatic tone of the conclusion is steadfastly comic.

In conflating *Measure for Measure* with the much more securely comic *Much Ado*, Davenant was faced with a task which went further than a simple rewriting of plot and moderating of personalities. In order to make the play 'fit' for a Restoration audience, its verse form and imagery needed close attention. Writing about Davenant's adaptation in *An Account of the English Dramatic Poets* (1691), the critic and biographer Gerard Langbaine remarks how 'where the language is rough or obsolete, our author has taken care to polish it'. Few readers or audiences today would agree that Davenant managed to 'polish' any part of the original, though most would concede that his dramatic language is a good deal more straightforward than Shakespeare's. The sacrifice paid for such clarity, however, is considerable. In cutting a fair proportion of the complex and disturbing lines of dialogue, Davenant effectively removes the very qualities which modern audiences find fascinating. Some disturbing expressions, such as Claudio's likening his own pursuit of desire to 'rats that ravin down their proper bane' (1.2.129), are taken out, as are some of the images of corruption and putrescence in Angelo's major soliloquy at the end of Act 2 Scene 2. The erotic language associated with Isabella is sanitized, so that she is said to have a '*sweet* (rather than a *prone*) and speechless dialect' (1.2.180) and is asked by Angelo to offer up the treasures of her '*youth*' rather than her '*body*' (2.4.96). The speech in which she talks of stripping herself in readiness for punishment and death is also considerably toned down, as is her response to Angelo's sexual demands. Such editing serves to make Isabella a less sexually vital, and therefore less troubling, character in the play, one who can be safely married off at its conclusion.

Davenant's linguistic dilution succeeds in taking the savage edge off *Measure for Measure*. Moreover, his decision to write the entire comedy in blank verse, with a generous helping of rhyming couplets to work up its most sentimental moments, transforms the language of the original into something altogether more conciliatory. It is clear, though, that certain aspects of its staging left a vivid impression on Samuel Pepys who, in his diary entry for 18 February 1662, declared it a 'good play and well performed, especially the little girl's ... dancing and singing'. Other theatre-goers were less convinced, one in particular describing it as 'two good plays to make one bad'. The play's extremely short run would suggest that its detractors were probably in the majority.

Further Thinking

- ➤ The psychology of Angelo has been compared to that of Iago in *Othello*. Could you find any textual evidence to support this?

- ➤ In *Shakespeare: The Invention of the Human* (1999), Harold Bloom, one of America's most controversial literary critics, argues that Isabella is Shakespeare's 'most sexually provocative female character' (365). How would you respond to such a claim?

- ➤ Knowledge of key Bible texts provides a useful foundation for reading literature. Look over the first four chapters of Genesis and pick out any details which relate to Shakespeare's plays (*Hamlet* and *The Tempest* in particular).

Afterlives...

The Pre-Raphaelite painter, William Holman Hunt, captured the scene when Isabella tells her brother of Angelo's proposition in a picture entitled *Claudio and Isabella* (1853). The dilemma of the play is strikingly represented here, with strong moral contrasts being drawn through the depiction of the siblings. You can view the painting and find out more about it at www.tate.org.

5

Hamlet: A play of 'perpetual modernity'

Unlike some of Shakespeare's plays, *Hamlet* has never fallen out of favour with audiences, performers or scholars. Down the centuries it has withstood the vicissitudes of theatrical fashion, critical interpretation and school curricula, with 'To be or not to be' remaining one of the most quoted lines in Western literature – one which has been known to finds its way into various areas of popular culture. In *Forms of Attention* (1985), Frank Kermode puts the tragedy's enduring appeal down to its 'perpetual modernity' (62), a quality that allows it to be remade in the image of each new generation.

This chapter

- considers the rise of film in literary studies and the attraction of *Hamlet* for film makers
- explores early modern attitudes to revenge
- examines the dramatic impact of questions in the play
- analyzes how film directors have represented the Ghost on screen

The rise of the Shakespeare film

Thanks to the technological advances of the second half of the twentieth century, screen versions of Shakespeare's plays have become increasingly accessible. Since the invention of the VCR recorder in the late 1970s, teachers and students have been able to replay Shakespeare films *ad infinitum*, enabling a depth of analysis difficult to achieve with the more ephemeral mode of stage performance. However, it is only in the last ten years or so that Shakespeare on film has become an integral part of the mainstream literature curriculum in schools and colleges. If examiners of the 1980s and 1990s complained that celluloid Shakespeare got in the way of students' 'true' understanding of the text, nowadays, writing confidently about cinematic interpretation will often gain candidates as much credit as citing the views of established critics. The increasing acceptance of film as an intellectually valid focus for Shakespeare study has likewise been seen in higher education. In a recent report published by the English Subject Centre (*Teaching Shakespeare*, Neill Thew, 2006) 88 per cent of lecturers who responded to the survey of under-graduate Shakespeare teaching said that they made use of film resources in their classes, and an increasing number of today's university English courses include modules on Shakespeare and the cinema.

Watching Shakespeare's plays on screen differs markedly from watching them on stage. One of the most obvious differences is that a film is fixed and inviolable; yes, the projector might break down, but the performance itself remains securely captured. A stage performance, on the other hand, always holds potential for disruption. Acting against the noise of mobile ringtones and raucous school parties is a familiar hazard for most stage actors. Some even experience direct communication from individual members of the audience. The actor and director Mark Rylance, for example, lately recalled in an interview with Mark Lawson how, during the early days of Shakespeare's Globe theatre, a man shouted out 'Get on with it!' as he delivered the 'Agincourt' speech from *Henry V*. And if audiences can disrupt the actors, so the actors can disrupt the spectators. Daniel Day-Lewis walking off stage mid-way through performing *Hamlet* in 1989 was not only a memorable case in point – it also highlighted the ultimate power of the player. Once in the spotlight, the stage actor is free to follow or disregard the director's advice, a freedom which Laurence Olivier clearly found intoxicating:

> The actor on stage is all-powerful ... There is nothing the director or author can do once the house lights dim ... The actor can choose to do or say anything he likes, he is the governor, he cracks the whip.
>
> (*On Acting*, 1986, 246)

The film performer has no such licence: if *he* wilfully disregards the director's vision, his performance is destined for the cutting room floor. For some, the intimacy and tension of being in the same moment and space as the actors is lost in the viewing of a film in the cinema or, even more so, on a laptop or Smartphone. Arguably, though, the film spectator enjoys a different form of intimacy with Shakespearean performance in being able to rewind, pause or fast-forward a performance and through engaging with DVD 'extras' such as off-cuts and interviews with the cast.

Any adapter of Shakespeare for the screen is faced with several taxing questions. How can a play that would run for well over three hours in today's theatre be fitted to a cinema timeframe closer to Shakespeare's 'two hours' traffic' of the stage? How should a medium able to produce hyper-realistic effects deal with an early modern text? How are violent deaths, the heat of battle and raging storms – often only verbalized or presented fleetingly in Shakespeare's script – to be realized? Should dramatic conventions such as asides and soliloquies be abandoned, or 'translated' into the filmic mode? Perhaps, though, the most exacting question of all is how to deliver the lines of the text. Cinema, with its capacity for amplification, enables actors to pronounce Shakespeare's words much more naturalistically than they could on stage. Ian McKellen and Ralph Fiennes both have experience of playing the same Shakespearean role on stage and screen. Talking about Richard Loncraine's 1995 film version of *Richard III*, McKellen remarked that Shakespeare 'frequently captured a conversational tone ... ideal for cinema', a view echoed by Fiennes, responding to questions about his directorial debut film, *Coriolanus*: 'One of my notes to myself ... was "Don't over inflect". The speech needed to be naturalistic.' Though these two highly accomplished actors make the job of rendering late sixteenth-century language accessible for modern audiences sound straightforward, it would be foolhardy to believe that it can be managed without extensive editing. The majority of Shakespeare films contain fewer than half the original lines, Kenneth Branagh's 'conflated text' *Hamlet*, with a running time of four hours and two minutes, proving a brave exception.

Shakespeare films are not limited to direct adaptations based on the play text or straightforward recordings of stage productions. Some of the most admired works in the canon of Shakespearean cinema include creative re-workings by Akira Kurosawa and Grigori Kozintsev, whose films diverge from the original text into quite new territory. Others, such as *She's the Man,* a modern American take on *Twelfth Night*, or *West Side Story*, a 1960s updating of *Romeo and Juliet*, take Shakespeare as an inspirational starting point. There is also a well-established sub-genre of films which make aspects of Shakespeare's life or works their main focus, two of the most successful being Merchant Ivory's *Shakespeare Wallah* (1965) and John Madden's *Shakespeare in Love* (1998). Rather less successful, both in the eyes of the critics and at the box office, was Roland Emmerich's *Anonymous* (2011) – an ill-fated attempt to propound the theory that Edward de Vere was the true author of Shakespeare's works.

Hamlet has proved perennially popular with film makers. Though the first screen version was as early as 1900 (a three-minute film featuring Sarah Bernhardt as Hamlet), it would take until the middle of the century for the first landmark *Hamlet* to be produced. Olivier's 1948 *film noir* vision of the tragedy proved enormously influential, not least for realizing on screen Ernest Jones's Oedipal reading of the drama. Though generally considered a success, it did not meet with the approval of the critic L. C. Knights:

> It was a good film, as films go, but no one who knew Shakespeare could fail to be impressed by the thinness of effect achieved by the obtrusiveness of the medium. Not only was the mind distracted by the lace of Hamlet's collar or the precariousness of his perch when speaking the 'To be, or not to be' soliloquy, the photographic realism inhibited ... any but the crudest response.
>
> (*Some Shakespearean Themes*, 1960, 22)

Knights's comments are typical of the resistance to filmic treatments of 'high art' which persisted throughout much of the twentieth century. The catalogue for the 1964 Shakespeare quarter centenary exhibition, for example, put forward the view that: 'Shakespeare's plays were filmed on the theory that they would benefit from a wider "stage". Unfortunately, early cinema technique was not sufficiently developed to cope with them '. And this was by no means an opinion confined to traditionalists. In an interview published in *Sight and Sound* a year later, Peter Brook spoke of the 'sad history of Shakespeare on the screen', describing the majority of the one hundred or so Shakespeare films to date as 'unspeakably bad' ('Shakespeare on Three Screens', *Sight and Sound*, 34.2, 1965, 66). Yet at the same time as Shakespeare on screen was being declared a failure, one of the masterpieces of the genre was in production: Kozintsev's *Hamlet* (1964). Moving away from Olivier's relatively domestic Elsinore to a strongly political landscape, a totalitarian state, where soldiers and spies lurk in every recess, the film recalled for its first audiences the brutal realities of Stalin's regime, not long since passed. Dubbed the 'Russian *Hamlet*', it received commendatory reviews, even from conservatives. One such, the actor and critic Robert Speaight, considered it 'masterly', averring that 'Not many foreigners – and by foreigners I naturally do not include Americans – really understand Shakespeare ... Kozintsev is a notable exception to this general failure' (*SQ*, 19, 1968, 90).

From time to time, Shakespeare on screen still incurs the wrath of textual purists or the disdain of those who regard film as deserving only the lowliest of places in the hierarchy of the arts. Increasingly, though, such attitudes are at odds with the public mood and with the interdisciplinary approach of contemporary literary studies. Far from being a threat to the literary status of the play, film is now regarded as crucial to its survival. As Kenneth Rothwell points out in the conclusion to his authoritative survey *A History of Shakespeare on Screen* (2004): 'Shakespeare remains incarnate in the trinity of page, stage and screen ... Thrice armed, he is unlikely to go away' (274).

Revenge and the early modern audience

The revenge motif has featured in all three main literary genres for centuries. In modern times, what Shakespeare's contemporary, the philosopher Francis Bacon, defined as the 'wild justice' of revenge is more likely to be represented on screen than on stage. Whether unfolded through the daily or weekly increments of the soap opera, the rapid trajectory of the action film, or the more slow-burn drama of psychological disturbance, stories of characters seeking redress for past wrongs continue to compel us. Revenge was one of the major themes of early modern tragedy. Plays such as *The*

Spanish Tragedy by Thomas Kyd, *The Revenger's Tragedy* by Thomas Middleton and John Webster's *The Duchess of Malfi*, are all notable examples of the highly popular genre of 'revenge tragedy'. Central to such dramas is a protagonist who is compelled to avenge the murder of a family member or lover – and to meet his own destruction in the process. Typical dramatic features include ghosts (often malign and mouldering) and graveyards, scenes of feigned or genuine madness, grotesque acts of violence, and a final scene which notches up a heavy death toll, far in excess of the catalyst crime.

While it is impossible to know for certain how early modern audiences felt about revenge, they would doubtless have been aware that it was condemned by both church and state. The Bible offers texts expressly prohibiting blood revenge. In the Old Testament, Psalm 9 praises God for His ultimate 'righteous judgement' (9.4), while in the New Testament, Paul insists that avenging evil is not a task for the individual, but for the state authorities 'instituted by God' (Romans 13.2). Audiences would also have been aware that the state authorities of the day were clamping down hard on acts of private vengeance, such as those condemned so emphatically by the Prince in Shakespeare's *Romeo and Juliet*. Members of the aristocracy were no longer free to settle their disputes via one-to-one combat (duelling was a particularly fashionable menace), a diminution in power which, combined with the loosening of hierarchical structures that came with a flourishing market economy, caused them considerable anxiety. The spectacle of the avenger taking the law into his own hands provided audiences with a thrilling example of personal agency, as well as a stark reminder of the heavy price individuals paid for it.

Shakespeare's first tragedy, *Titus Andronicus,* was an early contribution to the revenge genre. While it pleased its original audiences, for centuries now it has been placed on the sidelines of the canon, in part for its savage violence, but also on account of its aesthetic infelicities. *Hamlet* is usually regarded as an example of revenge tragedy at its most sophisticated and morally complex – more than compensating for the earlier play's shortcomings. Though features of the genre such as a ghost, feigned madness, and a graveyard scene are retained, it holds back from the gratuitous violence of *Titus Andronicus*, more concerned with exploring the moral ambiguities surrounding acts of vengeance than satisfying the baser instincts of an audience. Whereas some revenge plays, such as *The Revenger's Tragedy*, are generically self-regarding, the prevailing mood of searching introspection found in *Hamlet* draws attention to the ethical and religious complexities of the genre's central motif.

Critical consensus until quite well on in the twentieth century was that *Hamlet*'s primary audiences would have been at one in expecting the hero to avenge his father's death. A. C. Bradley asserts that the 'conventional moral ideas of his [Hamlet's] time ... told him plainly that he ought to avenge his father' (*Shakespearean Tragedy*, 1904, 99). Such certainty has been gradually eroded by scholars such as Eleanor Prosser, whose *Hamlet and Revenge* (1967) led the way in insisting that early modern attitudes to revenge were 'far more complex'(4). Hamlet's own uncertain response to revenge might be seen as representing this complexity. Traditionally, the dramatic avenger is presented as torn between orthodox belief and natural sensibilities, but this is not the case with Hamlet: the feelings he articulates are rather more difficult to categorize. As critics frequently point out, his disgust at his mother's concupiscence appears to be at the heart of his emotional turmoil, so that his duty to avenge his father could be viewed as a form of displacement activity, a means of hiding feelings of sexual revulsion behind the mask of the more socially acceptable feelings of the angry avenger and dutiful son.

On first hearing of his uncle's crime, Hamlet presents a resolute willingness to avenge his father, and though he acknowledges that divine law forbids 'self-slaughter' (1.2.132), he never articulates any Christian concern about the prospect of slaughtering Claudius. His first encounter with the Ghost sees him courageously ignore Horatio's 'do not go with it' (1.4.62) and, once the paternal exhortation to revenge the 'foul and most unnatural murder!' (1.5.25) is spoken, to declare his dedication to the task with all the zeal of a religious convert. However, by the end of the second act, Hamlet has made no coherent plan of action, save putting on a play to prove his uncle's guilt. Whereas in the third act of most revenge dramas the avenger plans a precise, often elaborately brutal killing, or indeed, succeeds in carrying one out, Hamlet engages with the aesthetics of drama and with two fictional avengers: Pyrrhus and Lucianus.

With his '*dread and black complexion*' (2.2.393), Pyrrhus is the epitome of the bloody avenger. His pause before striking the death blow is borne out of a moment of distraction, as he hears the crash of falling Ilium, seeming more an opportunity for him to renew his vigour, than a sign of irresolution. In comparison, Hamlet's protracted pause appears more that of a cerebral scholar, whose habit of contemplation seems unfitted to the inexorable propulsion of revenge. That is not to say that he ever consciously rejects the role of avenger. He frequently rebukes himself for his inaction, sometimes taking on the bellicose lexis of the killer. He rails against Claudius, the 'bloody, bawdy.../Remorseless, treacherous, lecherous, kindless villain' (2.2.515–6); yet no sooner are the words pronounced, than he falls to self-examination, berating himself for indulging in talk over action, for being an 'ass'. Indeed, Hamlet's language frequently reveals that his instincts swerve away from violent deeds. His declaration 'Now could I drink hot blood' (3.2.380) loses its force by being governed by the conditional tense; likewise, when an opportunity to kill Claudius presents itself, he declares only that he '*might*' (3.3.73) do it, not that he *will*. Far from being a studied stance of superiority, a Baconian assertion of the civilized over the barbaric, Hamlet's predisposition to verbalize and think, rather than act in the white heat of fury, is a matter of some shame to him.

Where Act 3 offers fictional parallels to Hamlet the avenger, Act 4 provides two from real life. Hamlet's mistaken killing of Polonius – through an arras, not face-to-face – marks him out as an avenger *manqué* and instigates the play's second cycle of revenge, led by a much more efficient avenger: Laertes. Nothing gives this son 'pause' before pursuing his father's killer; he quickly gathers up an army of followers, bursts through the doors of the castle and has to be physically restrained. Unlike Hamlet, he is completely at home with the well-worn diction of the vengeful son: he 'dare[s] damnation' (4.5.132), casting aside any scruples of conscience or theology. Fortinbras, too, is a son who can block out the rational 'When honour's at the stake' (4.4.55), carrying out a revenge plan that goes beyond the familial to the world of war and politics. Audiences today are likely to compare Hamlet favourably to such counterparts, finding in his sensitivity and intellect a finer representative of humanity. However, such a Romantic view of Hamlet tends to overlook less attractive features of his behaviour: his cruelty to Ophelia, his callous response to Polonius' death and its aftermath, and his efficient dispatching of Rosencrantz and Guildenstern.

Hamlet's revenge finally comes about not from his own strategy, but from that of his intended victim, Claudius. The hectic speed of the closing scene ensures that Hamlet bears little resemblance to the stereotype of the calculating avenger; he fights in an arena where all odds are stacked against him, killing only as a responsive act and leaving any public announcement of his uncle's regicide unspoken. Ultimately, he fails to live up to the revenge ethic of Old Hamlet's generation or the ideal expressed by Bacon that the man who holds back from taking revenge 'is superior ... it is a prince's part to pardon'. As the curtain falls, human thought and behaviour have been shown to be highly complex, ever-shifting and impossible to encompass in moral codes or state edicts.

'Who's there?' Questions in *Hamlet*

Beginning with a spare two-syllable question which has intrigued audiences down the years, *Hamlet* moves on to consider questions of human existence that can never be definitively answered. What lies beyond death? How should justice best be served? Is human kind really so different from the animal? And it is perhaps the play's treatment of such abidingly debateable questions which lends it what F. S. Boas termed an 'atmosphere of obscurity' (*Shakspere* [*sic*] *and his Predecessors*, 1896, 384), prompting him to label it a 'problem' play, alongside *Measure for Measure, All's Well that Ends Well* and *Troilus and Cressida*.

The dialogue and soliloquies of *Hamlet* contain a more than usually high proportion of questions. Number alone is not necessarily significant, of course; a play set in a schoolroom is likely to feature an abundance of questions, as would a scene featuring a missing person returning after an absence of many years. Nor are questions inherently more significant than plain statements. Certain types of questions, such as direct requests for information, or phatic queries about someone's well-being, operate solely as a means of establishing an everyday naturalism. In *Hamlet*, though, such 'empty' questions are often freighted with greater significance. The opening line is a good example of a direct question that resonates throughout the rest of the tragedy, and Claudius' phatic questions spoken in the court help to characterize him as a slick politician, who knows how to draw on established forms of social discourse to project a certain public image. In performance, interrogative inflections frequently contribute to the dramatic mood. Hamlet's eager desire for the Ghost to resemble his father is conveyed through the question 'His beard was grizzled, no?' (1.2.238), the negative question-tag carrying with it a sense of fervent excitement. The iteration of questions can also help to express heightened emotion. The last line of Hamlet's first speech to the Ghost, for example, contains three short

questions: 'Say why is this? Wherefore? 'What should we do?'
(1.4.57), creating a sense of urgency and uncertainty, the final
question anticipating the play's preoccupation with the idea of
action itself.

ⓘ *Read 3.2.86–128 and look closely at the questions posed in the extract. Now think about the following questions:*

- Look at Claudius' question at line 88. Does it have
  any significance beyond the phatic?
- Hamlet's treatment of Ophelia in this extract has often
  been regarded as cruel. How might his questioning
  here add to such an impression?
- How does Hamlet use questions to serve his intention
  to appear 'idle'?

This is a very public scene, one that has been initiated
and organized by Hamlet, and which could be seen as
a departure from his usual melancholy. Yet the questions
which generate so much of its drive and energy are primarily
motivated by defensiveness, aggression and distrust, rather
than any genuine desire to know anything about or from the
addressees. Claudius' opening question seems a purely phatic
phrase, a polite formality at the start of an event. Usually
when someone in a social situation is asked how they are, the
questioner is adhering to a certain convention, expecting to
receive an answer along the lines of 'Fine, how are you?' Here,
though, Claudius' question seems to hold more significance,
not least because it refers us back to a previous meeting when
the step-father posed a rather more confrontational question
to his stepson: 'How is it that the clouds still hang on you?'
(1.2.66). Given what has happened between these two points
in the play, it is likely that Claudius asks how Hamlet 'fares'
in order to gauge his mental state; he has been unnerved by his

behaviour in the court and is anxious to monitor and contain it. Hamlet's initial response, 'Excellent i' faith!', keeps within the social code; however, this is immediately followed by his wresting of the word 'fare' from the original question and punning on its association with food, comparing himself to the chameleon, a creature popularly believed to live on air. In his riddling appropriation of Claudius' seemingly empty question, then, Hamlet makes a thinly veiled accusation that he is being deprived of his right to the throne ('promise-crammed'), couched in metaphor that depicts him as hollow and unfed, in contrast with the 'bloat King' (3.4.180) he addresses. Claudius' response, 'I have nothing with this answer', not only draws attention to his disapproval of Hamlet's violation of linguistic social rules, but also epitomizes the prevailing tensions of the scene. Verbal communication between characters might be rapid and fluent here, but it is by no means easy or even, at times, comprehensible.

Turning his attention from the King to Polonius, Hamlet seems to recover a manner more fitting for a prince hosting a royal event. Evidently putting politeness before genuine interest, he questions Polonius about his youthful acting career, only to seize on the answer and subject it to his characteristically astringent word-play. The mask of the decorous host is quickly dropped as Polonius' Julius Caesar becomes a 'calf' (a term commonly denoting a stupid person) and the counsellor is once again made to fit into Hamlet's category of 'tedious old fools' (2.2.214).

Having employed word-play to alienate Claudius and Polonius, Hamlet then turns his attentions to Ophelia. Their ten-line **stichomythic** exchange (108–17) is often picked out as an example of Hamlet's gratuitous cruelty, what Kenneth Branagh has described in interview as his 'piggery', and it is in exchanges such as this that some critics discern a genuine madness in the hero. If Hamlet's aggressive manipulation of Claudius' question and Polonius' answer can be seen to connect with his problematic identity as the avenging Prince, his lewd, bitter treatment of Ophelia seems to relate more to his disgust at sexuality. This feature of Hamlet's psychology is not one that 'passes show' (1.2.85); it is explicitly expressed several times in the play – and not only in the isolated moments of soliloquy. Here Hamlet renews his invective against what he sees as women's uncontainable sexuality, linking back to the previous scene in which he exhorts Ophelia to seek the celibate life of the cloister. His first question to Ophelia 'Lady, shall I lie in your lap?' carries an overt sexual connotation and a degree of phallic threat. Ophelia's brief response is a pithy refusal of his outrageous suggestion, one which Hamlet quickly turns against her. Rather than reading her answer as a sign of chastity, it is taken merely as proof that she has understood the obscene quibble in the question and in so doing, conformed to the misogynistic stereotype of female sexual 'knowingness'. Hamlet's next question further probes her familiarity with bawdy through the phrase 'country matters', with its vulgar pun contained in the first syllable. Ophelia parries this attack by withdrawing, by making herself a cipher, someone who thinks 'nothing'. Yet even this self-annihilation is not enough to protect her from Hamlet's onslaught, as he takes the word 'nothing' and exploits its multiple associations with the male and female genitalia, at the same time moving adroitly from the case of *one* woman, Ophelia, to *all* 'maids'. The stretch of stichomythia comes to an end with Ophelia's line 'Ay, my lord', the first word of which is a repetition in **homophonic** form of the 'I' in Hamlet's preceding question; yet another attempt to block off discourse and with it, potential insult and hurt.

Rather than being regarded as a sign of genuine psycho-sexual disturbance in Hamlet – a relatively modern viewpoint – his baiting of Ophelia could be seen as no more than a calculated means of displaying his 'antic disposition' to the court. Failing to show any regard for a young woman's propriety and feelings, and provoking her with indecencies is, after all, a compelling sign of insanity, especially in such a highly public situation. Yet however we construe the reasons for Hamlet's behaviour, an audience cannot help but feel uncomfortable, even alarmed, by his treatment of Ophelia here. Certainly, some of the sexually transgressive elements of this scene anticipate not Hamlet's but Ophelia's madness later in the play, where her altered mental state is suggested in part by her singing of ribald ballads to royal company.

In the final third of the extract, Hamlet delivers the last two of his eight questions. Bitingly sarcastic and heavily rhetorical, these are not the questions of a madman; rather, they show the mental control of the hero as he brings the focus back to remembrance of the dead, his own revenge, and the significance of the dumb show to follow.

Ghosts on screen: Almereyda's *Hamlet* (2000)

A good four hundred years have elapsed since the Ghost of Old Hamlet made its first appearance on the Globe stage. Since then belief in the supernatural has steadily declined, thanks in part to the gradual separation of faith from scientific understanding. While the question 'Do you believe in ghosts?' can still be asked with some degree of seriousness, any strong belief in the spirit world is usually regarded as a sign of credulity or mental illness. Shakespeare's audiences, though, would have had a strong sense of the numinous and a genuine fear of the otherworldly.

The vast majority of English theatre-goers would have belonged to the Church of England (the only recognized Protestant denomination) and would have been compelled by law to attend its Sunday services. And while there may well have been some who held fast to their pre-Reformation Catholic beliefs, state regulation increasingly ensured that these were not aired in public. *Hamlet* is, on the face of it, set in a Protestant world, its hero a student at the impeccably Protestant university of Wittenberg, *alma mater* of Martin Luther. The spirit world, however, is decidedly more

Catholic. While the word 'Purgatory' is never spoken, it is strongly implied by the Ghost's description of its crimes being 'purged away' (1.5.13) as a consequence of being denied the last rites of the Catholic faithful. The existence of Purgatory was passionately denied by Protestants, defined in the twenty-second of the Thirty-Nine Articles of Religion, established in 1563, as 'a fond [foolish] thing ... grounded upon no warranty of Scripture'. Shakespeare's presentation of a ghost taking a brief respite from the Purgatorial fires was, then, a controversial one, especially given that a proclamation of 1559 had required all plays to be licenced by the Revels Office, warning against works wherein 'matters of religion ... shall be handled'. While there wants evidence to argue that *Hamlet* is a validation of the old faith's belief in Purgatory, it does, as Stephen Greenblatt points out, come closer than any other play of the time to presenting this middle passage as a 'frightening reality' (*Hamlet in Purgatory*, 2001, 236). For a true Protestant, a ghost from Purgatory was by definition a false apparition, a certainty which *Hamlet* insists on destabilizing as characters and audience alike are prompted to question whether the spectre is indeed Hamlet's father or 'goblin damned' (1.4.40).

Chief among the challenges of adapting *Hamlet* for the screen is how to present the Ghost to an audience a good deal more materialist than Shakespeare's. A survey of a few of the *Hamlet* films produced in the last fifty years or so suggests that the director's choice of point of view is crucial in interpreting the nature of the Ghost and his relationship with his son. Captured mainly in **low-angle** shots, the Ghost of Branagh's version towers above Hamlet, immediately suggesting an over-bearing authoritarian father. Zeffirelli's spectre, on the other hand, is a much less imposing figure. Shown mainly from Hamlet's point of view in predominantly **medium-long and long-shots**, this fustian-clothed figure has a wan and vulnerable air and is much more likely to elicit Hamlet's 'Alas, poor ghost' (1.5.4) than Branagh's armour-clad equivalent. Likewise, how far the director follows Shakespeare's cue in making the Ghost a fully material presence requires careful thought: if the figure is too realistic, it risks being undistinguishable from the everyday world of Denmark; if too 'ghostly', it risks appearing absurdly out of place in what is essentially (in mainstream cinema at least) a realistic medium. Tony Richardson found a simple way round the problem by omitting the Ghost entirely from his 1969 film version of a highly successful stage *Hamlet*. The presence of the Ghost is felt only by way of a blinding light thrown on the figures it confronts and their startled reactions to it. In contrast, Olivier and Kozintsev offer the viewer a much more concrete presence, their Ghosts being clad in full armour; however, both guard against too much realism by allowing only the merest glimpse of Old Hamlet's face and by manipulating the chiaroscuro effects of black and white film to create a supernatural effect.

In all of the films mentioned so far, the action of *Hamlet* is set either in the play's stated time and place or, in Branagh's case, a less distant past. The setting of Michael Almereyda's adaptation, however, is contemporaneous with its own production: Manhattan in 2000. In this hypermodern adaptation, Shakespeare's Wittenberg intellectual is transformed into an amateur videographer, struggling to cope in a society dominated by a corporate mentality and a ruthless media machine. Ethan Hawke's Hamlet carries around a Fisher-Price Pixelvision camera – a children's toy adopted by avant-garde film makers – and employs various other new technologies to record his inner and outer worlds, bringing to mind Oscar Wilde's definition of the hero as yearning to 'be the spectator of his own tragedy' (*The Complete Letters of Oscar Wilde*, 772).

Introducing a ghost into such an unrelentingly postmodern world was always going to be a challenge for a film maker. Yet rather than limiting the challenge by cutting down the Ghost's screen time, Almereyda increases it through the addition of a number of invented scenes. Sam Shepard's Old Hamlet appears both in an interpolated scene in Horatio's flat and at points in the text when the Prince declares that 'readiness is all' (5.2.200). And where the low-resolution black and white images created by Hamlet's PXL–2000 might seem the obvious choice to capture a ghostly presence, the director opts instead for the colourful clarity of Super 16mm film, bringing the spectral directly into the realms of the real. Showing little inclination to use cinematic tricks to create a sense of the supernatural – save the occasional transformation of the entirely solid Ghost figure into a transparent one – Almereyda creates a highly realistic apparition, clothed in a leather trench coat (with a hint of the military about it) for its first appearance and later in dinner suit and smart overcoat.

In the introduction to the published screenplay of the film, Almereyda writes that he wanted to build a 'visual structure to accommodate Shakespeare's imagery and ideas' (*William Shakespeare's Hamlet: A Screenplay Adaptation*, 2000, x). So Purgatory becomes a Pepsi machine into which the Ghost dissolves – an arresting image of the twenty-first-century nightmare of global branding and consumer culture – and the human surveillance of Elsinore becomes the automated presence of a hotel's CCTV camera, capable of capturing images of both the living and the dead. Hamlet first sees the revenant on the balcony of his hotel room, which serves as a liminal space – neither this world nor the next. The Ghost crosses over the threshold of the glass door into Hamlet's room seconds after delivering the line 'Mark me' (1.5.2), a choreography of utterance and entry which underscores the continuing authority of the patriarch. As the scene progresses, so Almereyda moves away from the alternating reaction shots most commonly employed to capture this crucial encounter on film to bring father and son together in the same frame. Yet for all the intimacy this allows, the direction maintains a tension between physical tenderness and physical aggression. Recounting his Purgatorial suffering (against the backdrop of television images of the earthly flames of the Gulf War), Old Hamlet gently touches his son's face, only to bear down on his shoulders a second later, as if rehearsing the very deed he insists his son carry out. Throughout the scene and elsewhere, the Ghost clutches a handkerchief to his ear to staunch the poison still leaking from it, at certain moments touching Hamlet with this same handkerchief, connecting him physically with the deed and marking him out as avenger. Only at the close of the scene do we have a moment of unalloyed familial affection, as the father embraces his son tenderly, before returning to the balcony – and the afterlife.

Almereyda's *Hamlet* has been dismissed by a minority of film academics as pretentious and self-regarding, with some mocking the director for citing as his scholarly inspiration Harold Goddard's somewhat outdated study, *The Meaning of Shakespeare* (1951). Yet most critical judgements have been positive, even laudatory. Maurice Hindle regards the film as capturing 'much of the dramatic essence of Shakespeare's *Hamlet*' (*Studying Shakespeare on Film*, 2007, 198), and David Bevington holds it up as a prime example of 'how a low-budget, modern-setting adaptation can be made to illuminate Shakespeare's text at least as effectively as the more costly and showy enterprises of Zeffirelli and Branagh' (*Murder Most Foul:* Hamlet *Through the Ages*, 2011, 187). Whether Almereyda's *Hamlet* will remain in the canon of Shakespeare films, or whether its hypermodernity will make it age rather more rapidly than versions favouring more traditional settings, remains to be seen.

Further thinking

➤ Some literary critics argue that the auditory and visual power of film means that the viewer cannot escape from the carefully framed viewpoint of the director. With this in mind, would you say that film adaptations of Shakespeare limit interpretative possibilities?

➤ The revenge motif is present to varying degrees in a substantial number of Shakespeare's plays. Pick out revenge elements in a tragedy, a comedy and a romance and compare their dramatic treatment.

➤ Make a list of allusions to literary and film texts in Almereyda's *Hamlet* (there is a huge number of them, so it is unlikely that anyone's list will be complete). How far do they serve to illuminate Shakespeare's *Hamlet*?

Afterlives ...

Perhaps because of its perceived high seriousness, *Hamlet* has attracted more than its share of burlesque treatments. One of the most memorable is to be found in Chapter 31 of Charles Dickens's *Great Expectations* (1860), which relates the hero's visit to a more than usually amateurish performance of the tragedy. Dickens knew the play extremely well, perhaps enabling him to manipulate its detail all the more successfully.

6

Othello: Sex, race and suggestibility

Tracing the history of *Othello* in performance is in some respects to trace the history of attitudes to race over the past four centuries. The slave trade, racial segregation and state apartheid all asserted themselves after the text's original production and form an inevitable filter through which audiences today view the play. Not surprisingly, the drama brings us to consider some uncomfortable questions, even in what is generally considered to be a multicultural age.

This chapter

- examines a relatively new critical approach that advocates rooting our study of Shakespeare in the material present
- considers the presentation of sexuality in the play in the context of early modern attitudes
- analyzes how *Othello* makes its readers and audiences conscious of the workings of language
- explores how one of the major directors of Shakespeare on film visually translates the imagery and themes of the tragedy

Presentism: 'The new kid on the Shakespeare block'

For none of us can step beyond time. It can't be drained out of our experience.

(Shakespeare in the Present, 2002, 3)

So wrote Terence Hawkes in a work that is commonly regarded as the 'presentist' manifesto. As a critical practice, presentism takes the here-and-now as the inevitable starting point of textual investigation, insisting on the inescapability of current perspectives. While such a theoretical label might imply an adversarial relationship to historicism, its proponents insist that it is by no means advocating a relapse into the belief that literature holds universal, unchanging truths, or an assumption that the present is always superior to the past. As presentists see it, new historicism has developed into a critical orthodoxy, guilty of overstating the alterity of Shakespeare's time and of privileging the past over the present. An over-zealous attention to the minutiae of the recorded early modern world, so presentists argue, has left us fearful that our response to a Shakespeare play might be risibly anachronistic (though it must be said that the anachronistic is more troubling for us today than it would have been for Shakespeare and his audiences). One possible consequence of this is that the aesthetic impact of literary texts is sidelined in favour of what Kiernan Ryan has typified as 'the endless studies bent on shackling Shakespeare to everything from maps and money to cooking and cosmetics' ('*Troilus and Cressida*: The Perils of Presentism' in *Presentist Shakespeares*, Hugh Grady and Terence Hawkes (eds), 2007, 168). Presentism strives to re-attach us to the literary work, to restore the pleasure and freedom of interpretation, while remaining 'committed to a theoretical situatedness in our own cultural and political moment' (Hugh Grady, 'Shakespeare Studies, 2005: A Situated Overview', *Shakespeare,* 1, 114).

Othello seems to invite a presentist reading more than the other major tragedies, its world being relatively more familiar to us than that of kings and princes. Its focus on a relationship between a black man and a white woman also makes it of particular interest to twenty-first-century audiences for whom race continues to be a highly controversial issue. Although some critics argue that Shakespeare's age was 'pre-racial' and, consequently, to view *Othello* through the lens of current race relations is wrong-headed, presentists such as Evelyn Gajowski encourage a critical reading situated in the moment, so as to 'gain a heightened awareness of the narrative of human history as an ongoing, imbricated (and imbricating) process' (*Presentism, Gender, and Sexuality in Shakespeare*, 2009, 7). The contemporary resonance of *Othello* came strongly to the fore when Barack Obama gained victory in the 2008 US presidential election. Connections were made, and continue to be made, between the fictional hero's eloquence and that of the first African American president, between Othello's situation as the saviour of the Venetians and Obama's as the man promising to bring vital change to the United States. In 2009, a seminar addressing the question 'Is Obama an Othello for our times?' was held at the Warwick Arts Centre. Whilst acknowledging the dangers of making too literal-minded a comparison, panellists explored correspondences between Obama's and Othello's Islamic roots and the weight of the representational force that both the fictional and the real-life hero carry. They also agreed that, though it is tempting to regard the racist attitudes reflected in a drama of 1604 from a certain altitude of 'knowing better', there are still plenty of potential Iagos in a country where racial divides remain active and powerful.

Presentism calls for a heightened awareness that our approach to a play such as *Othello* will inevitably be influenced by the period in which we live. Such awareness is not, however, to be gained simply by focusing on what we find 'relevant' to our present circumstances. Any study of the play's treatment of race will require alertness to the fact that notions of racism have differed vastly over the centuries and even the past few decades. The same applies to the interprative focus on the play. That race is a principal area of critical interest in the twenty-first century is evident from the introductions and notes provided in the most up-to-date scholarly editions of *Othello*, though it was not until the 1960s and 1970s, a time which saw the establishment of the Commission for Racial Equality and the Race Relations Act in Britain, that sustained critical studies of Shakespeare and what was then termed 'colour' began to be published. And even with the influence of ground-breaking articles such as G. K. Hunter's 'Elizabethans and Foreigners' (*SS*, 17, 1964), it would take until the 1980s for the postcolonial criticism which informs so much of today's discussion of *Othello* to emerge.

The critical practices which have been most influential on recent readings of *Othello* – postcolonial theory and feminist theory – are, in fact, inherently presentist, situating their approach to the play in current gender and race politics. A presentist approach to *Othello* generates a rich diversity of interpretation. Some critics promote the play as a compelling example of Shakespeare's ability to see beyond immediate circumstances to a vision of a better world where love transcends difference. First staged at a time when inter-racial marriage would have been viewed by most audience members as aberrant, the lovers' courage in defying the decorum of Venetian society is seen as an ideal to be aspired to, an argument against bigotry, reaching out to what Bakhtin termed a 'superaddressee', one 'whose absolutely just responsive understanding is presumed ... in distant historical time' (*Speech Genres and Other Late Essays*, Caryl Emerson and Michael Holquist (eds), 1986, 126). There is plenty in *Othello* to support such a view: it is the first early modern drama to present a Moor who has anything other than despicable features, let alone one who – for the first two acts of the play at least – is presented as noble, eloquent and respected by European society. Karen Newman, in her article '"And wash the Ethiop white": Femininity and the Monstrous in *Othello*', goes so far as arguing that 'Shakespeare's play stands in a contestatory relation to the hegemonic ideologies of race and gender in early modern England' (in *Shakespeare Reproduced: the Text in History and Ideology*, Jean E. Howard and Marion F. O'Connor (eds), 1987, 157).

Regarding Shakespeare as a prescient proponent of an anti-racist agenda is undeniably appealing, yet as Emma Smith points out in her succinct and comprehensive study of the play: 'it is disquieting to have to acknowledge that, on occasion, his plays fail to buttress contemporary tolerant opinion' (*Othello*, 2005, 39). How the hero's transformation from eloquent warrior to vengeful murderer is accounted for is central to an interpretation of the play's racial politics. Mid-point in the drama and about half-way through what is commonly known as the 'Temptation Scene', Othello soliloquizes:

> Haply for I am black
> And have not those soft parts of conversation
> That chamberers have, or for I am declined
> Into the vale of years – yet that's not much –
> She's gone, I am abused, and my relief
> Must be to loathe her. O curse of marriage
> That we can call these delicate creatures ours
> And not their appetites!

> (3.3.267–74)

It is a speech that captures in miniature the ambivalent nature of the play. We hear in the rhythms and hesitations of the lines Othello's movement from self-doubt to a fleeting rally of confidence, followed by a retreat into the generalizing habit of misogyny. Othello considers his colour, his culture, and his age to be viable reasons for his wife's infidelity, his articulation of *three* possibilities complicating a straightforward reading of his situation. Nonetheless, the primary position of 'black' in the speech, its inseparability from the lack of 'soft parts of conversation', and his apparent dismissal of age as a significant factor (though the grammar is ambiguous here) all point to skin colour as the hero's chief 'disadvantage'. If read as confirmation that a Venetian world view has finally infiltrated the hero, these lines support an idea of Shakespeare as a playwright both of and beyond his age, who gives us in *Othello* a glimpse of what *might be* before reminding us of what *is*. The audience is encouraged to place blame not on the black 'outsider', but on the white majority whose values have corrupted him.

By way of contrast, Michael Bristol's contention that *Othello* is a 'comedy of abjection' (*Big-time Shakespeare*, 1996, 175–6), with Othello placed as its central comic monster, renders the speech one of the play's carnivalesque moments, played before an audience 'for whom a racist sensibility was entirely normal' (181). It is a view which, as its author concedes, presents a severe challenge to modern sensibilities in its suggestion that, far from being a text which dramatizes the possibility of racial equality, it is instead 'a highly significant document in the historical constitution both of racist sensibility and of racist political ideology' (182), an insight that can only be gained from the vantage point of the present.

Unsurprisingly, given its broad sweep and the combative stance of some of its advocates, presentism has its detractors. John Holbo, for example, sees it as 'a species of error' (*Literature Compass*, 5, 2008, 1097), falsely projecting elements of the present onto the past and overstating the multi-perspectival nature of history. Yet grounding the study of literary texts in the present has long been, and continues to be, the most rewarding – not to mention the most feasible – option for teachers of Shakespeare at school level. Presentism invites the undergraduate student to revisit such pre-university readings in the light of a more sophisticated and conscious critical practice.

Sexuality in *Othello*

Nineteenth-century editors who set about making Shakespeare suitable for family reading found *Othello* to be one of their toughest challenges. The preface to the tragedy in Thomas Bowdler's 1831 edition of *The Family Shakspeare* [*sic*], recommended it be transferred 'from the parlour to the cabinet', presumably to be kept under lock and key for 'adults only'. Almost two centuries on, the presentation of the erotic in what E. A. J. Honigmann describes as a 'sex-drenched play' (Arden 3, 52), continues to attract a more than usually diverse range of interpretation.

Considering an early modern dramatization of sexuality from the vantage point of our own time requires a degree of caution. That sexual desire and practices are the same the world over and impermeable to changing times might seem commonsensical. However, as the history of just the past half century clearly shows, what is deemed 'natural' human behaviour is not set in stone, but defined by social, cultural and economic factors. That sexuality is as much a construct as an essential biological drive is an intellectual position which has dominated critical practice in recent years. One of the most influential exponents of this idea is the cultural historian, Michel Foucault (1926–84). In the first part of his three-volume history of sexuality, he insists:

> Sexuality must not be thought of as a kind of natural given which power tries to hold in check, or as an obscure domain which knowledge tries gradually to uncover. It is the name that can be given to a historical construct ... a great surface network in which the stimulation of bodies, the intensification of pleasures, the incitement to discourse, the formation of special knowledges, the strengthening of controls and resistances, are linked to one another, in accordance with a few major strategies of knowledge and power.
>
> (*The Will to Knowledge*, 1990, 105–6)

Foucault regards Shakespeare's time as the turning point in the history of sexuality, a time when sexual behaviour started to be shaped by forces such as the judicial system and the medical profession – forces which would grow increasingly powerful throughout the eighteenth and nineteenth centuries.

Iago is the play's self-styled sex expert. Playing on his status as experienced married man, he offers Roderigo his 'wisdom' on the inherent instability of erotic desire and the need to control 'carnal stings' (1.3.331). He puts his linguistic powers to work to plant a variety of lewd visual scenarios into the imagination of his victims: Desdemona and Othello 'making the beast with two backs' (1.1.115) (to torment Brabantio); Desdemona and Cassio 'paddling' palms (to torment Roderigo); and Cassio laying his thigh over Iago and kissing him, in the middle of an erotic dream of Desdemona (to torment Othello). Indeed, to acquire a 'feel' for the bawdy of early seventeenth-century England one need look no further than Iago, whose locker-room vernacular places him squarely in the military world, ensuring that all take him for the blunt soldier, never stopping to question what might lie beneath his plain-speaking exterior.

What clearly does lie beneath, though, is a seething hatred for his master. The image of Othello conjured up by Iago beneath Brabantio's window conforms to the contemporary dramatic stereotype of the libidinous, predatory Moor, passed down from medieval morality plays, and supplemented by empirical 'evidence' found in early modern travelogues. Shakespeare's depiction of Aaron the Moor in *Titus Andronicus* conforms in most respects to stage type, announcing his lascivious plans to 'wanton' (1.1.520) with Tamora, Queen of the Goths in his very first speech. The opening act of *Othello* could be read as a direct challenge to such representations of the Moor figure. Iago's crude description of the black Othello 'tupping' (1.1.88) the white Desdemona seems to have been set up for contradiction, as the so-called sex-beast proceeds to deal calmly and authoritatively with Brabantio's insults and with the pressing concerns of the imminent invasion.

Desdemona's frank admission of her sexual feelings for Othello in front of the Senate further challenges the stereotype of the lascivious Moor. Asked to confirm if she 'was half the wooer' (1.3.176), she declares:

That I did love the Moor to live with him
My downright violence and scorn of fortunes
May trumpet to the world.

(1.3.249–51)

In rejecting wealth, convention and sexual reticence at this juncture, Desdemona is confounding an entire belief system. For an aristocratic Venetian such as Brabantio, consensual sex between a black man and a white woman goes against 'all rules of nature' (1.3.102) and can only be explained if the Moor, true to his stereotype, is found to have administered 'mixtures powerful o'er the blood' (1.3.105) to get his evil way. That his daughter can publicly contradict this 'natural' explanation is a shock from which he never recovers.

Shakespeare leaves the audience in no doubt that Desdemona is sexually attracted to Othello. The imagery used to describe her reception of his travellers' tales is that of the appetite, commonly associated – both then and now – with erotic desire: 'She'd come again, and with a greedy ear/Devour up my discourse' (1.3.150–1). Here, in one of the play's numerous role reversals, she plays the part of the courtly lover, giving Othello a 'world of sighs' (1.3.160) in reward for his exotic stories, as well as the hint that he should woo her. That Desdemona feels physical desire for a man is not in itself unusual – women at the time were commonly held to be sexually rapacious – but that she should be free and open about her longings for a Moor is highly transgressive.

If Desdemona resembles Juliet in anticipating pleasure in the 'amorous rites' (*Romeo and Juliet*, 3.2.8) of the marriage bed, her choice of an ethnically different lover is where any similarity ends. Iago understands his society's deep-rooted fear of miscegenation and realizes that, while the Duke might have considered the national threat of Turkish invasion as more pressing than that of a single inter-racial marriage, once peacetime resumes, so too will normative attitudes. As if putting language back into kilter, he appropriates the word 'violence', that he has heard Desdemona use to convince the Senate of her love for Othello, to convince Roderigo to the contrary. The attraction was not love but 'a violent commencement in her' (1.3.345), which is bound to burn itself out. Moreover, as if rewinding the events of the play's first act, he persuades Roderigo that Desdemona's 'delicate tenderness will find itself abused' (2.1.229–30) and that she will veer to one of the 'curled darlings' (1.2.68) that should have been her initial choice. As far as most Venetians are concerned, 'natural' feeling is that which corresponds to societal norms: a woman 'naturally' desires a man of her own class and colour – and preferably one chosen by her father. What seems to lurk beneath this suppression of female agency, however, is a strong fear of the uncontrollability of women's sexuality, and it is this fear that Iago plays on in his intimate conversations with Othello.

There can be no doubt that Iago's instilling of European misogynistic attitudes into Othello plays a major part in transforming him from a loving husband to a violent wife abuser and that it is not, as some commentators have seen it, a simple matter of a superficially 'civilised' man reverting to primitive type. Nonetheless, the play raises questions about how far Othello has what the African American author and political activist, W. E. B. Du Bois (1868–1963), described as a 'double-consciousness, this sense of always looking at one's self through the eyes of others' (*The Souls of Black Folk*, 1903, 11), a potentially corrosive perspective, with or without the malicious intentions of an Iago. Just a few lines after Desdemona has declared her passionate love for her husband to the Senate, Othello presents his feelings in somewhat contrasting terms. He insists that it is to please Desdemona, and not to satisfy the erotic desires of a new husband, that drives him to request his wife accompany him to Cyprus:

> Vouch with me, heaven, I therefore beg it not
> To please the palate of my appetite,
> Nor to comply with heat, the young affects
> In me defunct, and proper satisfaction,
> But to be free and bounteous to her mind.

(1.3.262–6)

The lines can be read as a prime example of Othello's 'double-consciousness'. Aware of how he appears through the eyes of a typical Venetian, he attempts to present himself as sexually 'defunct', as unlike the prejudiced view of the hypersexual Moor as he can be. Yet they could equally well be read as the shrewd words of an experienced general in a tight spot. Where there is a tendency in our day to equate a strong sexual libido with masculinity, the early modern view was rather different: too much sex weakened the male both physically and mentally. In declaring his resistance to the delights of conjugality, then, Othello preserves his role as saviour of the nation, a role that has helped make his marriage acceptable to the state in the first place.

One influential critic, Valerie Traub, reads these same lines as expressing the speaker's sexual anxieties, anxieties which are 'culturally and psychosexually over determined by erotic, gender, and racial anxieties, including … the fear of chaos he associates with sexual activity' (*Desire and Anxiety: Circulations of Sexuality in Shakespearean Drama*, 1992, 36). Others have read them as an indication of the sexual inadequacy which lies at the centre of the couple's marital problems, with much critical fuss being made about whether or not the marriage is ever consummated. Some critics go so far as blaming Desdemona's murder on the frustration and anger which result from the sexual failure of the wedding night. Ultimately, though, theories about the consummation of the marriage can never go beyond mere conjecture. In Shakespearean drama, as in real life (the sex trade and pornography permitting), sexual activity is hidden away; we cannot, to use Iago's memorably alliterative phrase, 'grossly gape on' (3.3.398).

If the consummation issue has sometimes led critics to be over-literal, consideration of the sexual overtones of Desdemona's murder have yielded rather more sophisticated analyzes. It is a commonly held view that the killing of Desdemona materializes the early modern association of death and sex. In Elizabethan English 'to die' could mean to orgasm, a metaphor which carried with it a sense of oblivion and annihilation far removed from our modern use of the verb 'to come'. In stage and screen performances, Othello often suffocates Desdemona in a manner evoking the throes of orgasm, a necro-erotic coincidence which seems to be underscored, even ritualized, in the rhetorical patterning of Othello's dying words:

> I kissed thee ere I killed thee: no way but this,
> Killing myself, to die upon a kiss.

> (5.2.356–7)

While Othello's words seem to echo Romeo's in Shakespeare's earlier *liebestod*, they are altogether more disturbing and involved. The psychosexual nature of this later hero calls for far greater attention than that of his more youthful and more straightforward predecessor.

Othello and the power of language

The nature and significance of language is keenly explored in all of Shakespeare's plays and poetry, though *Othello* is especially notable for its insistence on making the audience hyper-conscious of the words they hear spoken. As the play progresses, so the usual transparency of verbal communication begins to thicken and, rather like when we are made to think about the operation of breathing, the process is rendered strange and unnatural.

Early modern attitudes to language were closely associated with biblical texts. In Genesis, Adam is given the power to name 'every living creature' (2.19), so that speech becomes a crucial sign of man's dominion over the animal kingdom. On the other hand, the proceeding story of the tower of Babel (11.1–9), tells of the loss of the 'original' Adamic language: a linguistic system wherein words were integral to the things they stood for, rather than an arbitrary appellation. Language was seen, then, as both a privilege and a curse, a contradiction that generated an ambivalent attitude to speech and writing.

The Venice of *Othello* is circumscribed by text and speech codes. The Duke promises the outraged Brabantio recourse to the 'bloody book of law' (1.3.68); Iago rails at the fact that 'Preferment goes by letter' (1.1.35); and Brabantio speculates that his daughter is bewitched because he has *read* of 'some such thing' (1.1.172). The elopement of Desdemona unsettles not only the decorum of Venetian society, but also its linguistic sureties. The Duke's speech to the aggrieved father, expressed in a series of rhyming couplets (1.3.203–10), is met by a sarcastic mirror language:

> So let the Turk of Cyprus us beguile,
> We lose it not so long as we can smile;
> He bears the sentence well that nothing bears
> But the free comfort which from thence he hears.
>   [...]
> But words are words: I never yet did hear
> That the bruised heart was pierced through the ear.
>
>   (1.3.211–20)

Here, for all his anger, Brabantio retains the linguistic control associated with the Venetian aristocracy in order to respond to the Duke in kind, his verbal imitation at the same time exposing the leader's speech as no more than a rhetorical brush-off.

Iago is both resentful and protective of the eloquence and bookishness of Venetian aristocratic society. He sneers at Cassio for being a 'bookish theoric' (1.1.23), while evincing equal contempt for the military Othello's 'bombast circumstance' (1.1.12). Clearly disturbed that an outsider can take on Venetian discourse, he casts doubt on his ability to sustain it. Referring back to Othello's wooing of Desdemona through 'bragging and telling her fantastical lies' (2.1.221), he asks Roderigo to consider whether she will 'love him still for prating?'(2.1.222); and, after he has exposed the fault lines in the hero's non-native language, derides his 'unbookish jealousy' (4.1.102), relishing the uncovering of what he sees as the Moor's inadequate learning.

Iago is often viewed by critics as the consummate rhetorician, whose social class denies him the opportunity to show off his linguistic virtuosity in public, obliging him instead to test it out in private situations. Cassio makes the fatal, if understandable, error of regarding Iago as more 'soldier than … scholar' (2.1.166). Placed in a position of superior knowledge thanks to Iago's frequent soliloquies, the audience realizes that nothing could be further from the truth. He confides to them that he 'must show out a flag and sign of love/Which is indeed but sign' (1.1.154–5), the **hendiadys** ('flag and sign') emphasizing the doubleness which he professes.

Iago's sophisticated understanding of language allows him to disrupt the linguistic confidence and decorum of others. His verbal manipulations are exercised first on a relatively easy target, Roderigo, then on the rather more challenging figure of Cassio and, finally, on his 'prize' victim, Othello. In one scene, Iago attempts to force Cassio out of his 'gentlemanly' habit of speaking:

CASSIO: She's a most exquisite lady.
IAGO: And I'll warrant her full of game.
CASSIO: Indeed she's a most fresh and delicate creature.
IAGO: What an eye she has! methinks it sounds a parley to provocation.
CASSIO: An inviting eye; and yet methinks right modest.

(2.3.18–23)

Played out here is a tussle between two modes of discourse: that of courtly love and that of a crude demotic. Iago's following up of words such as 'exquisite' with the suggestive metaphor of 'full of game' is not only an invitation to Cassio to lower his social standing by taking on the idiom of common misogyny, it also draws attention to register and tone. Is the language of courtly love no more than a verbal cover-up for brute physical desire? Though Cassio's reference to Desdemona's 'inviting eye' seems to edge closer to Iago's mode of speaking, the second part of the line, strengthened by the strong **medial caesura**, blocks Iago's strategy, putting him firmly back in his place – but not for long. Iago's next tactic of loosening Cassio's tongue with alcohol will see him brought down to speaking 'parrot' (2.3.275).

Iago expends his greatest linguistic efforts on destroying the confident articulateness of Othello. In the course of the play, he weaves false scenarios which, according to Terry Eagleton, succeed in 'punching a gaping hole in reality' (*William Shakespeare*, 1986, 66) and erode Othello's faith in Desdemona. At other times, he proceeds through the lightest of conversational touches. Take, for example, his treatment of Othello after Cassio's exit from visiting Desdemona:

IAGO: Ha, I like not that.
OTHELLO: What dost thou say?
IAGO: Nothing my lord; or if – I know not what.

(3.3.34–6)

Here, what we presume to be a mumbled remark combines with Iago's use of **aposiopesis** in line 36 to plant doubt in Othello's mind – a calculated omission setting him on his tragic course.

⑦ *Read 3.3.93–132 and analyze:*

- how the audience is made increasingly conscious of the relation between words and meanings
- the verbal means by which Iago manipulates Othello

One word which is put under close scrutiny here is 'honest'. As William Empson pointed out in his essay 'Honest in *Othello*', 'there is no other play in which Shakespeare worries a word like that' (*The Structure of Complex Words*, 1951, 218). In the course of events, the adjective is deliberately spotlighted, its meaning rendered labile. The repetition of 'honest' in this particular scene underscores Othello's choice: to believe in the honesty of Cassio, and by association his wife, or to take on board the insinuations of 'honest Iago'.

Just as the word 'honest' is batted back and forth by the speakers, so the word 'think' is repeated in mirrored speeches. In operation here is what the linguist Roman Jakobson termed the 'metalingual function': a checking by one speaker that he is using the same verbal code as his fellow speaker. Just as someone might ask an interlocutor to explain what is meant by a particular word or expression, so Iago's reiteration of 'think' at the start of line 108 suggests a need to confirm that he and Othello have a shared understanding of the monosyllable. Under Iago's control, the verb shifts from signifying belief in Cassio's honesty to an empty word used merely to humour the cuckolded general: 'Why then I think Cassio's an honest man.' This transition is aided by Iago's dextrous manipulation of language at line 128. The placing of 'I think' immediately after 'I dare be sworn' weakens the initial certainty, its parenthetical positioning holding it at a sceptical remove from Iago's affirmation that Cassio 'is honest'.

As what is commonly known as the 'Temptation Scene' progresses, so Iago seems fired up by his own verbal power, sounding more and more like the master out of the two men. This status exchange reaches its completion with Othello's 'sacred vow' (3.3.464), **perfomative language** that enacts his subordination to Iago. From this time forward, Iago can sit back and observe the effects of his linguistic labours. When Lodovico, shocked at having witnessed Othello strike Desdemona, asks Iago if he can offer any insights into his master's behaviour, he is told:

> You shall observe him,
> And his own courses will denote him so
> That I may save my speech.

$$(4.1.278-80)$$

Iago's withdrawal from language after his eventual capture signals his ultimate defeat and carries an irony entirely characteristic of the tragic mode, not least as the final syllable he pronounces is 'word'. In an age when speech was viewed as a God-given gift, separating man from the animals, his silence further signals that he has retreated from humanity itself.

Orson Welles's *Othello* (1952)

Orson Welles was one of the most innovative adapters of Shakespeare, though of his three Shakespeare films, *Othello* is probably the least well known. Filmed in numerous locations in Morocco and Italy, the production took more than three years to complete, a prolongation which played havoc with continuity – not to mention the nerves of the cast. Forty years after it took the *Palme d'Or* at Cannes, a restored version was released with a re-recorded musical score and properly synchronized dialogue, with many of its original flaws ironed out. Not only did the restored version use 1990s technology to improve the film quality, it also made it more commercially available, helping to bring about a reappraisal of what Jack J. Jorgens judged to be 'an authentic flawed masterpiece' (*Shakespeare on Film*, 1977, 175).

One of Welles's most daring directorial decisions was to start the film where the text ends. Living up to his own imperative that 'any movie has to have a great opening', the first five minutes or so draw the viewer in with striking camera work inspired by the pioneering cinematography of Sergei Eisenstein. Othello and Desdemona are carried on biers to the sound of Latin chants and dissonant piano chords, creating an atmosphere fitting for the grand sweep of tragedy. Iago looks down on this funeral scene, from his incarceration in a cage suspended above the scene: a disturbing image that renders him both animal-like and omniscient. In disrupting the play's linearity in this way, Welles establishes the ineluctability of the bloody outcome, creating his own macabre version of the Prologue which prefaces the action of *Romeo and Juliet*.

The film-goer is taken back to the opening of the play-proper by way of a narrative voiceover, adapted from Shakespeare's principal source, a story taken from Giraldi Cinthio's *Hecatommithi* (1565). Welles proceeds to edit and shape the text to his own ends, cutting the whole to just over ninety minutes of screen time. Micheál Mac Liammóir, the Irish actor who played Iago, writes in his highly entertaining memoir of the film's production: 'to-morrow we do a long speech ... it comes in Act One, Scene One, God knows in the film where it will be' (*Put Money in thy Purse*, 1952, 137). And he had every reason to fear the disorientating effects of Welles's textual rearrangements, the excision of the villain's soliloquies being one of the most significant manipulations of the text. Welles no doubt realized that if the soliloquies were played straight to camera, or via voiceover, the balance of the film could be adversely affected (Iago is the third longest role in Shakespeare). He chooses instead to demonstrate the duplicity of the Ensign in scenes between Roderigo and Iago, selecting a few key lines from the asides and soliloquies to transplant into their conversations. The impact of this is to remove the audience's complicity with Iago, placing them more in the role of distanced spectators.

Welles's adaptation moves away from the common conception of *Othello* as a 'domestic tragedy' to present a predominantly outdoor, military world. **Establishing shots** of battlements and rows of armoured troops underline the orderliness of army life; the military presence is also felt in the 'off-duty' drinking scene where Bianca carouses with her lover sporting a soldier's helmet. Othello seems very much part of this world at the start of the film – before its **image system** works to convey his psychological breakdown and fall from military grace. **Diegetic** sound motifs, such as the raging sea and the cries of seagulls, and the **non-diegetic** pounding of piano chords and discordant choric singing express his emotional turmoil and mark moments of crisis. The black-and-white film not only serves as a means of expressing the play's imagery of light and dark – and by association the racial difference between Othello and Desdemona – it also allows for the expressionistic use of shadows and silhouettes, suggestive of doubleness, uncertainty and a lack of clear-sightedness.

Welles's **metonymic** technique conveys the play's imagistic patterns and thematic concerns with impressive economy and impact. The drama's iterative metaphors of entrapment are captured in the visual textures of the film. Iron grilles and gates, slatted ceilings and floors, and the cage that appears ominously at significant moments, all build up a sense of incarceration and threat, the criss-cross shapes even being picked up in miniature in Desdemona's hair net. We are reminded of the question of Othello's Christianity through the huge cross which is held aloft before the funeral procession, by the altar piece in the crypt where the murder takes place and, on a smaller scale, by Desdemona's rosary. The firing of a cannon (both weapon and phallus) signals the consummation of the marriage, as well as the moment when the husband becomes fully convinced of his wife's infidelity: a visual representation of the difficulties of sustaining a marital relationship in a male, military environment. Clothing reinforces the hero's increasing vulnerability to Iago's influence. Resplendent in robes befitting a Moor of 'royal siege' (1.2.22) at the start of the film's main action, he moves to the equally impressive armour of the feted military leader. However, we soon see Iago in the process of removing his Captain's armour, at the same time as informing him of the 'pranks' (3.3.205) of Venetian women. Once stripped of his steel carapace, Othello appears physically more vulnerable and socially less elevated, dressed in a plain hooded cape: the aristocratic Moor brought down to the nomadic outsider.

The ocular imagery of the play is adapted especially well for the filmic mode. Outdoor scenes show bright sunlight and wind impede characters' vision at crucial moments, while in indoor scenes sight is clouded by the smoke of incense or the mist of hot water. Othello's faltering sense of self is succinctly portrayed as, while listening to the insinuations of Iago, he gazes in a mirror as if for the first time seeing himself as others see him. Later, by way of ironic parallel, we see Roderigo attempt to see himself in the makeshift mirror of the Turkish bath house, only to find his image clouded by steam. And just after Othello has sworn himself to Iago forever, Welles includes a split-second shot of two blind street beggars singing in unison, an image which seems to connect to what is by this point the hero's almost total blindness to the truth of his own situation.

Welles's blacked-up face and the film's refusal to make overt the racial issues of the play is not entirely in tune with the sensibilities of our own more multi-ethnic age. But this should not be allowed to detract from its very considerable filmic achievements, not least its success in capturing some of the essential elements of the Shakespearean text in 'brilliant angular forms cut as it were out of blinding sunshine and shadow' (*Put Money in thy Purse*, 159–60).

Further thinking

➤ Some presentists argue that recognizing your own feelings towards an emotionally demanding text can serve as a valid and stimulating point of departure.

Select any scene from a Shakespearean tragedy which you find particularly affecting and try to define your responses to it. If you can, ask fellow students to read the same scene so that you can compare your reactions.

➤ The handkerchief in *Othello* has attracted a wealth of critical comment. Lynda E. Boose, for example, argues that it 'not only spans the major issues of the play but also reaches into man's deepest cognitions about his sexuality, his myths, his religion, and his laws' ('Othello's Handkerchief: "The Recognizance and Pledge of Love"', *ELR*, 5, 1975, 374). Can you think of stage properties of comparable significance in other Shakespearean tragedies?

➤ Some critics have found in *Othello* affinities with the comedies. What links could you find between *Othello* and the comedies covered in this book (try to think beyond character to aspects of structure and language)?

Afterlives ...

One of the best-loved and best-known operatic treatments of Shakespeare is Giuseppe Verdi's *Otello*, which premiered at Milan's La Scala in 1887. Verdi worked with one of Italy's most esteemed composers and poets, Arrigo Boito, to produce what has been described as the 'perfect' opera. The libretto distils the play to fewer than 800 lines and omits Act 1 entirely, opening with the triumphant arrival of Otello in Cyprus. But what is lost without the play's Venetian perspective? And is the operatic Desdemona a figure of passivity and resignation?

7

King Lear: 'That things might change, or cease'

King Lear has long been considered the most troubling and problematic of the tragedies. For nearly 150 years it was only performed in Nahum Tate's re-written version. Where Samuel Johnson found it disturbing, the Romantics saw it as sublime: 'the most perfect specimen of dramatic art in the world' (P. B. Shelley). The twentieth century responded to the play variously, as Christian allegory, or as politically apocalyptic.

This chapter

- looks at Marxist criticism as a way of approaching the text
- considers early modern attitudes to authority and duty
- examines some differences between the play's Folio and Quarto texts
- discusses Grigori Kozintsev's film adaptation of *King Lear*

Marxist readings

So distribution should undo excess
And each man have enough.

(4.1.73–4)

Marxism is the political philosophy of Karl Marx (1818–83) and Friedrich Engels (1820–95) and it goes without saying that the influence of Marxism and Communism on more than a century's history has been immense. The following synopsis identifies some of the key concepts of Marxism as an ideological means of exploring literary texts. Both writers were, first, commentators on the brutalizing industrial conditions of the mid-nineteenth century: Engels' *Condition of the Working Classes in England in 1844* analyzes capitalist production in the newly-developing cotton trade. For Marx and Engels, society and individual human experience is materialist: controlling economic factors constitute the 'base' organization of society; ideas, philosophies and artistic expression are defined as 'superstructure'. The inherent tensions and contradictions within these class relations create dialectic – history is never static. The materialist outlook extends also to religion: to Marx, existence is wholly earthbound; there will be no heavenly compensation for societies' inequalities and injustices. For their contemporary Victorian Christian writers, the sufferings of life are ultimately redeemed by a higher spiritual reality. Marx, however, defined religion as 'the sigh of the oppressed' or, famously, 'the opiate of the people'. In 1848 Marx and Engels published *The Communist Manifesto* which moves from political analysis to revolutionary conflict, arguing in favour of class struggle for a fairer society which would abolish private ownership, and share equitably the means of production, distribution and exchange. In the twentieth century, the idea of the superstructure (or hegemony) as shaping all individual notions of self in the world, was further defined; in Britain, the Marxist literary critic Raymond Williams arguing that

> [In] any society, in any particular period, there is a central system of practices, meanings and values … [which] constitutes a sense of reality for most people.
>
> (*Culture and Materialism*, 2005, 38)

As the writing of Marx and Engels is rooted in the social conditions of the time, similarities with contemporary fiction can frequently be found (Elizabeth Gaskell's novels of Manchester life would be a good example). There are shared concerns, even where the ideology fundamentally differs. But can Marxist theories be applied retrospectively to texts such as Shakespeare's plays? In terms of Marxism as a critical methodology, a number of relevant connections emerge:

- *historic*: a Marxist critic sees literary production, just as any other cultural expression, as shaped by and expressive of its social and political world, in particular by the material conflicts of that world. Shakespeare's theatre, then, can be seen as dramatizing its contemporary world, rather than 'essential' or 'universal'.

- *theoretic*: a Marxist critic delves into a text with a commitment to uncovering layers of hidden meaning, discovering a buried agenda of struggle and resistance. Feminist studies such as Coppélia Kahn's 'The Absent Mother in *King Lear*' (New Casebooks, 1993) would be a good example.

- *presentist*: modern readers and audiences bring their own knowledge and experience to the play so although Marxist readings are historicist, there might be a powerful new political significance for modern readers with a concomitant commitment to challenging and changing readers' and audiences' attitudes.

Marxist critics of *King Lear* would not, on the other hand, engage with ideas of (pastoral) 'Nature' other than in terms of a specific political point about Elizabethan enclosures or failed harvests. Nor would Marxist critics hide behind generalizations about the play's 'mystery' or argue, with A. C. Bradley, that the 'only real thing in it is the soul, with its courage, patience, devotion.' Christian interpretations of the play expounded by early twentieth-century writers such as Bradley and Wilson Knight were questioned and found wanting from the mid-twentieth century when political readings emerged. Critics found in *Lear* an expression of unredeemed devastation suited to post-war trauma. It no longer seemed possible to identify in the play a benign resolution. For the Marxist Jan Kott, *Lear* 'is the decay and fall of the world':

> [There] is neither Christian heaven, nor the heaven predicted and believed in by humanists. *King Lear* makes a tragic mockery of all eschatologies: of the heaven promised on earth, and the heaven promised after death ... both the medieval and the renaissance orders of established values disintegrate. All that remains at the end of this gigantic pantomime is the earth – empty and bleeding.
>
> (*Shakespeare our Contemporary*, 116)

'Her price is fallen'

The opening of the play lends itself to materialist analysis because of Lear's fatal confusion between love and material value. The spectacle of Lear's public demand for assurances of love is uncomfortable viewing: adult married women should not be called upon to produce sickly-sweet speeches for daddy. Lear's opening declaration is all too revealing: 'Know that we have divided in three our kingdom'. The legalities are apparently already accomplished, the performance of filial affection is what is now required. Lear desires some gratifying competitiveness from the trio:

> Which of you shall we say doth love us most
>
> (1.1.51)

The hyperbole from Goneril and Regan is immediate, almost unthinking. Goneril's words are also strangely meaningless: 'more than ... Dearer than ... Beyond what ... No less than … As much as … Beyond all …'. Each blank verse line commences with a comparative term while concluding that speech is 'unable'. Lear wants to quantify love and this is exactly what Goneril understands. She is instantly rewarded. There are, interestingly, no answering words of love or gratitude. Lear simply accepts this fulsome flattery and 'shadowy forests … plenteous rivers and wide-skirted meads' change hands. The profession of love has its equivalence in material goods – as Goneril expects. In the source play, *The True Chronicle History of King Leir and his three daughters,* the old king is obviously anticipating something special from Cordelia: 'drop down nectar from thy honey lips' (*King Leir*, Globe reprint, 2005, 1.2.76) Shakespeare ratchets up the tension, making Lear's request yet more competitive and more brutally commercial:

> what can you say to draw
> A third more opulent than your sisters?

(1.1.85–6)

Her 'nothing' is her dismissive reply to his demand for a display of rivalry. His revenge is the auctioning of Cordelia: she must be equally mortified and humiliated in the public sphere. He expects that she should suffer corresponding rejection now 'her price is fallen'. Cordelia is now reduced to an unwanted, and unsalable, object: 'she's there and she's yours'. And it is perhaps telling that he has sought rivalry between his potential sons-in-law as well as in his own immediate household. Lear's scheme recoils when France restores 'value' to Cordelia, 'this unpriz'd-precious maid', the **oxymorons** emphasizing the contradictions of her position:

> Fairest Cordelia, that art most rich being poor,
> Most choice forsaken and most loved despised …

(1.1.252–3)

The disastrous confusion of love and marketable goods is not over, however. A similar equation between affection and things can be seen when Goneril and Regan reduce the crucial status symbols of Lear's regality:

> Thy fifty yet doth double five and twenty,
> And thou art twice her love.

(2.2.448–9)

In Marxist (or Marxist-feminist) terms, Lear's mistake is not just commodifying Cordelia, objectifying her as a piece of mercantile property that can be sold to the highest bidder. No, love itself is commodified here: no more than a means of exchange, and quantifiable in terms of knights, land, products.

'Take physic pomp'

A Marxist critique of *Lear* would pay close attention to the play's language of surplus and inequality. This is important to both Lear and Gloucester in their pained reflection on suffering and injustice. Gloucester's thoughts are the more accessible, inspired by the revelation that a mad beggar might offer him more compassion than courtly nobles. Indeed, in the scene of his torture and blinding, the question of class is emphasized. The servant who attempts to stop Cornwall in his actions sees his interference as 'better service' than a lifetime of feudal loyalty. The ensuing fight between the two men is brought to a violent end by Regan 'Give me thy sword. A peasant stand up thus!' (3.7.79). Class seems more important to her than love. The sadism of 'Let him smell his way to Dover' is countered by the two remaining servants who express their disquiet and fetch remedies for Gloucester's bleeding eyes. Morality in this scene is expressed and enacted by those who are powerless and alienated. The Old Man (who also protests his lifetime of service) continues this motif. He is reluctant to entrust the wounded Gloucester to a naked beggar but responds with excessive generosity to Gloucester's request for 'some covering for the naked fellow'. The Old Man's charity cannot be 'valued' by the two parties involved here: one is blind; the other (apparently) deranged. A few rags would suffice but what Gloucester hears is:

> I'll bring him the best 'pparel that I have,
> Come on't what will.

> (4.1.52–3)

The Old Man's gesture symbolizes generosity itself – it has no prospect of reward and is performed partly as a protest against the cruelty of his 'betters'. Gloucester's response to such conflicting external voices is a clarion call for greater equality: 'So distribution should undo excess / And each man have enough' (4.1.73–4).

Lear's words are strikingly similar: he too defines justice through the redistribution of wealth:

> Take physic, pomp,
> Expose thyself to feel what wretches feel,
> That thou may'st shake the superflux to them
> And show the heavens more just.

> (3.4.33–6)

The pursuit of justice in Lear's mind extends beyond this, though: in his madness he is consumed with the desire to judge – as sole ruler and arbiter. In the storm, he establishes a parodic courtroom with the naked Edgar as 'robed man of justice' and the Fool as 'yoke-fellow of equity'. Fool and madman metaphorically represent the state of justice in Lear's kingdom. And the scene is juxtaposed immediately with the corrupt 'trial' scene of Gloucester where Cornwall exemplifies all the cynicism of power:

> Though well we may not pass upon his life
> Without the form of justice, yet our power

Shall do a courtesy to our wrath, which men
May blame but not control.

(3.7.24–7)

In the great scene between Lear and Gloucester (4, 6), Lear
moves towards an extraordinary statement of radicalism:

None does offend, none, I say, none. I'll able 'em ...

(4.6.164)

The entire, mighty hierarchical structure of monarchy, nobility,
formalized legal system – authority itself – has become 'A dog's
obey'd in office'. Lear moves beyond his earlier empathy
for those who are poor and cold; he desires an anarchic
breakdown of existing hierarchy. For Lear to move from the
instant judgements he makes at the beginning of the play to an
assertion that there is no crime; no one is guilty, is unparalleled.
These are revolutionary statements. Marxist readings of *Lear*
would identify inequality as central to the text: it is not
unhistorical to make this connection; rather it is a joining-up
of the play's preoccupations with the audience's own political
knowledge. Tragedy arises in *Lear* not because of implacable
gods or through inherently mysterious workings but as a direct
consequence of social conflict and its repercussions.

Early modern ideas of authority and duty

every inch a king.
When I do stare, see how the subject quakes.

(4.6.106–7)

It is extraordinary to reflect that Lear's words were first spoken
before James I. The play was performed in the banqueting hall

at Whitehall on Boxing Day, 1606. The spectacle of a king divesting himself of his clothes, ardently seeking the company of a Fool and a beggar, possibly, in his madness, provoking grotesque laughter, would certainly challenge James's view of the monarch's divine authority. Yet, at the beginning of the play, Lear is as autocratic as James, a king whose extreme consciousness of his own superiority led him to compare himself with God:

> Kings are iustly called Gods, for that they exercise a manner or resemblance of Diuine power vpon earth; for if you wil consider the Attributes to God, you shall see how they agree in the person of a king.
>
> (*Political Writings*, James VI and I, 181)

This is exactly the attitude to royal authority assumed by Lear and dramatized in all the exchanges of the opening scene. Courtiers dance attendance upon the king; foreign princes woo his daughter. Both James I and Elizabeth understood the effectiveness of royal pageantry and display as a means of establishing and reinforcing sovereignty. Critic Leonard Tennenhouse discusses the elaborate iconography and display James commanded for his coronation, including the medals and coins that depicted him dressed as a Roman emperor (*Power on Display: The Politics of Shakespeare's Genres*, 1986). Fancy dress was, to both Elizabeth and James, the outward declaration of majesty. James was also notorious for his courtly extravagance. Lear's 'train [of] men of choice and rarest parts' (1.4.255) is, then, consistent with the expectation and performance of authority. The play at its outset could be said to exemplify Stuart absolutism together with the flattery and deference James himself demanded. Kent, for example articulates his unswerving deference to his liege lord:

> Royal Lear,
> Whom I have ever honoured as my king,

Loved as my father, as my master followed,
As my great patron thought on in my prayers ...

(1.1.140–3)

Indeed, Kent desires only to maintain the status quo: 'Reserve thy state' is cautionary advice against abdication. James I would certainly approve: his ambition was to unite his kingdoms and consolidate his power. But the intemperate rage Lear directs against Cordelia descends on Kent in language which reveals the egotism at the heart of power: 'Come not between the dragon and his wrath.' Lear believes that his authority is so absolute that it is not possible to revoke his judgement:

That thou hast sought to make us break our vows,
Which we durst never yet, and with strained pride
To come betwixt our sentences and our power,
Which nor our nature, nor our place can bear,
Our potency made good ...

(1.1.169–73)

The play defies and rejects Lear's concept of authority, showing how tyrannical demands and habits of submissiveness undermine moral judgement and common sense. Where Kent courageously opposes Lear, Gloucester is silent even if he disapproves. Later, though, Gloucester exerts his own moral judgement rather than persist in the habit of subjugation:

My duty cannot suffer
T'obey in all your daughters' hard commands.

(3.4.144–5)

His words point out that abuses of authority are not located in one individual. Regan and Goneril both assume that they are above the law: the latter proclaims, 'the laws are mine ... / Who can arraign me ...?' (5.3.156–7). Regan expects to be both judge and executioner in the scene of Gloucester's torture: 'Hang him instantly!' are her opening words (3.7.4). Lear's absolutism has created a political world that is seen to be corrupt and demeaning.

Perhaps the greatest irony of the play is that the king we see crowned with flowers has acquired a new authority, a vision that penetrates beyond any known structures of power. Like Isabella in *Measure for Measure*, he sees the superficiality of rulership – 'But, man, proud man/Dress'd in a little brief authority' (*MM*, 2.2.118–9). This is the heart of the play's complexity and originality. Lear sees that where 'Robes and furred gowns hide all' (4.6.161) justice is untenable. He understands, also, that words can be lies where power encourages flattery: 'they told me I was everything; 'tis a lie' (4.6.103–4).

In the original play, 'Leir' rules once more and here, too, the moral forces of Kent, Edgar and Albany are dedicated to restoring authority to Lear. Yet he has no desire to resume power: his finest moment, recognizing Cordelia, fumbles towards the simplest sense of self:

> as I am a man, I think this lady
> To be my child Cordelia.

> (4.7.68–9)

In terms of monarchical authority, the final exchanges of *Lear* are exceptional. There is no triumphalist Malcolm displaying the severed head of Macbeth; there is no warlike drum announcing the arrival of Fortinbras. Shakespeare briefly allows the audience to believe in the possibility of resolution as Albany attempts to pursue the good ending:

> we will resign
> During the life of this old majesty
> To him our absolute power;
> [...]

> All friends shall taste
> The wages of their virtue and all foes
> The cup of their deservings.

(5.3.297–303)

But he is defeated; Lear is beyond caring now Cordelia is dead. Albany makes an attempt to nominate Kent and Edgar as co-rulers, but that fails too. In its devastating depiction of the tragedy of Lear's authority, the play ends by backing away from bestowing the crown on anyone at all.

> I loved her most, and thought to set my rest
> On her kind nursery.

(1.1.124–5)

Early modern notions of familial duty would certainly dictate filial obedience. The biblical command to 'honour thy father and mother' combined with new ideas of patriarchy had the effect of elevating the male role within the household. King James I concludes his discussion of the 'divine power' of kings with an analogy of the family:

> Kings are also compared to Fathers of families; for a king is trewly *Parens patriae*, the politique father of his people.
>
> (*Political Writings*, James VI and I, 181)

It might seem a paradox of early modern Protestant England that patriarchal power increased. Lawrence Stone cites many examples of the expected submission to parents in the home:

> [The] stress on domestic discipline and the utter subordination of the child found expression in extraordinary outward marks of deference which English children were expected to pay to their parents in the sixteenth and early seventeenth centuries. It was customary for them when at home to kneel before their parents to ask their

blessing every morning and even as adults on arrival at and departure from the home.

(*The Family, Sex and Marriage in England 1500–1800*, 1982, 122)

The quotation illustrates how unthinkable it is for Lear to kneel to Cordelia in response to her request for blessing: 'look upon me, sir/And hold your hands in benediction o'er me!' (4.7.57–8). But his gesture redeems his earlier 'be gone/ Without our grace, our love, our benison' (1.1.266–7). Stone's study of the period argues a number of factors: on the national scale, the monarch had displaced (or expected to displace) old Catholic loyalties to the Papacy and its hierarchies of priests, bishops and cardinals. But this obtained also in the microcosmic world of the family: the priest was no longer set apart from society in his sacramental world of the Latin Mass and his avowed celibacy. So the male 'head' of the household gained new moral and spiritual authority, often leading his family in household prayer and biblical study. Conduct books of the time paint a picture of the family in explicitly political language: a good example might be John Dod's and Robert Cleaver's *A Godlie Forme of Householde Governement* (1630) where the household is 'a little commonwealth, by the good government whereof, God's glory might be advanced.' Within this scheme, the 'chief governor' is the father, authoritarian and all-powerful. Parents from middle and upper classes certainly expected to select marriage partners for their offspring, a choice that would be based on mercenary values rather than romantic ones. Furthermore, this was not restricted to parental control of daughters' lives but extended also to sons. Severe attitudes to discipline and punishment were ubiquitous and both boys and girls were routinely beaten.

In *Lear*, an oppressive model of family life is exposed and then brutally destroyed from within. As feminist critics have observed, the 'absent mother' means that the dictatorship of the father is unmitigated. Shakespeare dramatizes a world where all affective duty breaks down: the key point here being the connections between Lear's world and Gloucester's. In neither family is there an affectionate marriage or sibling loyalty. The opening words of the play, 'knave ... whoreson', demonstrate the inadequacy of Gloucester's duty towards his son. Resentment and rivalry between siblings might be expected in such circumstances but it is not exclusive to Edmund; it soon emerges in Goneril's words about Cordelia:

> He always loved our sister most, and with what poor judgement he hath now cast her off appears too grossly.
>
> (1.1.292–3)

Any loyalty between Goneril and Regan will be short-lived as their sexual competitiveness takes over. Goneril is totally cynical in accomplishing her ends by any means; her aside – 'If not, I'll ne'er trust medicine' – is crudely sardonic. Edgar desires the courtly satisfaction of the duel against Edmund; Goneril just poisons her sister. At a time of tightly-argued rules of duty and obedience, the chief players here hate, destroy and are, themselves, destroyed. For Kiernan Ryan, the early modern world of enforced duty and imposed authority can only be tragic:

> *King Lear* makes it clear that love within the patriarchal family, however pure it seems, is doomed to be infected by domination, dependency, resentment and guilt.
>
> (Penguin text of *King Lear*, 2005, xlix)

Quarto and Folio texts

Why are there two different versions of *King Lear*? Did Shakespeare himself revise the later version, making his own changes to the playscript? Is it significant that the earlier version was described as a 'history' of Lear rather than a tragedy? Above all, do these questions matter? Any page of Arden Shakespeare presents readers with the drama itself, explanatory commentary below the text and, beneath that, an area once described as 'barbed wire', a prickly area to be avoided. The purpose of these marginal references is to supply all the various textual possibilities that exist from different versions of the play. Many are insignificant; some are fascinating. Perhaps the best example of a textual variant in Shakespeare's work is the opening of Hamlet's first soliloquy:

O that this too, too *solid* flesh
O that this too too *sullied* flesh
O that this too too *sallied* flesh

(1.2.129, my italics)

All of these are valid textual readings: the first expresses Hamlet's despair that he cannot simply dissolve away and cease to exist; the second implies flesh that is dirty or contaminated and 'sallied' (Arden 3) has implications of besieged or assailed. These are significant differences. Every editor of a Shakespeare text needs to make decisions about what to include and which readings to favour. As an acting text, both theatre directors and actors exercise choices in the light of their interpretation.

Quarto and **Folio** are terms which refer to the published form of Shakespeare's theatre texts. Quartos were the small-size text of individual plays, some of which appeared in Shakespeare's lifetime. They were assembled from the hand-written working drafts used in the theatre, in some cases involving the original manuscript. 'Good' quartos were printed from 'fair copy' and regarded as authoritative. The term 'bad quartos' refers to texts which were based on actors' recollections of plays, often for the purpose of producing a version which could be profitably sold to a theatre company. Manuscript sources could be hastily copied; badly-written and full of minor errors. There was no standardized spelling at that period. Quartos, then, were often far from being the author's single and definitive text; the modern sense of a perfect finished work is simply not appropriate to this period. There is debate as to how far Shakespeare himself was ever involved in the publication of early manuscripts. The First Folio is, famously, the collection of thirty-six plays published in 1623, seven years after Shakespeare's death. It was compiled by two editors, John Heminge and Henry Condell, fellow actors and friends of Shakespeare.

King Lear first appeared as a quarto text in 1608, entitled *M. William Shak-speare: His True Chronicle Historie of the life and death of King Lear and his three Daughters* (see Arden 3, 112). A substantially different text entitled *The Tragedie of King Lear* was printed in the First Folio, 1623. Many modern versions conflate the two texts, incorporating approximately 100 Folio lines not in the Quarto and some 300 Quarto lines not in the later Folio, on the basis that the writing is all Shakespeare's. It is possible that the earlier text is the version that Shakespeare first wrote and that the 1623 version shows his own revisions. If so, this would offer a unique insight into the author's creative and theatrical thinking. It might imply the evolution of a text: from author's original manuscript through the collaborative contributions of the acting company to a final, altered play. The existence of two versions raises the questions of whether to privilege one text over the other or continue the tradition of merging the two. As well as minor textual differences, there are also entire scenes which only appear in the earlier Quarto version. These include:

- The 'trial' scene in the hovel: from Edgar, 'The foul fiend bites my back' to Lear, 'why hast thou let her 'scape?' (3.6.17–55).

- The two servants who comment on the blinding of Gloucester: 'I'll never care what wickedness I do … Now heaven help him!' (3.7.98–106)

- The quarrel between Goneril and Albany: from 'I have been worth the whistling' to 'Monsters of the deep' (4.2.29–51) and later, 54–60 and 63–70 in the same scene.
- The whole scene of Kent and the Gentleman discussing Cordelia's 'smiles and tears' (4.3)
- Edgar's account of Kent's death (5.3.203–20)

These scenes are dramatically powerful; Albany's rejection of his wife is morally satisfying, as is the brief moment of humane compassion from the servants. The imagery used of Cordelia introduces redemptive possibilities: she is 'sunshine and rain', her tears 'pearls from diamonds ... holy water from her heavenly eyes'. Did Shakespeare choose to omit the latter since the following scene introduces the audience immediately to the goodness of Cordelia in similar terms: 'All you unpublished virtues of the earth/Spring with my tears' (4.4.16–17)? Or is it possible that Shakespeare desired to prune the text of instances of kindliness in order to darken the tragedy?

Two small details were added to the Folio text:

- Lear urging the Fool to enter the hovel: 'In boy, go first' (3.4.26)
- Lear 's words on justice (4.6.161–6)

There is poignancy in Lear's concern for the Fool, interrupting the political rhetoric addressed to 'houseless poverty/naked wretches'. It establishes his concern for those who suffer with him and shows his changing attitude to his loyal Fool, earlier threatened with the whip. His attack on wealth and hypocrisy and defence of all criminals – 'None does offend' – could be seen as enforcing this motif in the play. There is no simple 'right answer' to these textual questions; it is widely accepted that both Q and F are Shakespeare's writing yet the shape of the play and the balance between good and evil is altered, making the later Folio a bleaker play.

The History of King Lear by Nahum Tate, 1681 ('Reviv'd with Alterations')

The post-Restoration audience found Shakespeare's devastating conclusion simply too disturbing to accept. In Samuel Johnson's words:

> Shakespeare has suffered the virtue of Cordelia to perish in a just cause, contrary to the natural ideas of justice, to the hope of the reader, and, what is more strange, to the faith of chronicles ... I was many years ago so shocked by Cordelia's death, that I know not whether I ever endured to read again the last scenes of the play.

Johnson debates whether the cruelty of the play is 'too savage and shocking' to be enacted on stage and argues that the 'extrusion' of Gloucester's eyes 'seems an act too horrid to be endured in dramatick exhibition.' He debates the rival merits of Tate's or Shakespeare's conclusion and defers to majority taste:

> [The] publick has decided. Cordelia, from the time of Tate, has always retired with victory and felicity.

Tate produced a greatly reduced version of Shakespeare's play. Major differences appear from the opening: Edgar woos Cordelia from the beginning of the play; Edmund ('Bastard' in Tate's text) also admires her, although he is also seen 'amorously' with Regan. In the final scene, Albany and Edgar intervene just as Lear and Cordelia are to be hanged, and Albany resigns troops and rulership to Lear. Edmund has been slain by Edgar; Regan and Goneril have poisoned each other; Cordelia remains to be Queen. Gloucester and Kent return to be welcomed into the general celebration. The final speeches, affirming truth and justice, could not be further from Shakespeare's. In looking at Tate's language, though, it is worth remembering that Shakespeare was the first to take liberties with the existing tale. No one watching the first performances would have expected to see Lear entering with the dead body of Cordelia; every source, historical or literary, reinstates Lear at the end and reunites him with Cordelia. In that respect, Tate is closer to the original tale than the *King Lear* which is now familiar; it is Shakespeare who has re-written and troubled the known ending.

⟨?⟩ *Now make your own editorial choice: below are two extracts from the final scene of the play, as published in the Quarto and Folio versions, plus Tate's ending.*

- Look at the differences in the language of Q and F; what is suggested in Lear's final words?
- In the Quarto, the final lines of the play ('The weight of this sad time') are spoken by Albany rather than Edgar. Is this change important?
- Do you agree with the early twentieth-century views of Bradley who described the Folio as moving 'from despair to something more than hope'?
- Finally, read the extract from Tate. This is how the play ends in his version: what is your response to his conclusion?

Q, 1608

LEAR: And my poor fool is hanged. No, no life.
　　Why should a dog, a horse, a rat have life,
　　And thou no breath at all? O, thou wilt come no more.
　　Never, never, never. Pray you, undo
　　This button. Thank you, sir. O, O, O, O!
EDGAR: He faints. My lord, my lord.
LEAR: Break heart, I prithee, break. [*Dies*]

F, 1623

LEAR: And my poor fool is hanged. No, no, no life.
Why should a dog, a horse, a rat have life,
And though no breath at all? Thou'lt come no more.
Never, never, never, never, never.
Pray you, undo this button. Thank you sir.
Do you see this? Look on her, look, her lips,
Look there, look there. *He dies.*

Nahum Tate, 1681

EDGAR: Our drooping Country now erects her Head,
Peace spreads her balmy Wings, and Plenty Blooms.
Divine Cordelia, all the Gods can witness
How much thy Love to Empire I prefer!
Thy bright Example shall convince the World
(Whatever Storms of Fortune are decreed)
That Truth and Vertue shall at last succeed.

Kozintsev's *King Lear* (1970)

Shakespeare's words still ring, resonant and full. His verse is still blistering its hands today ... His plays seem to be written by someone close to us, by a man of our time.

(Kozintsev, *Shakespeare: Time and Conscience*, 1966)

Kozintsev's film of *King Lear* is a striking and imaginative transformation of the text and could be seen as a classic exemplar of Marxist interpretation. The life and work of Kozintsev spans twentieth-century revolutionary and Communist Russia. In his youth he was involved in radical Bolshevik agit-prop; *Korol Lir* was produced towards the end of his life after a career wholly involved in stage and screen. His first version of *Lear*, 1941, was a stage production in

Leningrad, just prior to the Nazi invasion and subsequently revived during the siege of the city. In Kozintsev's recollections:

> Shakespeare was with the people. On the street shells were exploding; frequently the audience and the actors had to leave for the bomb shelter ... Only a few instruments played the music of Shostakovich, a part of the set burned up ... The theatre shook ... The old king cursed injustice: he demanded that inhumanity be condemned.
>
> (cited, Joseph Troncale, 'The War and Kozintsev's Films: *Hamlet* and *King Lear*' in *The Red Screen: Politics, Society, Art in Soviet Cinema*, ed. Anna Lawton, 1992, 205)

By the time Kozintsev returned to *Lear* for the film version, he had also published *Our Contemporary: William Shakespeare* (translated as *Shakespeare, Time and Conscience*, 1966). A later collection of letters and diary extracts on the filming process reveals Kozintsev's profound meditations on the text and the film (*'King Lear', The Space of Tragedy: The Diary of a Film Director*, 1973). Maintaining a modern perspective rather than producing filmed costume drama, was always central to Kozintsev's intentions. So Pasternak's translation is in modern Russian; the subtitles reproduce lines from Shakespeare but the speech is twentieth century. The film maintains a tragic vision which is inherently Marxist; the tyranny of despotic rule sets events in motion, and the ensuing suffering is not exclusive to royal rank. Inspiration was drawn in part from Russian newsreels of the 'Great Patriotic War' (World War Two): destroyed villages and dead bodies in the snow, distraught and bewildered survivors; 'the people's grief' (*Lear*, 40).

⁇ *Some details to consider:*

- Gloucester's on-screen death and burial: why, perhaps, does Kozintsev substitute this for the 'cliff-top' scene?

- During the blinding of Gloucester, the camera cuts to Goneril lacing her boots and Edmund buckling on his belt. What is signalled by this movement away from the violent intensity of the moment?
- The role of the Fool: what does he add to the atmosphere at the end of the film?
- There is no final speech from Edgar. Why do you think Kozintsev chose to cut the last words of the play?

Lear's initial situation is presented from a Marxist perspective: 'At the beginning of the play, all life in him is frozen by the habit (or the necessity) of ruling' (*Lear*, 40). The play is not a simple folk tale of a man and his daughters but an insight into the falseness of royal power, deriving its strength from oppression and fear, susceptible to the demeaning relations of flattery. Equally, Gloucester's moral instincts are defeated by the habit of feudal deference: 'he is of one flesh with the social system' so even where he sees Lear acting wrongly, he cannot intervene. The individualism of Goneril, Regan and Edmund, on the other hand, exemplifies energies associated with 'the period of primary accumulation of capital' (*Time and Conscience*, 89). They desire and pursue the wealth and power of an old regime but employ methods that are newly capitalist. For Kozintsev, Shakespeare's Renaissance perspective is one which 'saw both the evil of the old order and the savagery of the new' (*Time and Conscience*, 94). The scene in the hovel (3.4) must, then, be the climax of Lear's moral awakening. Here, as in the film's opening, the screen is filled with the dispossessed. Lear's 'Poor naked wretches' is a speech addressed to those around him, seeking shelter in the straw, rather than an abstract self-accusation. And 'Off, off, you lendings' is a gesture of his complete identification with these outcasts, as well as the epiphanic revelation that his kingship has been no more than external trappings.

The film is not just a piece of Soviet propaganda, though. In terms of cinematic opportunities, Kozintsev was interested in what could be achieved beyond the possibilities of staging:

traitor Macdonwald and foreign invasion by the Norwegian Sweno. The tide of battle is clearly in Macdonwald's favour until Macbeth 'carves' his way towards him, his sword 'smok'd with bloody execution' as if he is the executioner performing the brutal act of disembowelling a traitor (the same image that Macbeth conjures when he refers to his 'hangman's hands' after Duncan's murder). The verb is disturbing with its implication that steam rises from the hot blood of Macbeth's victims. The decisive conclusion is likewise barbarous:

> he unseam'd him from the nave to th' chops,
> And fix'd his head upon our battlements.

> (1.2.22–3)

This clearly resembles the Elizabethan executioner's drawing and quartering of condemned traitors; as Neil MacGregor observes, 'human butchery was a part of life. Strolling across London Bridge to see a play at the Globe or the Rose, you would sometimes pass rows of traitors' heads impaled on spikes' (*Shakespeare's Restless World*, 2012, 260). Shakespeare's audience might well have attended popular executions. The dismembered head is, of course, horrifyingly **proleptic** of Macbeth's own dismal end. Yet the saintly King greets this with gratitude and the royal seal of approval: 'O valiant cousin! Worthy gentleman!' When the second wave of attack brings threats from Sweno, Shakespeare conflates years of Scottish history into a few lines of description to intensify the effect. The renewed assault introduces Banquo as Macbeth's fellow warrior: together they appear to 'bathe in reeking wounds' (40) where 'reeking' has similar connotations to the earlier 'smok'd'. Shakespeare uses the word identically in *Coriolanus* (1609) in a similarly martial context: 'to the battle came he where he did / Run reeking o'er the lives of men' (2.2. 118–9).

The Captain's final image has disturbingly religious connotations: Macbeth and Banquo seemed to 'memorize another

Golgotha'. This defies straightforward analogy: Golgotha means 'place of the skull'; it is the hill outside Jerusalem associated with the crucifixion of Jesus. Does the Captain mean simply that they create another place famed for brutal killing, or does he introduce connotations of spiritual horror? Golgotha, to Shakespeare's audience, would signify the furthest extreme of mankind's evil. To Duncan, though, these words 'smack of honour' and Macbeth must be instantly rewarded with the new, obviously ironical, title of Thane of Cawdor. In the context of warfare, this 'performance' of masculinity has been entirely successful, and is applauded as such. 'Theatre of war' is not a term used at the time but it is a resonant (and relevant) one: warfare as the opportunity for the practice and performance of modes of behaviour condemned outside that context. *Coriolanus* offers an identical classical comparison; both Coriolanus and Macbeth receive extravagant praise for wholesale slaughter. In their different worlds, they are linked by identical views of manly heroism where the physical courage required in brutal hand-to-hand warfare is the apotheosis of masculine honour. In *Macbeth* intense violence is perpetuated: each succeeding act of the play portrays a climactic moment of horrifying slaughter. And it is, of course, how Macbeth chooses to die: 'I'll fight, till from my bones my flesh be hack'd'. But it is also true of the way in which others define their masculine responses. When Macduff is told of the savage slaughter of his wife and children, Malcolm urges him to 'Dispute it like a man':

> Be this the whetstone of your sword: let grief
> Convert to anger; blunt not the heart, enrage it.

> (4.3.228–9)

In the final scenes, the young son of old Siward is described as if he has accomplished manhood in the nature of his death: 'He only liv'd but till he was a man/... /But like a man he died' (5.9.6, 9). His father enquires only about the manner of his death – 'Had he his hurts before?' – and then dismisses him: 'Why then, God's soldier be he'.

The warring medieval kingdoms that form the background to events – Scotland, England, Norway – were warrior communities. Duncan's observance and approbation of, rather than involvement in, the battle signifies his ceremonial and elevated role. He is too sacred to fight. Shakespeare creates a parallel in the English king (impliedly Edward the Confessor). His spiritual qualities are emphasized – he is 'full of grace' with a gift of 'healing benediction' (4.3.159, 156). Society has evolved beyond wholesale slaughter, as Macbeth observes:

Blood hath been shed ere now, i' th' olden time,
Ere humane statute purg'd the gentle weal ...

(3.4.74–5)

The aspiration to civilized values distances the king from the battlefield; warriors such as Macbeth and Banquo enact the masculinity of warfare on their behalf. In his study of masculinities, Robin Headlam Wells argues that there are two 'mutually opposed conceptions of manhood' in *Macbeth* that cannot be reconciled. The play is 'an anatomy of heroic values that offers no solution to the conundrum it dramatises' (*Shakespeare on Masculinity*, 2000, 137, 143).

It is not only the King but the women of the play who endorse warlike masculinity. Lady Macduff resents her husband's flight to England, leaving her defenceless:

He wants the natural touch; for the poor wren,
The most diminutive of birds, will fight,
Her young ones in her nest, against the owl.

(4.2.9–11)

Yet it is, in fact, Macduff alone who can distinguish between military and domestic masculinity:

> All my pretty ones?
> Did you say all? – O Hell-kite! – All?
> What, all my pretty chickens, and their dam,
> At one fell swoop?
>   [...]
> I cannot but remember such things were,
> That were most precious to me.

(4.3.216–23)

The association between martial masculinity and sexuality is an obvious one: in Act 4 of *Antony and Cleopatra* where Antony is, briefly, successful against Caesar, this is the erotic language of the lovers' triumphant greeting:

> ANTONY: O thou day o' th' world,
>   Chain mine armed neck! Leap thou, attire and all,
>   Through proof of harness to my heart, and there
>   Ride on the pants triumphing!
>
> CLEOPATRA: Lord of lords!
>   O infinite virtue! Com'st thou smiling from
>   The world's great snare uncaught?

(4.8.13–18)

He lays before her his victory and demands to be embraced as a warrior in full armour. Lady Macbeth also greets her husband in terms of the recent battle, 'Great Glamis! Worthy Cawdor!' whereas she addresses him with the intimate 'My husband!' as she waits for the confirmation of Duncan's death. When she upbraids him for abandoning his aspiration towards the crown, it is his love for her that she derides. She first attacks him with her escalating rhetorical questions, 'Was the hope drunk?' The implication that his hope wakes 'green and pale' carries the suggestion of a sickly hangover and also the 'green girl' – the fainting, adolescent maiden. Her conclusion is decisive and devastating:

> Art thou afeard
> To be the same in thine own act and valour,
> As thou art in desire?

> (1.7.39–41)

The audience must know at this point that Macbeth is defeated: her question provokes him to feel (or at least recall) desire, and then taunts him with the notion of sexual timidity. Given his status as conquering hero, it is scarcely surprising that he responds in terms of his superior masculinity, 'I dare do all that may become a man; / Who dares do more, is none' (1.7.46–7). But she parries with

> When you durst do it, then you were a man;
> And, to be more than what you were, you would
> Be so much more the man.

> (1.7.49–51)

She echoes his own language of manhood and exploits it, moving him beyond the immediate certainties of the battlefield towards the undefined act of the night. The denial of her own sexual identity is further confusing, incongruously evoking a vision of maternal love, as if she summons the fruit of their (successful) sexual union. And she has clearly judged well; by way of admiration he exclaims, 'Bring forth men-children only!' (73). It is horrifying to dwell on these words: his praise follows her image of infanticide; he makes real their sexual intimacy; he desires children who are 'men' – to further this masculinity of bloodshed. Macduff, on the other hand, speaking of his lost children, laments his 'pretty chickens'; 'my pretty ones' – his instinct is to feminize those (including a son) whom he has failed to protect. Macbeth has imbibed his wife's words and her thoughts to the extent that the 'act' itself is externalized by him: 'wither'd Murther ... with Tarquin's ravishing strides ... Moves like a ghost' (2.1.52–6). Early uses of the word 'ravishing' confirm meanings of both rape and predatory destructiveness. Yet it is Macbeth himself who links his state of mind with Tarquin's. In terms of Duncan's murder, the climax of this imagery of violence and sexuality must be his justification of his slaughtering of the guards – a detail not envisaged by his wife. His 'violent love' has overwhelmed him:

> Who could refrain,
> That had a heart to love, and in that heart
> Courage, to make's love known?
>
> (2.3.114–6)

But this is a massacre and the association between Macbeth's – presumably – unpremeditated action and the language of love used earlier by Lady Macbeth herself defeats her. It is precisely at the moment he says 'love' that she faints. She sees the truth. They cease to be united at exactly that moment when he reverts to the world of the battlefield, performing an act of uncontrolled savagery.

It is revealing that Lady Macbeth's persuasive language fails entirely at the banquet scene. She mocks his fears as no more than 'a woman's story at a winter's fire' (3.5.64); he is 'quite unmann'd in folly' (3.5.72). But the enemy confronting him here is the numinous, a spectral presence private to himself. Macbeth attempts to re-establish his identity in clichéd, masculine terms; reassuring himself that:

> What man dare, I dare;
> Approach thou like the rugged Russian bear,
> The arm'd rhinoceros, or th'Hyrcan tiger;
> Take any shape but that ...
>
> (3.4.98–101)

But Banquo's ghost terrifies him with possibilities that lie beyond his knowledge or power. By this point Macbeth's military code of honour has become no more than brutal individualism: 'for mine own good/All causes shall give way' (3.4.134–5). As critic Frank Kermode has suggested, excellence in warfare is what 'unmans' him when tormented by 'horrible imaginings' that '[Shakes] so my single state of man/[That] nothing is, but what is not':

> He is a brave man, a man of blood, Bellona's bridegroom; but like Coriolanus later he exhibits the defects of these qualities. He has an affinity with blood and darkness … He has his notion of virtus, the quality of being a man, and it serves him well in war; but it does not include the power to deal with the evil growing in his mind.
>
> (*The Riverside Shakespeare*, 1974, 1309)

In *Macbeth* Shakespeare dramatizes medieval Scotland as a world which demands a certain type of maleness, a role Macbeth can abundantly fulfil. Indeed, after his wife's death, the code of the battlefield is all that remains to him: 'Blow, wind! Come, wrack!/At least we'll die with harness on our back' (5.5.51–2). As Marilyn French has argued in *Shakespeare's Division of Experience* (1992), the role of gender in *Macbeth* is 'the keynote of the play, the "myth" from which everything else springs' (242). In Macbeth as tragic hero, Shakespeare dramatizes the man destroyed by the myth of manhood.

Macbeth the 'Jamesian' play

The literature of the early seventeenth century is termed Jacobean (in Latin, James is Jacobus) to designate the reign of James I. The term denotes the characteristic art and architecture of the period and has come, also, to suggest certain characteristics of the drama, most notably the genre of revenge tragedy. The majority of Shakespeare's plays are Elizabethan, but some of the greatest writing dates from the latter part of Shakespeare's career and critics are interested to question whether the late, Jacobean plays, could be said to share characteristic features. To what extent can a change in dramatic tone be perceived? To describe a play as 'Jamesian' is to introduce another consideration entirely: it signals not simply that the text is post–1603 but that the play dramatizes issues or ideas specifically connected with the new king.

Elizabeth's final years were troubled by the much-disputed question of succession: the Queen herself was famously unwilling to discuss her advancing years or name her successor. International diplomacy between Spain and sympathetic English nobles advanced the possibility of Catholic succession, or debated whether James might convert to Roman Catholicism. Some weeks before her death Elizabeth was said to have proclaimed 'I will that a king succeed me, and who but my kinsman the King of Scots'. James VI of Scotland was the child of Mary Queen of Scots and Henry Stuart, Lord Darnley, both of whom were descended from the Tudor dynasty, indeed they were first cousins, sharing the same grandmother, Margaret Tudor (Henry VIII's elder sister). James had the advantage, then, of a strong title and the firm Protestant conviction that would be necessary for Elizabeth's heir. In terms of *Macbeth*, the play's connection with the new king operates in two ways: James's own preoccupation with kingship and his obsessive interest in witchcraft. Critics have also found references to the contemporary Gunpowder plot in the language of the Porter.

James, Fleance and the *Basilikon Doron*

Macbeth seeks a second encounter with the Witches because he is tormented by their earlier prophecy: 'Shall Banquo's issue ever/Reign in this kingdom?' (4.1.102–3). He is shown a line of kings '[stretch'd] out to th'crack of doom', with a smiling Banquo acknowledging his paternity and lineage. In the distant future, some are seen to bear 'two-fold balls and treble sceptres', a reference taken to imply James's double coronation at Scone, the ancient coronation site of Scottish kings, and Westminster. Kermode sees this 'glorification of Banquo and of Fleance, founder of the Stuart line [as] an essential part of the Stuart political myth' (*The Riverside Shakespeare*, 1308). James would approve Shakespeare's source material, Holinshed's *Chronicle of Scotland*, as the Stuart dynasty is clearly identified:

> Banquho [sic], the thane of Lochquhaber, of whom the house of the Stewards is descended, the which by order of linage hath now for a long time inoied the crowne of Scotland, euen till these our daies.
>
> (Arden 2, 167)

To James, as absolutist ruler, monarchy is sacred so the notion of prophecy is inevitably appealing. The sanctity of kingship is pursued further in the play through the fleeting reference to Edward the Confessor, again drawn originally from Holinshed. Presented as a direct antithesis to Macbeth and his affinity with 'juggling fiends', Edward 'solicits Heaven', cures the sick and, significantly, passes on this gift to his successors:

> To the succeeding royalty he leaves
> The healing benediction. With this strange virtue,
> He hath a heavenly gift of prophecy;
> And sundry blessings hang about his throne,
> That speak him full of grace.
>
> (4.3.155–9)

Sally Mapstone, critic of medieval texts and early Scottish literature, observes that Shakespeare's closest borrowing from Holinshed is *Macbeth* ('Shakespeare and Scottish kingship: A Case History', *The Rose and the Thistle: Essays on the Culture of Late Medieval and Renaissance Scotland*, 1998). The scene between Malcolm and Macduff where Malcolm as true heir enumerates the 'king-becoming graces' was also derived from Holinshed (Arden, 176–7) and contributes to the discussion of monarchy. Early critics dismissed the scene as 'tedious' and found it difficult to account for the long dialogue between the two men; in fact there are troubling ironies in the vices Macduff regards as venial. Whether Shakespeare intends a glancing comment on James's less-attractive traits is unfathomable.

It would be interesting to know how far Shakespeare had had any acquaintance with James's *Basilikon Doron* (Greek for Royal Gift) originally written in 1599 and widely disseminated in England in 1603, on the eve of James's accession to the throne. The book is a manual on the nature and practice of kingship and addressed throughout to James's eldest son, Prince Henry, then aged five (died 1612):

> [My sonne] first of all things, learne to know and loue [God] ... first for that he made you a man; and next, for that he made you a little GOD to sit on his Throne, and rule ouer other men.
>
> (James VI and I, *Political Writings*, 1994, 12)

James exalts the nature of kingship, and proclaims the complete impossibility of overthrowing the ruling monarch, even if tyrannous:

> [A] wicked king is sent by God for a curse to his people, and a plague for their sinnes: but that it is lawfull for them to shake off that curse at their owne hand, which God hath laid on them, that I deny, and may do so iustly.
>
> (*The Trew Law of Free Monarchies, Political Writings,* 79)

Rebellion can never be justified and the much-cited 'divine right of kings' has arrived on English soil. Shakespeare's audience would know well how forcefully an absolutist monarch imposes authority: after the (Catholic) Gunpowder

Plot of November 1605, the plotters were swiftly pursued and arrested. The surviving eight men were tortured, sentenced in January 1606 and publicly hanged, drawn and quartered in the usual highly theatrical way. Extreme violence in this context demonstrates kingly power; it is to be feared, and its public manifestation silences opposition and enforces submission. As Alan Sinfield argues, 'Macbeth, like very many plays of the period, handles anxieties about the violence exercised under the aegis of Absolutist ideology' (' "Macbeth": History, Ideology and Intellectuals', *New Casebook* 1992, 123). Sinfield's essay analyzes the contradictions of a complacent Jamesian reading, pointing out that Duncan's state is chaotic before Macbeth's violent rule is imposed upon it. In the end, the ultimate taboo – the killing of the king – is violently performed twice within the play. To see the one act as blasphemous, the other as godly can only be problematic. James's own argument, that the tyrant must not be resisted, is not upheld in the play; while Duncan's proclaimed heir laments in England, Macduff advances war against Macbeth, killing him for reasons of personal revenge. For modern readers, history adds the ultimate footnote: James I argued Divine Right; in 1649 his son, Charles I, was executed by his people.

James and *Demonologie*

James's political writings articulate his desire to exercise control in a threatening context: Papists, Puritans, Nobles, are all described by him as challenging his authority. His fears included the paranormal: in his *Demonologie* (1597) he set out to establish that 'such devilish arts have been and are' and that witchcraft 'merits most severely to be punished.' He evokes a mortal world which is constantly embattled: even the virtuous should be ever-vigilant against the machinations of Satan whose aim is to undermine and destroy mankind. Witches, in James's world view, are motivated by 'the desire of revenge [or] worldly riches'. They desire 'either to hurte men and their gudes, or what they possess, for satisfying of their cruell mindes in the former, or else by the wracke in quatsoeuer sorte … to satisfie their greedie desire '. James singles out the power of prophecy and the ability to travel through the air as common to evil spirits, features of Shakespeare's witches. Clearly James felt personally threatened: he describes a bizarre sorcery involving a christened cat, dead body parts and a tempest which threatened his ship as it left Denmark for Scotland. A recent historical survey of the subject establishes that belief in witchcraft 'permeated every social and cultural level of late sixteenth-century Scotland' (L. Normand and G. Roberts, *Witchcraft in Early Modern Scotland*, 2000, 54). So intense was the pursuit of witchcraft and so appalling the torture practised, that the accused often confessed to the stories required of them in order to satisfy the 'ideological needs' of the accusers. This was particularly the case in Scotland: in England witch trials tended to be small-scale, localized and a means of directing malice or fear against – usually – a solitary old woman. Belief in witchcraft did not simply mean entertaining the possibility that evil spells might bring about harm; rather it meant fear of an entire world order. An inverted reality coexisting alongside normality and ruled by the exact opposite of godliness and order: 'nothing is but what is not'. Shakespeare conveys this in the opening riddling words of the witches, already set apart by their **tetrameter**:

Fair is foul and foul is fair
Hover through the fog and filthy air …

There seems no doubt that Shakespeare is tapping into more than just a generalized consciousness of demonology. There are too many details which resemble James's and other contemporary writings: bleak and barren wastelands by night are where witches gather; they are associated with prophecy and the ability to deceive through 'equivocating' half-truths; they raise storms, perform ritual dances and derive power from their familiars. The multiples of the mystic '3' are significant, as are the dismembered human and animal body parts. Above all, perhaps, the Weird Sisters embody a powerful female malignity.

No doubt, then, the new king would have been gratified to find his current obsession with the dark arts reflected in the play but is Shakespeare beating James's drum here? On stage and screen the witches are compelling and mysterious; evil is certainly located within the world of the numinous but, as every school child knows, Macbeth has already contemplated 'horrible imaginings':

> My thought, whose murther yet is but fantastical,
> Shakes so my single state of man,
> That function is smother'd in surmise,
> And nothing is, but what is not.

> (1.3. 139–42)

Furthermore, as Macbeth himself realizes, if their prophecies are accurate, then 'Chance may crown me/Without my stir'. As all early modern Protestants would understand, Macbeth, like everyone else, operates with free will. Milton's Satan acknowledges as much in his great soliloquy: 'Hadst thou the same free will and power to stand?/Thou hadst' (*Paradise Lost*, Book 4, 66–7).

There are unavoidable moral difficulties which disturb easy answers: first, to tie the prophecy of James's own lineage to this evil source is troubling; can the witches' revelations confirm the legitimacy of the Stuart dynasty? Second, in a play of violent retributive punishment, the witches alone remain unmolested. It would seem unlikely that this would be because of any squeamishness on Shakespeare's part: the authorities of the time pursued, tortured and executed women suspected as witches in large numbers. Within the theatre world women are not spared either: Shakespeare and other playwrights dramatize acts of sensational violence against women. In

Macbeth, as Polanski's film brilliantly emphasizes, the witches remain. To Terry Eagleton Shakespeare's witches are 'the heroines of the piece', exiles on the margins of Scotland's violence:

> [Inhabiting] their own sisterly community on its shadowy borderlands, refusing all truck with its tribal bickering and military honours ... they are poets, prophetesses and devotees of female cult, radical separatists who scorn male power and lay bare the hollow sound and fury at its heart.
>
> (*William Shakespeare*, 1986, 2)

Imagery in *Macbeth*

The extraordinary vigour and complexity of Shakespeare's language make his plays unique. He invariably chooses to dramatize existing stories or historical accounts so 'plot' is not where his originality necessarily lies, but the resonance of his imagery sets him apart, conveying unfolding levels of meaning and suggestion. Specific images linger in the mind and defy easy definition; returning to a play and re-investigating nuances of language seems always to suggest new possibilities. Phrases from *Macbeth* are memorably haunting:

> Will all great Neptune's ocean wash this blood
> Clean from my hand? No, this my hand will rather
> The multitudinous seas incarnadine,
> Making the green one red.
>
> (2.2.59–62)

Scholars of early-twentieth-century 'close reading' traced patterns of imagery through a particular play to suggest ways in which Shakespeare establishes the concerns and ideas of the drama as well as its overall tone and mood. Caroline

The conventions of the theatre and the structure of the play do not allow the whole fullness of life which the poetry embraces to be shown on the stage: many of the events are spoken of in the past tense, quickly skated over in the stage directions. In the cinema one can hold up the action in order to look closely into people's eyes and at the ever-widening panorama of events.

(*Lear*, 251)

The music of Shostakovich was central to Kozintsev's notion of fidelity to the play's 'poetic structure'. In his view, where cuts in the text had been made, the music re-introduced the imagery and style of the verse, 'carr[ying] on a dialogue with the characters' (*Lear*, 249). Perhaps the most striking incidence of the collaboration between Kozintsev and Shostakovich (they had also worked together on the 1941 stage version) is Kozintsev's crowd scenes accompanied by wordless choral singing. The wide-screen Soviet film format, the desolate landscape and the tramping vagrants create a powerful effect. The film is shot in black and white throughout in order to prevent any visual distraction. Nature is of immense significance here but must not be diluted into picturesque pastoralism. Indeed, here, too, a political ideology is to the fore: Kozintsev's view of Elizabethan England is one of roaming beggars, evicted from their homes by 'Dame Avarice':

Hordes of vagabonds, terrible caravans of human grief, roamed the country. They were ragged, exhausted from hunger, and vainly sought work. They dragged themselves along the roads, leaving by its edge the corpses of those who had no strength to go further.

(*Shakespeare: Time and Conscience*, 67)

He conflates these Shakespearean wanderers with twentieth-century fugitives, thus emphasizing the realities of a complex social world. Edgar as 'Poor Tom' is briefly a solitary outcast, soon joining a miscellaneous group of travellers. Towards the end of the film, as battle draws near, individuals and families are again on the march, sometimes trampled and overwhelmed by soldiers. The rare moments depicting an isolated individual stand out more acutely as a result, the most horrifying being the hanged body of Cordelia, framed by the overwhelming castle seen at the beginning of the film. And when battle is over, there is great poignancy in the small groups and families returning to the burnt-out shells of their homes to attempt to restore some semblance of their communal life.

Further thinking

➤ Experiment with applying Marxist ideology to different plays (perhaps *Measure for Measure* or *Othello*) thinking about the presentation of social inequalities and power relations.

➤ Ideas of authority are central to *Richard II:* think of the different ways in which it is theatrically presented.

➤ *Hamlet* is a play with a complex textual history. Find out about the variant placing of the 'To be or not to be' soliloquy and make your own judgement as to its dramatic appropriateness.

Afterlives …

King Lear is a play with a considerable 'afterlife': Edward Bond's *Lear* (1971) is an exceptionally brutal drama; Howard Barker's play *Seven Lears* (1989) is a political re-telling. Jane Smiley's novel *A Thousand Acres* (1991) sets the play in rural Iowa and imagines a disturbing back-story of incest and violence.

8

Macbeth: Kingship and witchcraft

> M*acbeth* is often regarded as the darkest of Shakespeare's tragedies, a vision of evil and alienation. It is unusually tied to ideas and anxieties of its time – perhaps because Shakespeare and his company are now the King's Men (from 1603) and under royal patronage.
>
> This chapter
>
> - examines the play from the perspective of recent work on masculinities
> - approaches the text as a product of the Jamesian era
> - explores aspects of the play's imagery
> - looks at Polanski's film of the play

Macbeth **and masculinities**

Masculinities is a late twentieth-century area of critical enquiry which has derived from gender studies and, as such, seeks to identify and question social and cultural constructions of gender. It is interdisciplinary, extending into sociology and psychology, as well as examining the representation of gender through theatre and performance history, and in the visual arts. How far gender is performative is a recurrent question. Textual critics, adopting this model of analysis, explore ideas of masculine behaviour, or gender specific ways of thinking within literary genres or individual works. Coppélia Kahn sees Shakespeare as 'critically aware of the masculine fantasies and fears that shaped his world, and of how they falsified both men and women' (*Man's Estate: Masculine Identity in Shakespeare*, 1981, 20). In fact, it could be argued that 'masculinities' as a concept has always informed discussions of Macbeth. Samuel Johnson's essay on the play (1765) is a useful point of departure: Macbeth's death is unlamented and 'every reader rejoices at his fall'. But Johnson singles out the concept of physical courage and the way in which Macbeth's morality is 'confuted' by the martial ethos of the play:

> [Lady Macbeth] urges the excellence and dignity of courage, a glittering idea which has dazzled mankind from age to age, and animated [the conqueror] ... Courage is the distinguishing virtue of a soldier, and the reproach of cowardice cannot be borne by any man from a woman.

The play itself throws the audience into confusion from the outset: battle here is not depicted in the glorious terms of *Henry V*. There are witches waiting for the end of the 'hurly-burly' and the opportunity to harvest their macabre spoils; their business is with anarchy and destruction. The King's role, conversely, is to represent all that is lawful and ordered, even godly, but as he questions 'What bloody man is that?' the complex relationship between rulership and extremes of violence has begun. The Captain's speeches are remarkable in two significant respects: the gruesome physicality of his descriptions, and the automatic association with valour. Neither the speaker nor the King acknowledges any troubling ambiguity in this respect. Indeed the Captain offers his account of battle as a tribute to his feudal lord. But the language of his narrative draws attention to inherent contradictions: he uses elaborate metaphor and convoluted syntax to describe blood and gore. In Shakespeare's conflation of Holinshed, Macbeth is fighting two waves of battle – an internal threat from the

power from their familiars. The multiples of the mystic '3' are significant, as are the dismembered human and animal body parts. Above all, perhaps, the Weird Sisters embody a powerful female malignity.

No doubt, then, the new king would have been gratified to find his current obsession with the dark arts reflected in the play but is Shakespeare beating James's drum here? On stage and screen the witches are compelling and mysterious; evil is certainly located within the world of the numinous but, as every school child knows, Macbeth has already contemplated 'horrible imaginings':

> My thought, whose murther yet is but fantastical,
> Shakes so my single state of man,
> That function is smother'd in surmise,
> And nothing is, but what is not.

> (1.3. 139–42)

Furthermore, as Macbeth himself realizes, if their prophecies are accurate, then 'Chance may crown me/Without my stir'. As all early modern Protestants would understand, Macbeth, like everyone else, operates with free will. Milton's Satan acknowledges as much in his great soliloquy: 'Hadst thou the same free will and power to stand?/Thou hadst' (*Paradise Lost*, Book 4, 66–7).

There are unavoidable moral difficulties which disturb easy answers: first, to tie the prophecy of James's own lineage to this evil source is troubling; can the witches' revelations confirm the legitimacy of the Stuart dynasty? Second, in a play of violent retributive punishment, the witches alone remain unmolested. It would seem unlikely that this would be because of any squeamishness on Shakespeare's part: the authorities of the time pursued, tortured and executed women suspected as witches in large numbers. Within the theatre world women are not spared either: Shakespeare and other playwrights dramatize acts of sensational violence against women. In

Macbeth, as Polanski's film brilliantly emphasizes, the witches remain. To Terry Eagleton Shakespeare's witches are 'the heroines of the piece', exiles on the margins of Scotland's violence:

> [Inhabiting] their own sisterly community on its shadowy borderlands, refusing all truck with its tribal bickering and military honours ... they are poets, prophetesses and devotees of female cult, radical separatists who scorn male power and lay bare the hollow sound and fury at its heart.

> (*William Shakespeare*, 1986, 2)

Imagery in *Macbeth*

The extraordinary vigour and complexity of Shakespeare's language make his plays unique. He invariably chooses to dramatize existing stories or historical accounts so 'plot' is not where his originality necessarily lies, but the resonance of his imagery sets him apart, conveying unfolding levels of meaning and suggestion. Specific images linger in the mind and defy easy definition; returning to a play and re-investigating nuances of language seems always to suggest new possibilities. Phrases from *Macbeth* are memorably haunting:

> Will all great Neptune's ocean wash this blood
> Clean from my hand? No, this my hand will rather
> The multitudinous seas incarnadine,
> Making the green one red.

> (2.2.59–62)

Scholars of early-twentieth-century 'close reading' traced patterns of imagery through a particular play to suggest ways in which Shakespeare establishes the concerns and ideas of the drama as well as its overall tone and mood. Caroline

Spurgeon's early study, *Shakespeare's Imagery and What It Tells Us* (1935), identified four areas of persistent interest: the 'borrowed robes' or ill-fitting clothes which suggest Macbeth's unfitness for honour or royalty; darkness and the patterning of light/dark throughout; the reverberating sound of grief 'yell'd out' across the universe, and, finally, sickness. Imagery, then, can unfold throughout the text, accreting layers of significance. It might, though, function discretely:

> They have tied me to a stake: I cannot fly,
> But, bear-like, I must fight the course.

> (5.7.1–2)

Macbeth's image implies that he is the victim of spectator sport as well as underlining the animal brutality of what is to come.

Figurative language works through replacement or parallelism; it is suggestive, not literal. Lady Macbeth's response to her husband's hyperbolic fear that his hand would stain the sea is dismissive: '[my] hands are of your colour; but I shame / To wear a heart so white' (2.2.63–4). She is attempting to be brisk and practical – wash your hands – while also implying that Macbeth is a coward. Or does the 'white' heart imply, bizarrely, a degree of innocence? And to what extent can the heart be 'worn' as if it is external to the self? Imagery can never be reduced to a formula: it is, by its very nature, elusive. It works through association, evoking connotations which may variously be connected with the senses; intellectual ideas; Nature; spirituality; notions of family or social bonds – the list must be as endless as the thoughts or feelings which flicker across the human mind.

In *Macbeth*, an excellent example of imagery that cannot be readily pinned down would be the following extract from one of Macbeth's key soliloquies. It must be said that this has attracted a vast amount of critical analysis; nonetheless it should be possible to approach it with a degree of imaginative openness.

⊙ *Read 1.7.16–25 closely and consider:*

- Macbeth's syntax: what does this suggest about his state of mind?
- the two principal similes
- metre: what is emphasized in the speech?

The syntax is convoluted because this is all one sentence with a series of images compressed within it. The similes can be easily identified – 'like angels, trumpet-tongu'd … like a naked new-born babe' – yet Macbeth's meaning is dense, even unfathomable. This is not to say that he himself is confused: he has just argued with complete clarity – 'I am his kinsman and his subject/Strong both against the deed'. But his thinking seems to leap into regions beyond custom or morality, forcing together images of angels, the naked new-born and the cherubim in ways that cannot be easily accommodated. Angels and cherubim are related, if not identical notions: the angels will plead Duncan's great virtues while the cherubim fly, unseen, around the universe riding the winds. Within this grand theological scheme is Pity, personified as the new-born babe – the most helpless and vulnerable expression of humanity, and one which is central to this play. Lady Macbeth is about to use a similar notion of innocent helplessness as the furthest extreme she can think of to impress upon her husband. Later, Lady Macduff's babes will be slaughtered at Macbeth's bidding. How does it function in Macbeth's mind here? There seems to be a contradiction in the idea of the babe 'striding the blast': an incongruously forceful verb. The 'blast' is likely to be the trumpet blast announcing the horror of the deed but in this play, with its language of storm and chaos, 'blast' could also carry apocalyptic suggestions. Certainly tears raining down to the extent that they drown the wind is both hyperbolic and tempestuous: grief more powerful than the elements.

The metre and alliteration draw attention to key words, too, so that pairs of oppositional phrases stand out:

'trumpet-tongu'd', 'deep damnation', 'naked newborn'. The overall effect is paradoxical: pity is at once vulnerable yet powerful. What Macbeth is literally saying is that Duncan's death will be greeted with universal sorrow; his expression of this cannot be confined within that simple statement.

⑦ *Now look at Macbeth's language after the murder of Duncan (2.3.89–94):*

- Is his horror genuine?
- Does his language here seem euphuistic?

Think about his puzzling description of Duncan's corpse: 'his silver skin lac'd with his golden blood'. Samuel Johnson saw these lines as 'forced and unnatural' so that Shakespeare could draw attention to Macbeth's hypocrisy. Is there an alternative possibility? Does Macbeth know that this is true – that 'grace' is indeed dead to him?

Polanski's *Macbeth* (1971)

Polanski's film is remarkable for its emphasis on extreme violence and brutality. Its portrayal of warfare and bloodshed is unflinching and the horror of the vengeful feuding against women and children equally unsparing. Polanski considerably augments the violence of the text; killing is vividly realized rather than off-stage. Additional murders and executions intensify the effect of primitive savagery. The death of Cawdor is made into a public scene; Macbeth kills not only young Siward but several other soldiers at the end of the play; the murderers of Banquo are summarily dispatched once they have brought their news to Macbeth's feast. The non-textual murder of Duncan is highly significant: the physicality of the deed is avoided by Shakespeare (quite possibly for political reasons) but here, Duncan wakes to see Macbeth, and the killing is both protracted and graphic. The butchered bodies of the guards are what prompts Lady Macbeth's fainting, a highly effective moment as it suggests that here, for the first time, she confronts the reality of what her husband has done – and what he is. The attack on Macduff's castle, seemingly connived at by a time-serving Ross, features the brutal slaughter of babies and young children, and rape of the women. Here, the masculinity of warfare and concomitant vulnerability of women and children is inescapable and horrifying. As Lady Macduff flees through the narrow passages of her castle, there is clearly no escape and sights and sounds appal – for several minutes nothing can be heard other than terrified female screaming. The courtly world itself is seen to be one which enjoys spectacles of cruelty: the bear-baiting which accompanies Macbeth's triumphant feasting makes Lady Macbeth shrink with horror, as she looks at the snapping dogs waiting to destroy the bear. The bodies of the beasts being dragged away is a sight which seems to brutalize and reduce the human losses. The film opens with the witches burying a severed arm and closes with Macbeth's head displayed on a pike above his castle. Viewers might well echo Macbeth's 'I have supp'd full with horrors'.

Two factors should be considered in debating the violence of Polanski's film: cinematic choices and Polanski's personal experiences. Much has been made of the murder of Polanski's wife, Sharon Tate and their unborn child, in 1969. But Polanski himself cites his childhood recollections of the Nazi occupation of Cracow; the casual savagery of the men who invade the peaceful domestic scene of Lady Macduff bathing her son derives from Polanski's remembrance of Nazi soldiers playing with, and taking, his childhood toy. The sadism of institutionalized power is terrifying because it is unrestrained. Cinematically, Polanski's intention is to maintain immediacy and realism: he questions how the (initial) scene of battle would appear for those involved and this is what he depicts. At the beginning of the film we see the end of battle and a soldier striking repeatedly at a dying man, a bleakly pointless act.

Polanski was influenced, in his interpretation of the play, by his countryman, Jan Kott, for whom *Macbeth* is a 'Death-Infected' play dramatizing the nightmare of 'History ... reduced to its simplest form, to one image and one division: those who are killed and those who kill' (70). For Kott, the killing of Duncan is Macbeth's 'Auschwitz experience' – the threshold beyond which killing is easy but also pointless. Politics is also implied in the smiling omnipresence of Ross: he is first Duncan's man, then he appears to approve and welcome Macbeth's kingship; he participates in the murder of Banquo; betrays his cousin and her children yet at the end of the play plucks Macbeth's bloodied crown from the ground and presents it triumphantly to Malcolm. He is history's essential time-server – a man with no moral integrity who survives through opportunism and ruthlessness.

In contrast with the play's savagery, Polanski makes the relationship between Macbeth and his wife touchingly youthful and passionate. He comments in his autobiography that the couple should not appear 'middle-aged and doom-laden' at the beginning of the play, rather they are a young couple with everything before them: '[they] don't know they're involved in tragedy; they think they're on the verge of a triumph.' There is a curious innocence in their first joyous encounter: the triumphant warrior returning to his love. Their soliloquies are conveyed through voice-over, often in close-up, so that the audience share their private thoughts and fears. Francesca Annis seems vulnerable and bewildered by her husband's later alienation from her; the nakedness of her sleep-walking scene reminding the viewer of Macduff's naked child while contrasting with the nakedness of the witches' coven. At the end, her broken body, hastily concealed, is left grubby and undignified. Polanski's script (written with Kenneth Tynan) omits Lady Macbeth's more violent imagery; two speeches are truncated with the effect of making her seem less evil as well as less in tune with the language of the witches. This is not a

Lady Macbeth who speaks of dashing out her baby's brains. When she appeals to Macbeth to fulfil his promise she seems tearful and ingenuous; dressed in white and promising him that they cannot fail.

The soundtrack of the film intensifies the effects of mysteriousness and wildness: a synthesizer creates the characteristic drone of the bagpipe as a sinister wail beneath the drum beats and discordant melodies played on strings and woodwind (created by the Third Ear Band). The film pre-dates CGI so the shots of landscape and castle also form part of the naturalism of the effect. The bleakness of the opening frames of a shore bathed in red light, and the wildness of the moorland enhance the play's atmosphere; here, the witches seem to merge with the landscape, remaining at the end of the play eternally available to those who seek them. Perhaps the most original scene is the final frame where a limping Donalbain mysteriously returns to Scotland; he too discovers the strange world of the witches concealed within the desolate landscape. So, impliedly, the entire cycle will resume.

Further thinking

➢ Explore any of the plays which treat the subject of warfare, thinking about language and ideology. How far does a martial masculine code shed light on *Othello*?

➢ Look at the language of Macbeth's final soliloquy, thinking about the ways in which different types of imagery interact. Now compare Hamlet's 'rogue and peasant slave' soliloquy (2.2.560–600). To what extent is Hamlet, too, trapped by masculine codes of behaviour?

➢ Analyze closely the opening frames of Polanski's *Macbeth*, paying close attention to lighting, camera work and the use of motifs.

Afterlives ...

U. A. Fanthorpe's poem 'Waiting Gentlewoman' (in *Side Effects*, 1983) is a dramatic monologue which voices the opinions of Lady Macbeth's unnamed lady-in-waiting. This high-class girl has serious doubts about the situation in the castle and in particular her boss: 'definitely/Not my type.' Tragedy and damnation reduced to class anxiety.

9

Antony and Cleopatra: The legendary on stage

The story of Antony and Cleopatra has undergone century after century of creative reworking in numerous art forms. In the early seventeenth century, Shakespeare's drama not only provided a fresh vision of the eponymous lovers and their political world, contributing to what was already an established body of literary treatments, it also invited audiences to consider the mythopoeic process by which historical figures take on legendary status.

This chapter

- explores the play from a postcolonial perspective
- considers what is known about the boy players of Shakespeare's day
- analyzes the dramatic function of its soliloquies
- looks at a recent all-male performance of the drama and its reception by audiences and critics

East meets West: A postcolonial view

How far is *Antony and Cleopatra* an early example of the stereotyping of the East as indolent, uncontrolled and feminizing? Can parallels be drawn between the play's depiction of the Roman imperial world and the colonial mentality which was beginning to emerge in Shakespeare's day? Was Shakespeare's Egyptian queen black? These are all questions which have been brought to bear upon the tragedy by postcolonial critics. Approaching a drama text from a postcolonial perspective involves being alert to the ideological forces which shaped its creation, as well as to those that have influenced how it has been analyzed and performed over the centuries. Although not fully fixed as a discrete reading practice until the 1990s, postcolonial criticism has already forged new and highly influential interprative pathways for Shakespeareans. Identifying the incipient stages of capitalism and European expansion as coterminous with Shakespeare's lifetime, postcolonial critics have read plays like *The Tempest* and *Othello* alongside contemporary documents such as travel journals and letters, some of which give accounts of voyages to the 'New World'. These readings have generated a wide range of views, with Shakespeare emerging as pro-colonial, anticolonial or committed to ambivalence.

A key text of postcolonial studies is Edward Said's *Orientalism* (1978), which explores how Orientalism as a Western cultural discourse represents the East as the inferior Other: indolent, sexually incontinent, feminizing and uncivilized. Although focusing mainly on post-Enlightenment times, Said notes that 'between the Middle Ages and the eighteenth century such major authors as ... Shakespeare ... drew on the Orient's riches for their productions' (*Orientalism*, 63). Certainly, Shakespeare was writing at a time that saw a developing relationship with the East through commerce, diplomacy and the arts, and whose dramas frequently dealt with Europe's fascination with the Orient. His vision of the East would have been informed by the travel literature of the time and, of course, by the picture of Egypt in his main source text, Plutarch's *Parallel Lives of the Greeks and Romans*, translated into English from the original Greek in 1579.

Critics writing in colonial times tended to view *Antony and Cleopatra* as a moral tale of the upright, 'civilized' West winning an inevitable victory over the effeminate East.

Unquestionably, there are aspects of the drama which could be seen to uphold this Orientalist perspective. Scenes in Egypt revolve around sleeping, eating, drinking, gaming and playing, with sexuality a favourite topic of conversation. Power resides in an almost exclusively female court, whose leader is shown to transform soldiers into 'women's men' (3.7.70). Rome seems to offer the moral corrective, a route-map to the physical and emotional self-restraint required for military success and personal honour. Caesar sets an ascetic example, refraining from excessive drinking during the treaty celebrations and lauding the younger Antony who once ate 'strange flesh/Which some did die to look on' (1.4.68–9), in stark contrast to the 'Eight wild boars roasted whole at a breakfast' (2.2.189) he is reputed to have preferred in his more mature years. Yet while Caesar seems immune to the lure of Egypt, his men display the fascination with the East which often shadowed Western disapproval. Maecenas and Agrippa are treated to Egyptian tales by Enobarbus who, as a practised code-switcher between the two geographical poles, acts as a kind of travel guide; Caesar's men both listen intently to his boasts of making 'the night light with drinking' (2.2.188) and to his extended paean of praise to Cleopatra – the greatest tourist attraction of them all.

That *Antony and Cleopatra* presents two diametrically opposed worlds is a view which prevails in the vast majority of theatrical productions, though close attention to the text reveals how it complicates rather than reinforces the usual East-West dichotomy. Egypt is assumed to be emotionally profligate and anti-rational, yet the story of Enobarbus, one of the most hardened of Roman soldiers, is one that suggests that the 'loyalty well held to fools' (3.13.43) can also be the path to wisdom. And if the Egyptians have to contend with the overflowing Nile, a geographical reality which associates them with mutability, so the Roman leaders have to contend with the changeability of their own people, who 'Like to a vagabond flag upon the stream/Goes to and back, lackeying the varying tide' (1.4.45–6). Those looking for moral lessons can, of course, look beyond such examples to the historical narrative that undergirds the play and find there the triumph of the austere Caesar over the self-indulgent Antony.

Read more circumspectly, *Antony and Cleopatra* could be seen as an exploration of transculturality. Cleopatra fuses Roman stoicism and Egyptian sensuality in her highly managed suicide, hybridizing the 'marble-constant' (5.2.239) Roman wife with the sensuous Egyptian mistress. At the same time as displaying the courage typically associated with the West, her gentle, almost pain-free death seems redolent of the sexual ecstasy of the East. Rather less self-determinedly, Antony takes on a perceptual richness that challenges Roman certainties:

Sometime we see a cloud that's dragonish,
A vapour sometime like a bear or lion,
A towered citadel, a pendent rock,
A forked mountain, or blue promontory
With trees upon't that nod unto the world
And mock our eyes with air.

(4.14.2–7)

Here he calls on the Eastern imagery of transformation and evanescence to express a vision of the world as constantly in flux, a vision impossible to articulate through the Roman imagery of rules, bindings and boundaries.

One other aspect of *Antony and Cleopatra* that has generated postcolonial readings of the text is the heroine's skin colour. Carol Chillington Rutter argues that: 'Shakespeare wrote a black narrative at the centre of *Antony and Cleopatra* ... marked by racial self-reference as explicit as Othello's. I "am with Phoebus' amorous pinches black," says the Egyptian, and the Moor, "I am black"' (*Enter the Body: Women and Representation on Shakespeare's Stage*, 2001, 62). Other frequently cited evidence in support of the theory that Shakespeare intended a black Cleopatra is found in references to her as 'tawny' and a 'gipsy'. Ania Loomba points out that 'Egyptians were widely grouped with other dark-skinned people of Africa and Asia as the descendants of Ham … Thus … Cleopatra's darkness is reinforced by suggestions that Cleopatra embodies Egypt'(*Shakespeare, Race, and Colonialism*, 2002, 114). Yet however convincing the textual evidence for a black Cleopatra might be, the roll-call of performers playing the part over the past half century or so (Vivien Leigh, Peggy Ashcroft, Vanessa Redgrave, Dorothy Tutin, Glenda Jackson, Helen Mirren, Judi Dench, Frances de la Tour, Sinead Cusack, Frances Barber, Harriet Walter) would suggest that theatre directors see her as fitting a long-prevailing Western ideal of female beauty as fair-skinned. Such casting practices have prompted critic Celia Daileader to put forward Cleopatra as the 'most consistently whitewashed of dark heroines' (*Racism, Misogyny, and the Othello Myth*, 2005, 28).

In *Things of Darkness* (1995) Kim F. Hall argues that Cleopatra's reference to herself as blackened by the amorous attentions of Phoebus 'conjoins her erotic nature with her darkness and … almost implies that she is black because of her sensuality' (97); looked at in this light, choosing a white performer to represent her severs a vital connection. The stage presence of a black Cleopatra visually reinforces a potentially radical element of the play. Instead of the conventional image of imperial conquerors signalling their victory by taking sexual possession of the subjugated nation's womenfolk, *Antony and Cleopatra* presents a white man taken sexual prisoner by a black woman. Cleopatra's 'conquering' of Antony is indicated through multiple perspectives. Philo opens the play declaring Antony to have been reduced by a foreign temptress to the status of a lowly servant, 'the bellows and the fan / To cool a gipsy's lust' (1.1.9–10). And Antony's speech and actions in the play constantly reinforce this image. Sometimes he seems an unwilling prisoner, striving to break free of his 'strong Egyptian fetters' (1.2.122), referring to himself as 'bewitched' and 'enchanted', both images which suggest the alterity of an alien female. At other times, it is as if his thraldom is an ineluctable reality of the heart. After the couple's defeat at Actium, he declares to Cleopatra:

> You did know
> How much you were my conqueror, and that
> My sword, made weak by my affection, would
> Obey it on all cause.

(3.11.65–8)

Yet one of the many complexities of the play is that Cleopatra never appears entirely certain of her role as 'conqueror'. Only in fantasy can she think herself triumphant:

> My bended hook shall pierce
> Their slimy jaws, and, as I draw them up,
> I'll think them every one an Antony,
> And say 'Ah, ha! You're caught!'

(2.5.12–15)

Shakespeare presents a power relation between his eponymous couple that would have unsettled original audiences. As a character in early modern drama, Cleopatra is unusual in being an independent ruler and the control she is shown to have over a Western ruler would have ruffled accepted ideas of gender and politics. Whether or not the threat of the foreign female is expelled in the course of Shakespeare's drama is one of the many questions which remain at its conclusion.

Acting the woman's part: Shakespeare's boy players

From the Restoration period onwards, male parts have been played by men and female parts by women, and any divergence from this established norm has come to be viewed as unconventional and theatrically experimental. That Shakespeare's female roles were played by male performers is one of the most obvious differences between the early modern stage and our own and one which has attracted considerable critical interest in the last thirty years or so. The amount of historical evidence available in this area of Shakespeare studies is relatively slight. The diaries of the theatrical entrepreneur, Philip Henslowe, biographical records of individual actors, and anti-theatrical tracts provide some guiding information, as do some of the published dramas of the time. Nonetheless, there are several major questions still to be fully resolved. Why were women prohibited from taking to the stage? What was the age range of the boys who played the female roles (and what did the term 'boy' actually mean back then)? Did men play some of the more mature women? What was the style of female impersonation? Did it aim at the same degree of naturalism as male performances? How did male and female playgoers respond to theatrical transvestism? Providing answers to such questions requires a good deal of conjecture and informed intuition: a critical process which inevitably results in a variety of competing theories.

It is known that other European countries such as Italy, France and Spain allowed female performers on the public stage and that theatre companies from the Continent played in London before the Restoration. A number of theories have been advanced to explain why the English were so slow to admit women to the stage, most of which revolve around issues of female power. Some put it down to a Protestant anxiety to fix women in their rightful place as good wives; others see it as a means of preserving 'jobs for the boys' and keeping females in a state of economic disempowerment. Others, however, argue that the reasons behind the prohibition are more psychological than economic or religious, borne out of the fear of a rampant female sexuality and the attendant consequences of displaying a woman's body on stage. There may also have been practical reasons; for example, women

were much less likely to be literate than men and thus unable
to read scripts.

It is generally accepted that women's parts would have
been played by adolescent boys. Apprenticed to a company at
around the age of ten, player boys would have developed their
acting skills through increasingly challenging female roles,
before moving on to male roles in their late teens. However,
it is thought that boys reached puberty one or two years later
than at the present time, so that the high voice and smooth
face that are the presumed prerequisites of female impersonation in Shakespeare's day would have endured well beyond
the mid-teens. Hamlet acknowledges the inevitable physical
changes in the boy actor in his welcome to the players:

> O old friend, why, thy face is valanced since I saw thee
> last! Com'st thou to beard me in Denmark? What, my
> young lady and mistress! By'r Lady, your ladyship is nearer
> to heaven than when I saw you last by the altitude of a
> chopine. Pray God your voice, like a piece of uncurrent
> gold, be not cracked within the ring.

> (2.2.360–6)

How would Shakespeare's audiences have responded to the
boy players? It is reasonable to assume that they would
have seen them as part of conventional theatrical practice
and would not have responded with the wolf-whistles that
sometimes accompany the entrances of cross-dressed actors
performing in today's all-male productions. But would the
presence of a male body in female attire have had no more
impact than the same actor playing a man? Lisa Jardine has
suggested that player boys would have allowed male spectators
to feel homoerotic desire, under the guise of responding to a
female character. Others, such as Jean E. Howard, argue that
the very fact that an actor could imitate (with what degree
of verisimilitude we will never really know) characters of the
opposite sex 'threatened a normative social order based upon

strict principles of hierarchy and subordination' (*The Stage and Social Struggle in Early Modern England*, 1994, 94).

It is clear from the anti-theatrical tracts of Puritan writers such as Philip Stubbes and John Rainoldes, that the gender confusion which came with cross-dressing was chief among what they saw as the immoralities of the stage. As biblical literalists they drew on the scriptures to endorse their objections, citing Deuteronomy's injunction that: 'A woman shall not wear anything that pertains to a man, nor shall a man put on a woman's garment; for whoever does these things is an abomination to the Lord your God' (22.5). While it can be assumed that regular theatre goers would not have held such extreme views, it is difficult to know for certain how they would have regarded the 'holiday' from the normative gender system which the stage offered. Would women have seen the easy switching between one sex and another as potentially liberating, freeing them from their 'naturally' inferior status? Or would the fact that men continued to take charge of constructing images of femininity have restricted any such feeling? And how far would men have seen in the boy actor the potential nightmare of feminization? In all likelihood every one of these possible responses and more would have been found among Shakespeare's audience.

Regarded through the ages as the cynosure of female attractiveness, Cleopatra, more than any other of Shakespeare's heroines, has caused actors and critics alike to reflect on the kind of boy who could have pulled off such an illusionary feat. It is also the woman's role which most explicitly draws attention to cross-gendered casting. After Antony's death, Cleopatra vividly describes the indignities she imagines will follow her political defeat.

> The quick comedians
> Extemporally will stage us and present
> Our Alexandrian revels; Antony
> Shall be brought drunken forth; and I shall see

Some squeaking Cleopatra boy my greatness
I'th'posture of a whore.

(5.2.215–20)

This self-reflexive reference to the boy actor is frequently quoted as evidence that a male child would have originally played this most strenuous of roles. In what appears to be a deliberate intrusion into theatrical illusion, the imagined player boy is derided through what in the final performances would have been the mouth of a player boy physically present, creating one of the several intriguing double perspectives of the drama. Cleopatra is both the whore that 'she is called in Rome' (1.2.112) and the dread Egyptian queen, who would rather die than suffer her 'greatness' to be parodied – and both are played by boys.

How far, then, did the practice of cross-dressing influence Shakespeare's writing of female roles? In *Squeaking Cleopatras: the Elizabethan Boy Player* (2000), Joy Leslie Gibson argues that Shakespeare took account of boys' smaller lung capacity, making female speeches shorter than male ones and inserting more pauses for breath. She also suggests that 'playwrights were skilful in limiting their emotional demands on the boys' (3). It is difficult to align such a theory with the role of Cleopatra. The second longest female part in the canon, it is comparable to that of King Lear or Macbeth and its emotional range is vast. Suggestions that Shakespeare moderated the sexual implicitness of his staging are equally at odds with *Antony and Cleopatra*. While the censor would inevitably have constrained the representation of sexual acts on stage, this is a play which makes frequent reference to kissing and embracing, both in speeches and stage directions. There is also the question of how far the boy playing Cleopatra would have striven to appear and sound sensual to early modern eyes and ears. Enobarbus's rapturous 'barge speech' stops short of describing her actual appearance: an omission which could be construed as Shakespeare's refusal to delineate a female beauty that can never be matched by a male actor. On the other hand, there is arguably no scene in the whole of Shakespeare that more explicitly engages with female appearance than that featuring the hapless messenger inventorying Octavia's height, face and hair colour for Cleopatra to measure herself against (3.3). Michael Shapiro points out in his extensive study of theatrical cross-dressing that 'We may never know exactly how much distance play-boys put between themselves and their female characters: they may have merely indicated these roles rather than representing women more or less illusionistically' (*Gender in Play on the Shakespearean Stage*, 1994, 37). What can be known from the text, though, is that it would have taken a boy of great talent, courage and stamina to have done justice to Shakespeare's Egyptian queen.

The Shakespearean soliloquy

The etymology of the term 'soliloquy' is relatively simple: of Latin derivation, the first part of the word means 'alone' (*solus*) and the second part 'to speak' (*loqui*). Defining the exact nature of a soliloquy in dramatic terms is rather more troublesome. It is commonly held that a speech only takes on the status of soliloquy if it is delivered by a character alone on stage. Yet some of the best known Shakespearean soliloquies are performed with one or more other characters present. In some cases, such as Hamlet's deliberating speech about whether or not to kill Claudius 'now 'a is a-praying' (3.3.73), the soliloquizer is aware of the other person's presence; in others, such as Malvolio's reading aloud of the forged letter, with three of the cast hidden behind a box-tree, he is not. And in *Antony and Cleopatra* the soliloquy which concludes with Enobarbus' death (4.9.6–26) is not only overheard by soldiers, it is also interrupted by their commentary on it. In all three instances, however, the speaker *assumes* he cannot be overheard: perhaps one of the most important markers of the soliloquy as a dramatic device.

How far, then, can an aside be considered a form of soliloquy? Clearly, some asides are intended to be addressed to a named character on stage. In *Antony and Cleopatra*, those which pass between Menas and Pompey in Act 2 Scene 7 seem intended to reveal the duplicity that lurks beneath the public face of politics, while the mocking asides shared by Agrippa and Enobarbus as they witness Antony and Caesar's leave-taking after the marriage treaty, illustrate how the mighty triumvirs are regarded by their subordinates. As the play moves on, though, the asides start to take on the dramatic force of soliloquy, those delivered by Enobarbus in Act 3 Scene 13 proving a case in point. Here, as well as performing the long-established choric function of the soliloquy in observing Antony's military decline, they also dramatize Enobarbus's personal dilemma as to whether or not he should desert his master – a relatively new feature of the mode. It might be argued that the relative brevity of the aside compared with the soliloquy, is a distinguishing feature, though like most attempts to pin down these dramatic devices, evidence to undermine such a distinction is easily found.

Perhaps even more difficult to pin down is the intended addressee of the solo speech. Wolfgang Clemen argues that the early modern soliloquy would have been intended for the audience:

> The open stage protruding right into the pit, with the audience on three sides, favoured close contact, even intimacy, and a secret understanding between the audience and the soliloquizing actor who was able to project his emotions by means of gestures, physiognomy and stage business.
>
> (*Shakespeare's Soliloquies*, 1987, 4–5)

This is a popular view and one supported by actors with experience of performing on the modern Globe stage. Indeed, today's Globe audiences seem to expect to be addressed directly – an expectation that can sometimes be difficult to manage. It might be fun for the groundlings to boo and hiss at Iago or Iachimo, but less fun for the players trying to capture the nuanced tonalities of Shakespeare's mature tragedies and romances. But while there are undoubtedly some soliloquies, especially those which contain questions, that seem to signal the audience as addressee, these are by no means in the majority, raising the question of how the more reflective type of soliloquy would have been, and should be, played.

The belief that Shakespearean soliloquies were written to be addressed to the audience has been challenged by a number of scholars, perhaps most redoubtably by James Hirsh. In a work of over 400 pages, he contends that, by Shakespeare's time, 'Audience address by characters in the midst of the action, a staple of medieval and early sixteenth-century drama, came to seem amateurish, undramatic, outmoded, and exhausted as a dramatic convention' (*Shakespeare and the History of Soliloquies*, 2003, 19). Hirsh also takes to task the idea that soliloquies were intended to reveal the unspoken thoughts of the speaker, arguing that they were written as external speeches, audible within the time and space of the fictional world on stage. With the realist mode having prevailed for well over a century, such a theory might be alien to the modern mind. However, Shakespeare's theatre was not naturalistic and that characters voiced ideas aloud to themselves (what Hirsh terms 'self-addressed speech') would seem to be a feasible suggestion.

⑦ *Bearing in mind the arguments outlined above, look closely at Antony's final soliloquy (4.14.96–105) and consider:*

- how the audience's knowledge that Cleopatra is still alive adds to the speech's impact
- the effect of the **apostrophe** to Eros

- the soliloquy's main dramatic function at this point in the play

There are numerous moments in Shakespeare's plays when a character displays painful emotion in response to an event or situation that the audience knows has not actually occurred. With the comedies, any feeling of unease at the sight of such unnecessary suffering is mitigated to some degree by its generic promise of a pleasurable resolution, but in the tragedies it can seem gratuitously cruel in its irony. *Antony and Cleopatra* is a play which demands that the audience regularly reappraise their view of the protagonists, both as a couple and as individuals, and this soliloquy is capable of provoking some highly complex responses. In the light of Antony's grief, which is surely no less painful for being based on a falsehood, Cleopatra's faked suicide appears all the more cowardly and self-serving, while his devotion seems more selfless than at any other point in the drama. At the same time, his failure to accomplish this final fatal act of swordsmanship – a stark contrast to the precise efficiency of Othello (another ageing military commander) or the determined speed of the adolescent Juliet – threatens to diminish his tragic status.

Addressing spectators in the process of committing suicide risks turning a moment of high tragedy into farce (think of Bottom's hilariously theatrical rendition of Pyramus' death in *A Midsummer Night's Dream*). The presence of the dead Eros provides a focal point for the actor-hero, allowing him to engage in a kind of dialogue through apostrophe. This helps both to control the physical action and to give occasion for Antony to demonstrate the kind of heightened awareness associated with the tragic hero's nadir, as he acknowledges the ironic reversal of the servant-master relationship. In addition, Antony's apostrophizing combines with his calling for help from the living off-stage, accentuating his solitariness at this moment of crisis.

Unlike Romeo and Juliet who die within moments of each other, Antony and Cleopatra die at different points in the play, indeed, in separate acts. One of the means by which Shakespeare keeps the lovers united in the minds of the audience during the interval between their deaths is by creating verbal echoes across the final two acts. The necroerotic image of the 'bridegroom in ... death' in Antony's final soliloquy finds its equivalence in Cleopatra's welcoming death as like 'a lover's pinch' (5.2.294) and his cry of 'dispatch me' finds a parallel in Cleopatra's apostrophe to the asp to 'Be angry and dispatch' (5.2.305). Hirsh's theory of the self-addressed soliloquy seems to fit well with Antony's final soliloquy. It is clearly not intended to be addressed to the audience and its style and matter do not lend themselves to an introspective delivery. In this respect the speech seems typical of a play whose method seems to discourage intimacy between the audience and the players.

Antony and Cleopatra is often regarded as lacking in the tragic intensity of plays such as *Macbeth* or *Hamlet*. This is due in part to a tendency to associate Shakespearean tragedy with interiority and in particular the inner struggles of the hero, often shown through soliloquy. Antony has a handful of soliloquies (though none as long as Enobarbus's death speech), but in none of these does he engage with his main dilemma: the choice between love and political power. A case in point is the soliloquy which comes just after he has finalized the marriage treaty with Caesar. His belief that the 'very dice obey' Caesar (2.3.32), comes not from any reasoned thought processes, but from the prognostications of a Soothsayer, and there is no attempt in the speech to present an alternative perspective before the conclusion is reached: 'I'th' East my pleasure lies' (2.3.39).

Depicting major historical events spanning over a decade, *Antony and Cleopatra* is an immensely fast-moving drama, with constant shifts of location. What Samuel Johnson described as the 'continual hurry of the action', leaves little room for soliloquy. Those that are included are often curtailed by the need for immediate action, whether to respond to Caesar's messengers, send Ventidius off to fight in Parthia, or to find a soldier willing to finish off a botched suicide attempt. That is not to say, however, that the soliloquies in the play lack dramatic impact or significance. Charmian's six-line soliloquy (5.2.313–18) is a theatrical *tour de force* which succinctly captures the ambivalent nature of the play. On the one hand, Cleopatra is elevated by her servant's absolute fidelity (as is Antony); on the other hand, her attempt to create an aesthetic in death is undermined. As death takes the Queen mid-sentence, Charmian is called upon to carry out her final duty: to straighten the crown which has slipped from its careful positioning. Viewed from an idealized perspective, this final soliloquy of the play proclaims a victory over death, whose sting has been replaced with the promise of 'play' and a better world, and whose status has been ennobled by the possession of a 'lass unparalled'. Viewed more cynically, it is mere myth-making, its illusion being abruptly broken by '*the* Guard, *rustling in*'.

The all-male *Antony and Cleopatra* at Shakespeare's Globe (1999)

Shakespeare's Globe is one of London's most established and popular cultural sites, attracting visitors and acting companies from all over the world. The desire to recreate as authentically as possible the performance conditions of the time stands at the heart of the project and first-time visitors to the Globe are usually taken aback by the sight of the old made new: the proximity of actors to 'groundlings', the strangeness of performance in broad daylight and the constant potential for disruption from the elements, the audience, or even the odd nosey pigeon landing on the stage.

The academic community has been closely involved with the Globe project from its early days, with one of the foremost scholars of the Shakespearean stage, Andrew Gurr, acting as its academic advisor. Nonetheless, the theatre's first few seasons were greeted with a degree of scepticism by Shakespeareans and theatre critics alike. Some were simply fearful that the enterprise would prove little more than a tourist attraction, while others were troubled by its commitment to what is usually termed 'authentic practices', deeming it both unachievable and backward-looking (the director William Poel had already attempted, and largely failed, to recreate Elizabethan staging a good century before). Such attitudes have mellowed over time and a number of Globe productions have been acclaimed by both theatre critics and Shakespeare scholars. One particularly successful production was the 1999 *Antony and Cleopatra*, a venture which took the company's quest for authenticity a step further in its employment of an all-male cast. For one audience member at least, this was a step too far. Giles Block, the production's director, recalled in interview how one man objected loudly from the yard at the casting of a male actor in the role of Cleopatra. Doubtless, this spectator had been seeking a theatrical experience which would capture a certain conservative idea of Tudor England, the stable universal truths of a playwright of genius, with an appropriately beautiful actress playing the world's most famous *femme fatale*. Instead, he was faced with theatrical cross-dressing: a muscular man in a wig of cascading ringlets, tightly-laced corset and swirling gipsy skirt.

That the sight of a male actor dressed as a woman can provoke such a public outburst in the late-twentieth century is a sign that the theatrical transvestite remains, or perhaps has become, an unsettling figure. Certainly, the announcement by the then artistic director of the Globe, Mark Rylance, that he was to play Cleopatra in an all-male production of *Antony and Cleopatra* attracted a great deal of interest from the press and, judging from some of the headlines, most of it was directed at how a thirty-nine-year-old man could transform himself into a legendary beauty. As the *Sunday Times* reviewer, Robert Hewison, commented: 'Dressing up in women's clothes is thrilling, because it is an act of transgression' and this element of thrill may well have contributed to the production's success.

The shock of the unfamiliar was audible in the laughter that greeted Rylance's first stage utterance, though most full accounts of the production emphasize how quickly spectators adjusted to the cross-gender casting.

The vast majority of press reviews focused on Rylance's performance as Cleopatra. For some reviewers it was a triumph; for others, the sexual ambiguity of a man in female costume seemed to overshadow all other considerations, the intemperate tone of some reviewers betraying their considerable unease with this blurring of gender roles. In terms redolent of the school playground, Nicholas de Jongh of the *Evening Standard* averred that 'Rylance might pass for one of those temperamental tomboy girls who later turn out lesbian', while the *Mail on Sunday*'s Rhoda Koenig likened him to 'a big girl who would get high marks in PE if she weren't so clumsy'. What emerges strongly from a survey of the reviews is that spectators had widely differing responses to all-male casting. At one extreme it was thought to have lowered one of Shakespeare's greatest tragedies to a parade of drag queens; at the other, it was considered a brave experiment aimed at understanding better how Shakespeare's theatre might have operated.

In striving for an authentic Jacobean performance, the company went beyond the casting process. Much historical research went into the design of Cleopatra's six hand-sewn costumes, intended to make visible her 'infinite variety': the 'gipsy queen' in brocade corset; the deserted mistress, artificially elevated in four-inch chopines as she triumphantly proclaims Octavia 'dwarfish'; the 'maid that milks' in simple smock after the death of Antony and, finally, regal in cloth-of-gold in the act of suicide. Just as costuming served a dual purpose in aiming for authenticity and enhancing the play's moods and movements, so too did the music. Musicians appeared throughout the performance, creating a sense of time and place in a play that spans two continents and covers the events of more than ten years. Moreover, in this open-air setting, where the effects achieved by an indoor theatre's lighting system are unavailable, music played a key part in controlling the dramatic atmosphere.

Antony and Cleopatra has long been considered a generically amorphous play, its Egyptian scenes lending it a ludic quality often seen to set it apart from the major tragedies. One much remarked upon feature of the Block production was its mixing of comic and tragic tones. As a theatrical environment the Globe is conducive to creating laughter; actors who perform there seem to thrive on the comedic effects they produce from communicating with the groundlings, and the large stage and sturdy pillars make it ideal for the rough and tumble of physical comedy. Managing to create and sustain a tragic tone in such a space is rather more challenging. The first half of Block's *Antony and Cleopatra* held the attention of the audience largely thanks to its comic brio, a feature which several reviewers thought to be to the detriment of the tragedy. The scene in which the dying Antony is hoisted up via a system of pulleys to take his last embrace with Cleopatra was felt to be particularly lacking in tragic decorum, provoking more giggles than tears in the audience. It must be said, though, that the play has always provoked ambivalent responses, teetering as it so often does on the edge of bathos. Although several reviewers criticized the comedy for overpowering the tragedy, some welcomed the shift in emotional weight, considering it to have offered a fresh perspective on the play. Writing in the *Guardian*, Michael Billington recommended the play be put on the generic transfer-list, a sentiment echoed by Bill Hagerty's pithy judgement on the play in the *News of the World:* 'Not tragic, but magic'.

That is not to say, however, that audiences were left unmoved by the play's final act. One scene picked out as particularly memorable for its intense emotional charge was that directly following Antony's death in which Cleopatra appears in a short, simple smock, with roughly cropped head and face scratched and bleeding. In a volume recording the Globe's first five years, Rylance writes of how the scene was inspired by a description of Cleopatra found in Plutarch:

'she had plucked her hair from her head ... also ... she had martyred all her face with her nails' (*Play*, 2003, 108). A stark contrast to her earlier resplendence and to the regal suicide to follow, this depiction of Egypt's queen brought low by grief was, as one reviewer put it, 'enough to make a grown man cry'.

Further thinking

➤ Think about the following soliloquies in the light of Hirsh's theory of the 'self-addressed speech' and the other competing theories discussed in the chapter:
  ➤ *King Richard III* (5.3.178–207)
  ➤ *Twelfth Night* (2.1.40–4)
  ➤ *A Midsummer Night's Dream* (1.1.226–51)
  ➤ *Cymbeline* (5.1.1–33)

➤ A spectator at a performance of *Othello* in 1610 wrote of the actor who played Desdemona that 'although she acted her part supremely well, yet when she was killed she was even more moving, for when she fell back upon the bed she implored the pity of the spectators by her very face'. What light does this rare review of an early modern performance throw on boy players?

➤ In *Antony and Cleopatra*, Shakespeare emphatically draws the audience's attention to the theatrical practice of cross-gender casting (5.2.218–20). Can you think of any similar examples in the comedies or romances?

Afterlives ...

John Dryden's *All for Love* (1678) is a dramatic version of the story of Antony and Cleopatra which, in the words of the author, aims 'to imitate the divine Shakespeare'. Though avowedly the work of an admirer, it is also a corrective to what Dryden saw as Shakespeare's disregard for the classical unities of place and time. Dryden's tragedy enjoyed far greater popularity than Shakespeare's throughout the eighteenth century and it is interesting to speculate on why it holds so little appeal for modern audiences.

10

King Richard II: The performance of majesty

R*ichard II* raised a number of highly topical and controversial issues for its original spectators. A drama of deposition, it played out on stage a reversing of the sacred ceremony of coronation, prompting audiences to question whether the language and symbolism of royal ritual and ceremony was any more than outward display.

This chapter

- attends to the play's interest in language through the lens of deconstruction
- considers the significance of clothing and costume in the early modern period
- analyzes the function of the play's dramatic verse
- examines the critical reception of Deborah Warner's controversial production of *Richard II*

Deconstruction and Shakespeare

Over the past decade or so, the term 'deconstruction' has migrated from the academy to the cultural mainstream. In its popular sense, to 'deconstruct' signifies a criticism or analysis of anything from a piece of writing to a political standpoint.

In its more specialized literary-theoretical sense, it denotes a critical practice grounded in the writings of the philosopher Jacques Derrida (1930–2004).The discourse of deconstruction is replete with images of instability – slipping, sliding, shifting and floating – expressive of its major contention that meaning can never be fully contained or fixed.

Deconstruction is a major area of post-structuralist thought; indeed, the two terms are often used interchangeably. As the term implies, post-structuralism is closely related to its forerunner, structuralism, a wide-ranging intellectual movement, which had a significant impact on several knowledge areas, including philosophy, the social sciences and literary studies. To understand post-structuralist thought, and deconstruction in particular, it is first necessary to have some grasp of the ideas of the Swiss linguist Ferdinand de Saussure (1857–1913), whose ground-breaking work in linguistics underpins the structuralist contention that all human thought and activity is constructed and not natural. At the core of Saussure's analytical framework is a simple idea: 'The bond between the signifier and the signified is arbitrary ... it [the signifier] actually has no natural connection with the signified' ('Course in General Linguistics' in *Literary Theory: An Anthology*, Julie Rivkin and Michael Ryan (eds), 1998, 79). What this means in practice is that a word like 'cow' (what Saussure calls the signifier) has a purely conventional relationship with the concept it conjures up in our minds (the signified). There is nothing essentially 'cow-like' about the word 'cow', either in its sound or appearance on the page; indeed, if there was agreement in the language community to refer to this milk-producing quadruped as a 'fismus', there is no reason why it should not signify just as well – as long as 'fismus' was not already in the linguistic system. This, according to Saussure, is because 'in language there are only differences *without positive terms* [Saussure's emphasis]' (Rivkin and Ryan, 88). We can tell 'cow' apart from 'wow' or 'sow' by the slight but crucial shift of the initial letter. The connection between word and meaning is, then, entirely relational: we understand something not so much by what it *is*, but by knowing what it is *not*.

If language is entirely arbitrary, removed from the way humans experience the concepts it defines, then it follows that it is also constitutive: it does not *reflect* the world around us; it *makes* it. What is assumed on an everyday, commonsensical level to be 'natural' is actually a formal organization of the world around us through the symbolic system of language. The demarcation between, say, spring and summer, green and blue, or day and night is a matter or convention and indeed, there are often times when the artificial nature of these linguistic markers become apparent such as when we encounter a language which chops up the world in a different way from our own (the classification of colours, for example). Reading, too, is part of a network of structures already in place before any kind of 'personal response' can take place; these include genres, conceptual and psychological frameworks and the system by which the text reaches the reader.

The precise relationship between structuralism and deconstruction is a much debated one. Put simply, deconstruction, and post-structuralist thought more generally, undermines any notion of a stable signifying system, offering a critique of objective knowledge, eternal truths and, in the case of literature, a unified text. One of the key structuralist ideas to be extended by deconstruction is Saussure's contention that all meaning inheres in difference and not in a fixed sign. Derrida's engagement with this idea brought into being one of the most hotly disputed terms of deconstructive practice: *différance*. A verbal pun, typical of the playful nature of so much of Derrida's writing, the term originates in the French verb '*différer*', meaning both to 'differ from' and 'to defer'. It is a neologism which captures both the idea that meaning is only created through the *difference* between one word (or sound unit) and another, and the concomitant idea that meaning is always *deferred*: when we pronounce a word it stands in place of something not present; when we write that word, it stands in the place of the word we pronounce. Not only does the

word stand for a 'deferred' presence, each one encountered
carries traces of what it is *not*, pointing to another signifier in
an endless chain of signification. The only way 'brown' can
be signified is through reference to other signifiers that denote
what it *is not* (so, according to the *OED*, *not* red, yellow or
black, but a mixture of all three). It follows, then, that the
signification of a literary text can never be fixed, nor can
readings ever be exhausted as any use of language (whether in
the text under examination or the metalanguage in which it
is discussed) is inextricably bound up in the endless chain of
signifiers and the multiplicity of meanings they generate.

The philosophical ideas that underpin deconstruction are
often highly abstract and may not appear directly applicable
to Shakespeare. However, literary scholars have employed
them to open up new and invigorating ways of reading the
plays, challenging the interprative habit of imposing a unifying
design on the text. *Richard II*, for example, is often seen as
a play organized around a series of oppositions embedded
in its structure, imagery and stage action and it is tempting
to ignore any 'loose ends' which cannot be tucked neatly
into this picture. Deconstructive critics would seek to interrogate such a reading by challenging its attempt to staunch
the proliferation of textual meaning, and by teasing out its
contradictions and uncertainties. Indeed, the indeterminacy
of Shakespeare's plays makes them especially amenable to
deconstruction, insisting as it does that a text can sustain
plural, often diametrically opposed readings. Furthermore,
the protean nature of Shakespeare's dramatic language (puns
for example) has offered plentiful opportunities for Derrida's
concept of *différance* to be explored.

Deconstructive critics have been particularly attentive to
the linguistic scepticism that is seen to run through the entire
Shakespearean canon. Numerous critics have hailed examples
such as Juliet's remark that 'a rose / By any other word would
smell as sweet;' (2.2.43–4) as signs that Shakespeare was a
Saussurean *avant la lettre*. However, as Jonathan Hope points
out in *Shakespeare and Language* (2010), 'Juliet ... is an

Aristotelian: she believes that names are arbitrarily attached to the things they designate by human convention' (2) and some in the play's original audiences would have recognized the connection with classical Greek thought. Yet, even if Shakespeare turns out to be more a man of his time than a forerunner of Saussurean linguistics, there is still a strong case to be made for his being more than usually interested in the relationship between words and meaning.

Deconstructing *Richard II*

Richard II is a play preoccupied with language and as such an ideal text for deconstructive reading. It makes frequent reference to forms of speech such as oaths and vows and to the power (or otherwise) of the spoken word. The word 'tongue', or words closely related to it, occurs thirty or so times in the text, often drawing attention to language and its usage (notice that 'tongue' was the most common term for 'language' in a culture where oral expression still dominated over the written). At the start of the play, Richard is supremely confident that his word is law and that the title of king is inseparable from the divinely ordained role of kingship. The power that inheres in Richard's 'breath' seems absolute, akin to God's when he breathes life into Adam:

> The hopeless word of 'never to return'
> Breathe I against thee, upon pain of life.

> (1.3.152–3)

It is a power that Bolingbroke publicly acknowledges:

> How long a time lies in one little word!
> Four lagging winters and four wanton springs
> End in a word; such is the breath of kings.

> (1.3.213–15)

However, acquiescence to the fixed signification of the word is short-lived as Bolingbroke topples words with deeds and renders the title of king a floating signifier.

John of Gaunt makes the first strike against Richard's confident belief in the marriage of the signified and signifier. The sustained punning which results from Richard's renaming of his uncle as 'aged Gaunt' (2.1.72) demonstrates the multiple meanings that can proliferate from a monosyllable. That the significance of a proper name can be so easily disrupted anticipates Richard's own loss of title and his reduction to 'nothing' in the play's final act. While Richard appears unmoved by any of the advice Gaunt offers him, he does note that it is possible to play 'nicely' (2.1.84) with names. In fact, Richard has his first direct experience of such play when his own title is transformed from King into 'Landlord of England' (2.1.113) by his dying relative.

As Richard's fortunes decline, so his faith in the unassailable power of the monarchical 'breath' becomes ever more severely challenged. On landing at Barkloughly castle, Richard's call to the natural world to destroy his enemies is pronounced with a theatricality that suggests his words are all alone sufficient. Yet as loss follows loss, he is driven to assert what was once assumed:

> The breath of worldly men cannot depose
> The deputy elected by the Lord.
>
> (3.2.56–7)

Assertion rapidly shifts to rhetorical questioning 'Is not the King's name twenty thousand names?' (3.2.85), and then to a dawning realization that his word is not absolute:

> O God, O God, that e'er this tongue of mine
> That laid the sentence of dread banishment
> On yon proud man should take it off again
> With words of sooth!
>
> (3.3.133–6)

Bolingbroke's attitude towards language differs markedly from Richard's. He understands that words are no more than labels to be moved around at will; he dismisses his father's suggestion to rename his exile 'a travel ... for pleasure' (1.3.262) as no more than a linguistic realignment, one that will have no real bearing on his situation. At the same time, he is quite ready to exploit the arbitrary nature of the signifier. In the course of the play, those around him have to adjust to his rapidly changing titles: Hereford, the Duke of Lancaster and, finally, King Henry.

As mentioned earlier in the chapter, *Richard II* is, on the surface at least, a play of contrasts and opposites and as such is worth examining in the light of Derrida's challenge to the binary oppositions which informed so much of structuralist practice. According to Derrida, Western thinking is structured around pairs of opposites such as man and woman, presence and absence, speech and writing. Deconstruction shines light on how each binary pair contains a superior partner, often indicated in the 'natural' order in which they are pronounced or written down; so, for example, it is more usual to place 'man' before 'woman' ('woman and man' sounds strange to most native English speakers). It sets out not to destroy or reverse such antitheses but to dismantle and examine them. The deposition scene (4.1) draws attention to the binary oppositions of high and low through Richard's analogy of the two buckets, chosen to convey the passing of power from one cousin to another. It is a wily metaphor by which he seems to reverse the hierarchical pairings of high/low and up/down which run through the play. The bucket rising high is obviously Bolingbroke, yet though its position carries the usual implications of high office and success, its 'lightness' connotes lack of substance, and the potential to be easily swayed; the heavy bucket on the other hand, while still figuring Richard's lowered status and heavy heart, also implies the weight of his natural authority, something that cannot be easily moved or *re*moved. What would seem to be a straight-forward reversal of binary opposites, however, proves more complicated on closer inspection. According to Richard's own analogical description, the heavy bucket should be 'down, unseen' (4.1.187), yet by his very recitation of it, he ensures that all eyes are turned on him.

Though deconstruction is perhaps less prominent today than it was in the 1980s and early 1990s, a number of its concepts and terminologies continue to influence today's critical practice. While it is often accused of being bewilderingly abstract and too intent on returning to its own first premises, its determination to expose the contradictory elements of a text (sometimes called the 'textual subconscious') often involves forensically close reading and an alertness to gaps and absences that can prove every bit as significant as what lies on the literary surface.

Clothes and the early modern theatre

Dress has always been a powerful semiotic, a system of outward display by which the individual can signal who they are – or at least who they would like to be thought of as being. One of the crucial differences between England today and the England of Shakespeare's time is that men and women are now more or less free to wear what they choose. High-street fashion copies the designer labels of the elite almost as soon as they hit the catwalk, allowing those on modest incomes to appear as on trend as their wealthier contemporaries. In the late sixteenth century, however, what people wore was restricted by economic circumstances, gender, religion and social status. Clothes were extremely expensive and were often included in the sum total of people's worldly goods, and willed to relatives or servants on their deaths.

Controlling what people wore was a means of maintaining social order. In 1559, Elizabeth I reinforced the sumptuary laws of 1533 and 1544, at a time when the rising middle class was acquiring the financial means to dress above their station.

The laws set down for each category of citizen the colour, textile and trimming of garments that could be worn; they specified the length of swords and the dimensions of ruffs and, in an attempt to discourage the purchase of imported goods, prohibited the wearing of certain foreign fabrics. Enforcing such laws proved extremely difficult and many who dressed above their status went undetected. However, not everyone escaped the full force of the law. One recent study of clothing in the early modern period cites a particularly memorable case of one who did not get away with 'dressing up':

> A Fellow of King's College was committed to prison in 1576 after a formal dispute with the Provost, when it was discovered that he was wearing 'a cut taffeta doublet ... and a great pair of galligastion hose' under his gown.
>
> (Ann Rosalind Jones and Peter Stallybrass, *Renaissance Clothing and the Materials of Memory*, 2000, 188)

Such modish aspiration was very much part of the spirit of the age. The Tudor court was a highly fashionable one with Elizabeth I at its sartorial centre. The Queen exhibited her sumptuous clothing both at court and to the wider public when she went on her summer travels through England (known as 'Progresses'). Courtiers were also required to display their fashion credentials if they were to cut a dash in courtly circles. As Polonius advises Laertes: 'apparel oft proclaims the man' (1.3.71).

The theatre provided an opportunity for anyone with the price of admission to see the fine fashions of the courtly world. It was a space where the usual sartorial rules were suspended, where boys could dress as queens, laymen as bishops, and actors of relatively slender means could play the king. While the stage sets were frugal, costumes were often lavish, with a substantial amount of a theatre company's budget being reserved for their purchase and upkeep. Andrew Gurr points out that an embroidered black velvet cloak, itemized in theatre records, cost £20 10s 6d, more than a third of what Shakespeare paid for his great house in Stratford (*The Shakespearean Stage 1574–1642*, 2009, 238). Managers needed to weigh up the enormous expense of costume against the enormous attraction it held for spectators. The only extant visual evidence of costuming practices is a drawing, believed to be by Henry Peacham, of a set for *Titus Andronicus*. Showing a mix of Roman and Elizabethan garb, with the most ornate outfits reserved for the main characters, the sketch suggests that the theatres took a fairly eclectic approach to costume, dictated by economic necessity. It is generally assumed that most of the cast would have worn contemporary dress, with the sartorial glamour and historically specific dress being reserved for the leading men.

Clothing is a highly significant feature of Shakespearean drama and can play a crucial role in the stage action. Costume allows heroines such as Viola to experience living in another gender and class; Malvolio's yellow stockings create comic uproar, while Cloten's ill-fated decision to dress in Posthumus' garments sets up one of the most gruesome moments in early modern theatre. Moreover, the plays abound with the imagery of clothes and fashion. Macbeth's title is said to 'Hang loose about him, like a giant's robe/Upon a dwarfish thief' (5.2.21–2), Benedick is accused of changing his friends as often as 'the fashion of his hat' (1.1.71) and Enobarbus responds to the death of Antony's wife by assuring him that his 'old smock' will bring 'forth a new petticoat' (1.2.175–6).

There are few such direct references to clothing in *Richard II*, but those that do appear carry considerable impact. Richard's contemptuous description of Bolingbroke's taking off 'his bonnet to an oyster-wench' (1.4.31) draws attention to the contrast between the two cousins: the one contemptuous of the lower orders, the other pragmatically aware of the importance of the common touch. And his declaration that 'The lining of his [Gaunt's] coffers shall make coats' (1.4.61) for soldiers, with its alliterative play and punning on the literal and figurative meaning of 'lining', portrays him as lacking the gravitas and maturity expected of a king, as well as forecasting a violation of the laws of inheritance which will lead to his downfall. The relatively high number of static scenes in *Richard II* allows audiences ample time to gaze on the actors, to appreciate through costume the shift from the courtly to the martial and from the splendidly regal to the abjectly ragged. The crown, orb and sceptre, insignia of monarchical power, act as material markers of Richard's descent in an unflinchingly drawn-out deposition scene: a vision of the 'unkinged' which would take on a brutal reality fifty years hence with the execution of Charles I. The striking contrast of the magnificent costume of the King at the start of the play with what we assume to be the habit of a beggar in Act 5 must have had a powerful visual impact on audiences, not least because, unlike the unrobed King Lear whose indigent state is shared by 'poor Tom', Richard's move from riches to rags is his alone. The sight of a destitute king would have had radical political implications, as well as reminding audiences of Christ's teachings on the ephemerality of material possessions. As one of Shakespeare's sources for the play, *A Myrroure for Magistrates* (1559) warns:

> Loe howe the power, the pride, and riche aray
> Of myghty rulers lightly fade away.

It is a warning that seems appropriate for a King who moves from the 'fashions in proud Italy' (2.1.21) to the rags of a prison cell, though Shakespeare's treatment of the fall complicates and questions its simple morality.

Shakespeare's all-verse drama

Richard II is one of only two Shakespeare's plays to be written entirely in verse (the other is *King John*). With its measured line lengths and metrical regularity, verse is an ideal medium for a play set in the medieval world of courtly ritual. However, it also proves highly adaptable to a diverse range of characters and establishes an extensive range of tonalities. The eloquent despair of Richard, the desolation of the widowed Duchess of Gloucester, the Machiavellian expediency of Northumberland, the maternal fervour of the Duchess of York, the choric pronouncements of the Gardener and the loyal simplicity of the Groom are all captured in blank or rhymed verse and sometimes a mix of both.

More than four-fifths of *Richard II* is in **blank verse**. The verse is termed 'blank' because of the absence of rhyme and is distinguished from prose by its regular **iambic pentameter** lines. The five-beat pulse of blank verse was particularly popular with playwrights of Shakespeare's generation and everything points to its being equally popular with audiences. As George T. Wright explains in his extensive survey of Shakespeare's metrical techniques, iambic pentameter is impossible to split into two equal halves as a 'midline pause, wherever it appears, leaves two stressed syllables on one side and three on the other' (*Shakespeare's Metrical Art*, 1988, 5).This property of the metre makes it less sing-song than, say, tetrameter, ensuring that its cumulative effect is neither soporific nor trivializing. The stress pattern of iambic pentameter is often said to be close to 'natural' speech intonations and thus an ideal choice for dramatic dialogue. However, scholars such as Robert Shaughnessy have challenged this truism:

> the unproblematised notion that the verse prioritizes the construction of 'character' through 'natural'-sounding speech foists a modern conception of selfhood, and of its articulation through the spoken word, onto texts that originated within a theatrical and cultural milieu ... in which these conceptions would have been barely imaginable.
>
> (*The Routledge Guide to William Shakespeare*, 2011, 361)

While it is always wise to be alert to the type of ahistorical thinking which Shaughnessy highlights, analysing the dramatic effects achieved through the sounds and inflexions of spoken dialogue on stage (or at least as they appear to modern ears) can be an illuminating process.

Blank verse is often defined in terms of a set of 'rules', making it seem a rather limited mode of expression. However, its rules are there to be broken and changes in line length and variations in stress patterns achieve striking, sometimes subtle, dramatic effects. It is commonly held that the ears of Shakespeare's original spectators would have been more attuned to such deviations from the norm than audiences of our own time, able to pick up an **alexandrine** line, an **unstressed ending** or a shift from iambic to **trochaic** metre. In a recent essay on *Richard II*, Brian Walsh lays emphasis on the actual process of listening to a verse drama, arguing that it can be a highly active and engrossing one:

> In straining to hear an expected end rhyme, in being surprised by one that appears seemingly at random, in being presented with a sudden pause in a speech, audiences of *Richard II* are put off balance throughout the play by the variegated sound patterns.
>
> ('The Dramaturgy of Discomfort in *Richard II*', *Richard II: New Critical Essays*, ed. Jeremy Lopez, 2012, 185)

The 'variegated sound patterns' of *Richard II* are managed through a number of techniques, one being the inversion of the stress pattern at the start of a line. Take, for example, Mowbray's speech lamenting the loss of his native language (1.3.154–73), where the sudden inversion of the initial iambic rhythm just over mid-way through the speech suggests anger threatening to break through:

> Within my mouth you have engaoled my tongue,
> Doubly portcullised with my teeth and lips,

> (1.3.166–7)

As with all poetic verse, sound variations also come from the **caesurae** which interrupt lines in one or more places. Notice how the caesurae in Richard's speech below create pauses pregnant with meaning, underscoring the absence of the responses he was once so sure of commanding:

> God save the King! Will no man say 'Amen'?
> Am I both priest and clerk? Well then, Amen.
> God save the King, although I be not he,
> And yet Amen, if heaven do think him me.

> (4.1.173–6)

Enjambement is another device which helps to vary the pace set by the blank verse pattern. Enjambed lines cross over from one line to another, often adding force to the first word of that which follows, or building momentum. Carlisle's lengthy homily in protest at the overthrow of an anointed king is carefully modulated through short sequences of enjambed lines dispersed throughout the speech:

> Disorder, horror, fear and mutiny
> Shall here inhabit, and this land be called
> The field of Golgotha and dead men's skulls.

> (4.1.143–5)

Here, the unstopped lines serve to drive home the inevitability of the civil turmoil prophesied by Carlisle. Yet speeches with a high proportion of **end-stopped** lines can also seize the attention of listeners. For example, the Duchess of York's speech imploring King Henry to pardon Aumerle's sedition (5.3.110–17) consists of mainly end-stopped lines which work together to aurally convey her obdurate refusal to budge.

The blank verse of *Richard II* is alternated or interleaved with rhyming verse. Although there had been a distinct swerve away from rhymed verse in the drama of the mid-to-late sixteenth century, Shakespeare continued to exploit its effects, especially in comedies such as *A Midsummer Night's Dream* and *Love's Labour's Lost*. In *Richard II* it fulfils the common dramatic function of indicating the end of scenes or concluding speeches, as well as creating more subtle resonances. Mowbray underscores the integrity of his case by concluding his speech with a complete rhyme:

> And when I mount, alive may I not light
> If I be traitor or unjustly fight!

> > (1.1.82–3)

And, not to be beaten, Bolingbroke responds in kind at the end of his next speech:

> And by the glorious worth of my descent,
> This arm shall do it, or this life be spent!

> > (1.1.107–8)

Gaunt's reaction to Richard shortening Bolingbroke's banishment (1.3.216–48) is made all the more powerful by the movement between blank verse and rhyme. The father's certainty of his own approaching death and of the injustice of his son's sentence is evoked by his insistent rhyming couplets, sustained over more than twenty lines of verse. The assurance of Gaunt's rhyming speech seems to discountenance the King who, at two points in the dialogue, attempts to disrupt it. But Gaunt's rhyme never falters and Richard's interjected, unrhymed line is simply capped and subsumed into the rhyming pattern.

> KING RICHARD: Why uncle, thou hast many years to live.
> GAUNT: But not a minute, King, that thou canst give.

> > (1.3.225–6)

While Richard's kingly status lends him the public advantage, Gaunt's age and familial authority give the scene a perceptible counter-current: the subject-Gaunt keeps himself in check through the constraints of rhyme; the uncle-Gaunt rebukes the nephew through the solemn and immovable quality of the same.

The magniloquent verse of Richard II is often viewed as the play's keynote. The Victorian academic and writer Walter Pater, seen by many of his generation as a grand master of English prose, admired Richard's 'golden language' (*Walter Pater: Three Major Texts*, ed. William E. Buckler, 1986, 512); the poet W. B. Yeats followed suit, comparing those critics who cast moral censure on Shakespeare's hero to schoolboys 'persecuting some boy of fine temperament, who has weak muscles and a distaste for school games' (*W.B. Yeats: Selected Criticism*, ed. A. Norman Jeffares, 1976, 99). This aestheticizing of Richard focused on his appreciation and command of language, seen by his admirers to grow all the more pronounced as his earthly fortunes decline. While most readers and audiences find little to admire in Richard in the first two acts of the play, some find themselves increasingly swayed in his favour through the rhetorical elegance of his language.

> ⁇ *Compare the possible impact of one of Richard's early speeches (1.1.152–159) to an extract from one delivered half-way through the drama (3.2.155–170). Look out for the effects created by:*

- rhyme
- enjambement
- caesurae
- modulations in the iambic stress

Immediately evident in the first speech, spoken in a highly ceremonial situation, is Richard's complete control. Each line is end-stopped and the regular caesurae lend the lines a stately formality. The sequence of three rhyming couplets and the symmetry of the proverbial 'Forget, forgive, conclude and be agreed', whilst all adding to this style of command, also carry an offhand levity: this is a king who pronounces decrees as if reciting a prayer rendered meaningless by over-familiarity. In contrast, Richard delivers the later speech seated not on his throne, but on the ground, a visual sign of his fall from power. Gone is the self-consciously authoritative tone of the earlier lines, to be replaced by verse whose vigour and variety engage and surprise the ear. The mesmeric effect of the **anaphora** in lines 157–9 is abruptly dispelled by '**All murd**ered.' The extra initial stress placed on 'All' and the strong caesura placed at the end of the phrase seem to mark the speaker's fearful anticipation of his own fate. As Richard's imagination dwells on the essential vapidity of kingship, it is as if he, as well as Death, is 'scoffing' at his earlier self: a king much given to 'monarchize'. The enjambement on line 160 seems to enact the crown circling the king's head, while the 'king' at the end of line 161 is brought into an enjambed collision with 'Keeps Death his court' at the start of the line which follows. Death's stealth and inevitable triumph are captured in the enjambement from line 169 to 170, the soft unvoiced **plosive** of 'pin' contrasting forcefully with its voiced equivalent 'Bores', and made all the more threatening by its being an irregularly stressed syllable positioned at the start of the line. The caesura after 'castle wall' indicates the precise moment of death, the mid-line pause allowing, perhaps, for the recovery of Richard's trademark flippancy detectable in 'and farewell, king!'

While audio adaptations of Shakespeare tend to be overlooked in today's predominantly visual culture, they can prove an effective means of studying poetic verse. *Richard II*'s rich verbal textures make it particularly well suited to audio performance, such as that directed by Jeremy Mortimer for BBC Radio 3. Starring Samuel West as Richard – a role he also played in the 2000 RSC production – the recording skilfully replaces the visual splendour of regal iconography and chivalric display with music and sound effects and features clear, well-modulated verse speaking. Listening to such a performance brings out the iteration of certain words and images, tonal modulations, rhetorical patterns and metrical variations, all aspects of Shakespeare's language which can be missed in a stage or screen performance.

'Girlie' Shakespeare: Deborah Warner's *Richard II* at the Cottesloe (1995)

Deborah Warner's production of *Richard II* was sold out long before its opening night. This was partly due to the fact that the cast included Fiona Shaw, one of the most acclaimed performers of her generation, and not a little to do with the fact that she was playing the male lead. Shaw and Warner had already collaborated on various productions and were seen as a formidable duo in their willingness to approach canonical texts with a fresh, irreverent spirit: their *Richard II* would prove no exception.

The press reviews of Warner's *Richard II* read like a concerted attempt to break up a beautiful friendship, with the majority heaping praise on the director and opprobrium on the lead player. Shaw was condemned for over-psychologizing, indulging in excessive gesture, breathing too heavily, massacring the verse and, with her cropped hair and aquiline profile, resembling a 'shorn Virginia Woolf'. In a review in the *Independent* (so excoriating it prompted a 'second opinion' from Paul Taylor in the same newspaper nine days later, defending Shaw 'from the baying critics') Rhona Koenig complained that 'Shaw's Richard … is a stereotypical girlie. Though crowned at 10, Richard was 30 during the events chronicled … and unlikely to be such a giggling prat'. Koenig had clearly missed the core idea of Warner's interpretation and Shaw's performance: the consequence of being a king at ten is arrested development and neurosis.

Warner's production foregrounded family relationships. Shaw talked in interview about inventing her own back-story, in which the royal cousins were childhood companions, Bolingbroke acting as Richard's main protector. While academics would be dubious about thinking about Richard as a 'real person' whose experience precedes the text, the actor's method, as evidenced here, is more psychologically grounded and the idea of the cousins' intimacy was central to performance. David Threfall, who played Bolingbroke, bore a strong physical resemblance to Shaw and familial fondness was demonstrated through Richard's kissing and embracing his cousin. According to literary critic, Peter Holland, one of the production's admirers, the deposition scene captured the relationship between the two with particular intensity:

> Richard entered with the crown in a shopping-basket and placed it on the floor between himself and Bolingbroke, undercutting the solemnity of the ritual by trying to play pat-a-cake with him. But the game was now excruciatingly painful and he responded to Bolingbroke's question, 'Are you contented to resign the crown?' … with an off-hand 'Aye', then turned and buried his head in the lap of the seated York and screamed 'No.' Miming the reverse coronation through tears, Richard prostrated himself full-length before the crowned King Henry, then punched at him until Henry embraced him and calmed him.
>
> (*SS*, 49, 1996, 266)

Warner's emphasis on family turmoil led to criticisms that she had neglected the play's political dimensions. However, critics could not deny that her presentation of kingship as little more than a charade had a sharply political edge and one that some of the more right-leaning newspaper critics found disturbing. The performance opened with Richard behind a gauze curtain, being dressed in his robes and handed his orb and sceptre: a dumb show suggesting that kingship is little more than a construct of ritual and clothing. This ceremonial figure contrasted starkly with the Richard who followed. For most of the drama he was dressed in white leggings and a short white tunic – making him resemble a mummy in the eyes of some critics and a model for fashion designer, Issey Miyake, in the eyes of others. By turns petulant, vulnerable and infantile, he was presented as a child in office, his feet not touching the ground when seated on the throne, and sucking his thumb as he prepared to recount 'sad stories of the death of kings ' (3.2.156) – a gesture that even the most well-disposed critics found a step too far. Other moments, such as when Richard comes to the ailing Gaunt, wearing a black-armband and carrying a wreath (hurriedly discarded when his uncle proves to be still breathing), pushed the implications of the text to their limit and portrayed a king who, in the words of Benedict Nightingale in *The Times*, was 'unfitted to rule anything larger or older than Enid Blyton's Famous Five'.

How far the production was informed by sexual politics was another major talking point and one which academics continue to debate. Both Shaw and Warner denied it had feminist impetus. In an interview for the *Independent* Warner explained how she cast Shaw because 'There's no one else I would want for Richard', while Shaw, in an interview with Carol Chillington Rutter, described her cross-casting as an 'experiment' (*SQ*, 48, 1997, 315), a means of liberating someone from gender. For the most part, though, reviewers did not focus on gender. As several of the better informed among them pointed out, cross-gendered casting was nothing new; there was a tradition of women playing male parts going back to the eighteenth and nineteenth centuries, when, on a stage considerably less wedded to realism than today's, women performed roles such as Hamlet, Romeo and Iago. Moreover, as Shaw remarked in an interview for the Open University, the role of Richard has 'gone off the cliff of effeminacy' – a woman playing him would seem to be a logical next step. The critical consensus was that Shaw had achieved an entirely androgynous performance, with Nicholas de Jongh of the *Evening Standard* commenting on how 'the theatre's power of make-believe seduces you into taking androgyny in your stride'.

Some academic critics were unwilling to accept Warner's avowed lack of feminist intention and argued that a woman playing a major male Shakespearean role inevitably signalled a gender-political stance. Elizabeth Klett asserted that 'Shaw's Richard was androgynous, embodying a wide spectrum of gender identities' (*Cross-Gender Shakespeare and English National Identity*, 2009, 34); others, such as Grace Tiffany, saw the production as ultimately reactionary, one which played into 'traditional notions of femininity as lack of emotional control, fickleness, finely tuned sensitivity, and weakness' ('How Revolutionary *Is* Cross-cast Shakespeare? A Look at Five Contemporary Productions' in *Shakespeare: Text and Theatre*, Lois Potter and Arthur F. Kinney (eds), 1999, 121).

Warner's *Richard II* was a highly ambiguous theatrical event, prompting radically different responses (the only aspect of the production reviewers were in one mind about was Hildegard Bechtler's stage set which transformed the Cottesloe into a highly flexible and multiperspectival space). Challenging audience expectations of kingship, masculinity and, perhaps most profoundly, Shakespearean performance, it succeeded in shaking up what its director and leading woman saw as a somewhat moribund theatrical climate. While a number of Shakespeare productions have since taken the casting of women in male roles a stage further by featuring exclusively female casts (most recently Phyllida Lloyd's 2012 *Julius Caesar* at the Donmar Warehouse in London), it is Shaw's performance which has left the greatest mark on theatre history.

Further thinking

➤ Can you think of other Shakespeare plays where the visual impact of clothing is crucial to its meaning and dramatic impact?

➤ John Gielgud (one of the most celebrated actors to have performed Richard II in the twentieth century) felt that the elaborate verse of the play prevented the audience from getting on intimate terms with the characters. How would you respond to this comment?

➤ Kathryn Hunter played the title role in a production of *King Lear* directed by Helena Kaut-Howson (Leicester Haymarket, 1997). What challenges would this role present for a female performer? How would they differ from those faced by Fiona Shaw in playing Richard?

Afterlives ...

In 1789, John Boydell set up the Shakespeare Gallery in Pall Mall, dedicated to exhibiting paintings of scenes from Shakespeare. One of the artists commissioned to produce work was James Northcote; his painting, *The Entry of Richard II and Bolingbroke into London*, vividly depicts a scene which is narrated but not actually staged in the play (5.2.1–40). The painting now hangs in the Royal Albert Memorial Museum in Exeter (www.rammuseum.org.uk) and provides a thought-provoking example of Shakespeare's words translated into brushstrokes.

11

Richard III:
History's monster or
charismatic villain?

Richard III was a popular figure on the Renaissance stage and continues to attract audiences in Shakespeare's savage and witty characterization. Arguments over the 'real Richard' and how far the play is an act of historical slander also thrive. The relationship between history, play and subsequent interpretation is complex.

This chapter

- discusses new historicism as a way of approaching the text
- engages with Elizabethan historiography and considers the nature of 'Tudor myth'
- analyzes characteristic features of Richard's rhetoric
- discusses the 1930s perspective of Loncraine's film

New historicism

Before defining new historicism, it might be helpful to give some consideration to what 'old' historicism might be. Briefly, the early twentieth-century historical approach took as its starting point the cultural supremacy of the literary work; historical and contextual investigations supplied no more than explanatory footnotes. Shakespeare's plays, in particular, were seen as shining stars in a firmament of 'background'. Details of Elizabethan theatre, politics and religion supplied discrete nuggets of information to elucidate specific lines or references in a given play. Equally, given the overwhelming dominance of Shakespeare and, in Britain, the popularity of the Tudors, educationally and culturally, a certain notion of History tended to be promulgated: generally, the 'Golden Age' of Elizabethan England, optimistic and expansionist, emerging from the superstition and oppression of the Middle Ages.

An historical approach of this kind might seem entirely laudable, acknowledging the significance of the text within its history and making the historical moment part of the process of writing. In formalist readings (text-only analysis) a literary work floats free from any cultural context, expressing 'universal' truths, or simply offering aesthetic challenges and pleasures. E. M. W. Tillyard was undoubtedly the chief exponent of the mid- twentieth-century historical method of enquiry and his *The Elizabethan World Picture* (1941) and *Shakespeare's History Plays* (1944) profoundly influenced post-war British and American teaching and scholarship. Eustace Mandeville Wetenhall Tillyard (1889–1962) was a key figure in shaping Cambridge University's English degree after World War I. His work on Shakespeare's histories was undertaken and published during World War II and was inevitably influenced by the anxiety and patriotism of that period. Modern British critics such as Graham Holderness (*Shakespeare: the Histories*, 2000) view Tillyard's role as inherently nationalist and conservative, upholding a passive acceptance of hierarchy and seeing England's history as Providential. Tillyard's writing is persuasive because it confidently offers a reading of the plays which is fixed and unambiguous – '*The*' essential Elizabethan view of the universe, as the title of his early monograph suggests. In this world, human affairs are governed by Providence and all human history moves teleologically towards the end point which is the Day of Judgement. Tillyard extracts a famous speech about order from *Troilus and Cressida* to establish his argument, proposing this as representative of both Shakespeare and his age; in this light, the plays become moral fables dramatizing the disastrous consequences of civil dissension.

Perhaps the opening point to make about new historicism is that it is completely opposed to the idea of text and 'background'. As a method of literary analysis, it developed principally in American universities from the 1980s (the comparable English approach tends to be termed Cultural Materialism). Unlike Marxist criticism or Freudian psychoanalysis, it does not operate with a specific doctrine as its basis; rather it is a set of critical techniques and strategies. In American studies, the key figure in defining new historicism (and first using the term) is Stephen Greenblatt and his early works describe a practice rather than a set of doctrines:

> an intensified willingness to read all of the textual traces of the past with the attention traditionally conferred only on literary texts.
>
> (*Learning to Curse: Essays in Early Modern Culture,*
> 1990, 14)

Breaking down the distinction between literary and non-literary texts inevitably challenges ideas of the canonicity of literary works; in Louis Montrose's much-quoted formulation: 'the historicity of texts and the textuality of history' (*The New Historicism*, ed. H. Aram Veeser, 1989, 20).

Differences between practitioners are inevitable – there is no 'manifesto' as such. But certain key premises can be identified:

- All expressive acts (writings, sculpture, legal documents, diaries) are embedded in a network of 'materiality'; literary and non-literary texts do not operate independently. The play is not the 'mirror of the age' but is instrumental in shaping the dominant ideas of its time.

- Literary texts do not 'transcend' their culture and there is no 'unchanging human nature' enshrined within them. The anthropologist Clifford Geertz has been influential in arguing that human beings emerge from their cultural moment – 'our ideas, our values, our acts, even our emotions, are ... cultural products' (cited in, Kiernan Ryan, *New Historicism and Cultural Materialism*, 1996, 8). The past is fascinating for its alterity (otherness) rather than its likeness to ourselves.

- History does not offer a single 'great narrative' or grand design (as implied by Tillyard) and historical continuities are invariably what later commentators read retrospectively into their chosen evidence. It is not possible to view the past objectively and it should not be venerated.

- In Greenblatt's own words: 'There can be no appeals to genius as the sole origin of the energies of great art' (*Shakespearean Negotiations*, 1988, 12). In other words, Romanticist notions of the poet are rejected.

In Britain, Cultural Materialism pursues similar historicist methods but, as Kiernan Ryan has observed, British writing tends to pursue specific political agendas:

[Cultural] materialism seeks actively and explicitly to use the literature of yesterday to change the world today. It is a brazenly engaged critical stance, committed to activating the dissident potential of past texts, in order to change the present conservative consensus.

(Ryan, 1996, xv)

Key to the political aspect of historicist criticism is 'State power and resistance to it' (Dollimore and Sinfield, *Political*

Shakespeare, 1994, 3): ways in which the dominant power establishes and perpetuates itself and the oppositional process of subversion and dissent. Leonard Tennenhouse's writing examines Renaissance texts in terms of authority and subversiveness, arguing that even Petrarchan lyrics or romantic comedies are 'openly and expressly political in the strategies by which they idealise State authority' (in *Political Shakespeare*, 120).

In both British and American criticism, early modern texts have dominated new historicist writing. Jean Howard thoughtfully suggests that modern scholars find in Renaissance texts 'their own sense of the exhilaration and fearfulness of living in a gap in history' (Richard Dutton and Richard Wilson, *New Historicism and Renaissance Drama*, 1992, 22). Historicist critics look with a troubled eye on the authoritarian structures of power that dominated early modern history. They scrutinize the texts of the period, finding a tension between texts that appear to operate in a collusive way, emphasizing the importance of order, or texts that challenge the status quo by critiquing established power structures and empowering marginalized voices.

One of the characteristic techniques of new historicism is the use of extraneous anecdote as a way into the text. This is far from old-fashioned 'source-hunting'; the arresting tale might be contemporary with the text, thereby offering a juxtaposition which sheds light on some aspect of the period, but it might be entirely remote and seemingly tangential. A typical example of this is Greenblatt's 'The Cultivation of Anxiety: King Lear and his heirs' where Greenblatt begins his discussion with a lengthy extract from the *American Baptist Magazine* of 1831 and the alarming first-person narrative of a Baptist minister breaking the will of his very young son. James Siemon draws on new historicist methods in his article '"The Power of Hope?" An Early Modern Reader of *Richard III*' (in *A Companion to Shakespeare's History Plays*, Richard Dutton and Jean Howard (eds), 2003). The discussion is entirely centred on the 'materiality' of text as Siemon analyzes the marginal comments of an anonymous reader (*c.* 1630) who annotated his/her Shakespeare First Folio. *Richard III* is selected for discussion precisely because it has seemed, in the past, to dramatize a Tudor mindset and Siemon sets out to demonstrate how unstable such a reading can be. The chief focus of attention is Richmond's speech to his immediate followers, before Bosworth:

> True hope is swift and flies with swallow's wings;
> Kings it makes gods, and meaner creatures kings.

> (5.2.23–4)

To establish the problematic nature of Richmond's couplet, and the seventeenth-century reader's response, 'power of hope', Siemon draws on the failure of Stuart foreign ventures; Calvin's definition of hope; the Percy family's motto 'esperaunce', all of which embed the annotated text in its original culture. The guiding premise is 'how little we know about early modern readers' (362) – an anti-essentialist view. Richmond's 'hope' at the end of the text, rather than the pious statement of Tudor stability, is seen as ironical. Providential readings of the play's conclusion are rejected; rather the play 'could be read as an extended ironic commentary on the falsity of worldly hopes for security and stability' (373). Tillyard's upbeat reading of Richmond's final speech is set against the concluding line of *Henry VI, Part 3*: 'here I hope begins our lasting joy' where the new king, Edward IV, addresses his baby son while Richard, aside, hisses 'I'll blast his harvest'. Power, at the end of *Richard III* is seen as tenuous and, in Richmond, unsure and coercive: 'What traitor hears me and says not amen?' In other words, agree with me, or suffer the traitor's death.

History and historiography: Early modern approaches

In Renaissance writing, the term historiography tends to mean, simply, history; it had not acquired its modern methodological connotations. So 'poetrie, philosophie and historiographie' might be opposed, as secular activities, to 'divinitie', the only study which would lead to God. The sixteenth-century engagement with the past was growing in sophistication, however: an aspiration towards historical impartiality can be seen warring with the colourful inventiveness of certain types of historical writing. For the purposes of this discussion, history refers to the events of the past, and historiography the different attitudes or strategies brought to the chronicling and interpretation of historical events.

Shakespeare's interest in history as dramatic subject matter is unarguable: ten plays in total from his earliest writing (probably *2H6*, 1590–1) to one of his final plays, *King Henry VIII* (1613). Plays such as *Macbeth*, *Julius Caesar* and *Coriolanus* also demonstrate Shakespeare's interest in chronicle sources, and the tragic struggle over succession. The eight key texts of English history invariably appear as two tetralogies spanning *Richard II* to *Richard III* and thus encompassing the Wars of the Roses, the bitter dynastic dispute of the fifteenth century. There is no evidence that Shakespeare himself saw the plays as a sequence, however, and it is worth remembering that the plays were not written in chronological order. *Henry VI, 1, 2 and 3* and *Richard III* begin his theatrical career, but are later in historical time than *Richard II*, the two *Henry IV* plays and *Henry V*. The First Folio regularized the titles and organized the plays according to historical time-line, creating an impression of orderly continuity which does not correspond with Shakespeare's writing. In purely dramatic terms, it is not difficult to see why this subject matter is appealing: war, divided loyalties, betrayals, scheming, murder, extremes of hatred and grief – a colourful canvas for the playhouses.

Powerful actors such as Alleyn and Burbage could be depended upon for major roles such as Richard III. Thomas Nashe (in *Pierce Penniless's Supplication to the Devil*, 1592) refers to an enthusiastic market for stirring tales on stage: he alludes to the tears of 'ten thousand spectators' over Talbot's death (in *1H6*) and although his numbers may be suspect, Philip Henslowe's records reveal that the takings for March 1592, when *1H6* was first performed, were the highest of the season. *Richard III* was popular both on stage and in print: the first quarto publication in 1596, entitled *The Tragedie of King Richard III* was, exceptionally, reprinted in at least five further editions before the Folio of 1623. Early modern readers seized upon a wide range of historical writing with enthusiasm, and dramatists were eager to exploit this interest. According to Ivo Kamps,'[more] than seventy historical dramas were written in England between the middle of the sixteenth century and the Revolution' ('The Writing of History in Shakespeare's England', Dutton and Howard, 2003, 4). Two unarguable points emerge: first the widespread enthusiasm for historical writing and, secondly, the complete lack of a univocal and consistent 'world picture'.

So far, so theatrically successful: 'History' as thoroughly marketable entertainment. But what expectations or prejudices did the Elizabethan audience bring to the performance, or reader to the text? Phyllis Rackin suggests that the second half of the sixteenth century is a transitional phase when radically different conceptions of historiography could be expressed, often by the same writer:

> Despite the widespread interest in history and the overwhelming chorus of praise for the benefits its study could confer, there was no clear consensus about its nature and purpose ... Three great innovations ... were changing English historiography ... a new interest in causation, a recognition of anachronism, and a questioning of textual authority.
>
> (Rackin, *Stages of History: Shakespeare's English Chronicles*, 1990, 5)

Text itself is perhaps the most telling area here: are textual sources 'true'? By the end of the sixteenth century a great deal more text was available; the printing industry was well established and small, cheap books proliferated. The old days of the great medieval chronicles, exquisitely hand-written and decorated, for monastic or noble libraries, had passed. The Protestant conviction that biblical text is the only source of truth had the unintended consequence of opening up the question of the validity of the text, as new translations offered subtly different readings. When Nashe defends the theatre, he argues that historical subjects inspire 'vertue' in 'these degenerate, effeminate days of ours'. Courageous deeds, patriotism, just political dealings; the stories from the past were expected to be instructive, but the didactic intention is two-sided, not simply enforcing a homily of obedience and respect for forms of authority, but also warning against tyranny and bad government. Looking across the two tetralogies, it is noteworthy that *Richard II*, the first play chronologically, deals with the usurpation of the 'anointed king'; at the end of the period, Richard III is defeated, and overthrown; he, too, sees himself as 'the Lord's anointed'. Throughout, the question of the good or effective ruler is central. There is no suggestion of unthinking obedience; the conflict and excitement of the drama comes from the struggle of individual choices, such as Hastings':

> I'll have this crown of mine cut from my shoulders
> Before I'll see the crown so foul misplaced.

> (3.2.42–3)

Shakespeare and 'Tudor myth'

Shakespeare had a number of key texts which might have inspired or influenced the writing of *Richard III*: Holinshed's Chronicles is a familiar source; Thomas More's *The History of King Richard III* (1543) contains details which occur in the play; Edward Hall's *The Union of the Two Noble and Illustre Families of Lancaster and Yorke* (1548) is the text that pursues a determinedly pro-Tudor line. The 'Tudor myth' is generally taken to be Henry VII's efforts to bolster his claim and establish undisputed sovereignty. His Lancastrian claim was weak. His mother, Margaret Beaufort, was a direct descendant from John of Gaunt, although through an illegitimate line retrospectively legitimized by Pope Boniface IX. Henry's grandfather, Owen Tudor, was simply the second husband of Henry V's widow, Catherine of Valois. Henry VII was de facto king, proclaimed on the battlefield, but Clarence's son had the stronger claim, and Richard himself had appointed his nephew John Earl of Lincoln as his successor. Tillyard, as Tudor myth-maker, looks for more than just an endorsement of Tudor rule: he argues in favour of a definitive linking of the events of history with God:

> Shakespeare accepted the prevalent belief that God had guided England into her haven of Tudor prosperity. And he had accepted it with his whole heart.
>
> (*Shakespeare's History Plays*, 1969, 210)

This is a classic example of the 'Providential' reading of history – the concept that God has a master-plan for all human affairs. To Tillyard, England must atone for the crime of Richard II's usurpation and murder: punishment descends through the generations of Lancastrians until Richard III, acting as God's scourge, is finally defeated and the Tudor peace is established. It is less than logical as a scheme of justice. If Bolingbroke must suffer for his crime, why is his son, Henry V, a triumphant vision of military success? If the Lancastrian line is damned, then why is Henry VI depicted as the saintly king? In *Richard III*, why should two Yorkist children be murdered for Bolingbroke's (Lancastrian) crime? Ivo Kamps draws attention to the contradictions:

> When we see the wicked prosper, it is a sign of God's provi-dence; when we see the good suffer, it is an indication of

God's providence. If we see the wicked punished, that too is a sign of God's providence, and if the good receive pity and mercy, this is also to be taken as evidence of God's providence.

(Kamps, 17)

It is certainly true that individual characters call on divine justice or interpret specific events as vindicating their own individual view of the working out of Providence – but that individualism raises the central problem: God cannot be on everyone's side. Shakespeare's incorporation of the ancient queen Margaret as a vengeful fury from the past illustrates this point effectively. The historical Margaret returned to France in 1476 and died in 1482. Shakespeare obviously cares far more for the effect of her haunting presence on stage than he minds about historical anachronism. In *Richard III* she acts as a reminder of the past and emphasizes the see-sawing between York and Lancaster in their desire for power and their ruthless destruction:

> Bear with me: I am hungry for revenge,
> And now I cloy me with beholding it.
> Thy Edward he is dead, that killed my Edward,
> Thy other Edward dead, to quit my Edward.
> Young York, he is but boot, because both they
> Matched not the high perfection of my loss.
> Thy Clarence he is dead that stabbed my Edward ...

(4.4.61–7)

Tillyard's view of 'the working out of God's plan' is profoundly troubling here: nothing in Christian theology suggests that the murder of the innocents is acceptable. Kelly's useful study establishes the complexity of rival Yorkist and Lancastrian myths rather than a single, univocal 'Tudor myth'.

We may add that if the concept of God's punishment extending beyond the sinner to his innocent children was difficult to accept, the concept of divine wrath extending for generations over a whole people for a crime committed in the remote past presupposes the kind of avenging God completely foreign to the piety of the historiographers of medieval and Renaissance England.

(Henry Ansgar Kelly, *Divine Providence in the England of Shakespeare's Histories*, 1970, 300)

But is Shakespeare concerned to create a deformed and black-hearted Richard to suit his Tudor audience? Richard himself is a charismatic and highly self-aware villain who delights in his Machiavellian scheming and double-dealing:

I am determined to prove a villain
And hate the idle pleasures of these days.

(1.1.30–2)

The very fact of the opening soliloquy is significant: Richard is the only eponymous hero to speak the first lines of the play; one of the largest roles in Shakespeare, he dominates the action throughout. Equally, the complex self-doubt of his final soliloquy suggests a link with the protagonists of the tragedies. The force of Richard's ambition and the ruthless brilliance of his manipulation of events owe more to the influence of Machiavelli and Renaissance ideas of political will than to Providence. And Richard's villainy did not spring from nowhere: he could perhaps be seen as the extreme version of the ambition and greed that exists in others. How many characters in the play, or across the tetralogy, are tainted by guilt? In *Richard III*, a long cycle (nearly ninety years) of bloodshed comes to an end. Richard has fought for the Yorkist cause for his father and his brother: internecine warfare has shaped his whole life. He has no difficulty recruiting powerful noblemen to his cause: Buckingham and Catesby engineer his accession and his supporters greatly outnumber Richmond's at Bosworth. In fact, it is a pervasively corrupt world, far from romantic notions of chivalry. Courtly love is parodied in Richard's wooing of Anne;

the Archbishop can be persuaded to hand over a young child in sanctuary; the hired assassin buries his conscience 'in the Duke of Gloucester's purse'. A more brutal, betraying and self-seeking world would be hard to find. But is Shakespeare depicting the past or does he evoke the Tudor world of his audience? A single instance might make a troubling connection: when Richard is priming Buckingham and Catesby to discern Hastings' loyalty, he is casually dismissive of opposition:

> BUCKINGHAM: Now, my lord, what shall we do if we perceive
> Lord Hastings will not yield to our complots?
> RICHARD: Chop off his head; something we will determine.

> (3.1.191–3)

Tudor monarchs were famed for executions: according to the Elizabethan writer William Harrison, a total of seventy-two thousand in the reign of Henry VIII (*Description of England*, 1577).

The notorious subject of Richard's physical deformity has often been seen as Tudor invention and certainly forms part of Shakespeare's characterization. No Shakespearean character attracts the range of bestial insult that Richard does, articulated throughout by the women. For Anne, in their first scene, he is 'Foul devil ... lump of foul deformity ... hedgehog ... homicide.' His own mother describes him as a cockatrice and a toad; to the vengeful Queen Margaret he is a 'cacodemon ... bottled spider ... hell-hound ... hell's black intelligencer.' Yet it is Richard who first introduces the subject; indeed he seizes upon it rather as Edmund in *King Lear* will choose to identify with 'bastard'. Shakespeare has no desire to soften the portrayal of Richard (historical sources such as the Croyland Chronicle refer to his intense grief at the death of his only son); rather, he chooses to exaggerate his energy, determination and his savage delight in his success.

In terms of Tudor myth, Shakespeare might have made far more of Richmond. In *Richard II*, Bolingbroke has a substantial role. Richmond is undeveloped as a character and appears like Fortinbras at the end of *Hamlet*: his role is to speak the clichéd words of restoration at the end of the play. But are these final lines joyous, or is there a troubling subtext for the Elizabethan audience?

> O, now let Richmond and Elizabeth,
> The true successors of each royal house,
> By God's fair ordinance conjoin together;
> And let their heirs, God, if thy will be so,
> Enrich the time to come with smooth-faced peace,
> With smiling plenty and fair prosperous days.
>
> (5.5.29–34)

The problem, in 1592, is that there are no Tudor heirs. The play could be seen as concluding with Tudor succession anxiety rather than the 'haven of Tudor prosperity'.

Much has been written about the Tudor blackening of Richard's reputation; there were, though, sources which defended him. A manuscript in circulation during the reign of Elizabeth praised him for his public virtues, good laws and lenient taxes. The (unknown) author suggests that if Richard had won at Bosworth, and his son had lived to succeed him, he would have been remembered as an honourable king. Later in the seventeenth century, William Winstanley included Richard in *England's Worthies*:

> this worthy Prince's fame [has] been blasted by malicious traducers, who, like Shakespear (*sic*) in his Play of him, render him dreadfully black in his actions, a monster of nature, rather than a man of admirable parts.

Is Richard a 'monster of nature'? As far as the performance of the play is concerned, every director and actor must make that judgement anew.

Richard's dramatic dialogue

In *3H6* Richard prides himself on his ability to dissemble: he can act any part and fake any emotion:

> Why I can smile, and murder while I smile,
> And cry 'Content!' to that which grieves my heart,
> And wet my cheeks with artificial tears,
> And frame my face to all occasions.
>   [...]
> I can add colours to the chameleon,
> Change shapes with Proteus for advantages,
> And set the murderous Machiavel to school.

> (*3H6*, 3.2.182–5,190–3)

One of the ways in which he commands the stage, taking charge of events and forcing people to comply with his will, is through his control of dialogue. Politically, he demonstrates all the volatile mood-changing of the tyrant, preventing opposition through terror. In the coronation meeting, Hastings believes that Richard is in a happy and relaxed state of mind, enquiring about strawberries, until he re-enters with an invented story of witchcraft, and within minutes is shouting 'Off with his head!' (3.4.75) Richard takes delight in his acting; he can effectively work the crowd with an appearance of humility; 'Will you enforce me to a world of cares?' He stirs up Edward's court, abusing Queen Elizabeth and her faction, but later appears the epitome of friendly candour:

> I do not know that Englishman alive
> With whom my soul is any jot at odds
> More than the infant that is born tonight.
> I thank my God for my humility.

> (2.1.70–1)

In close dialogue with one person, though, he reveals the full force of his intimidating personality. The wooing of Anne has often been described as a bravura performance; indeed, Richard congratulates himself on his dexterous handling of the scene.

Richard as the 'jolly thriving wooer' (1.2)

In analysing Richard's persuasive techniques in the long scene with Anne, it is worth remembering how the audience have just seen him; first in soliloquy, taking the audience into his confidence, and then with his brother, Clarence, where we see the immediate success of his plotting. He embraces Clarence, weeps, and then cruelly jokes at his expense:

> Simple, plain Clarence, I do love thee so
> That I will shortly send thy soul to heaven,
> If heaven will take the present at our hands.

> (1.1. 118–20)

In a similarly jovial fashion, he addresses himself to the business of wooing Anne:

> What though I kill'd her husband and her father?
> The readiest way to make the wench amends
> Is to become her husband and her father ...

> (1.1.154–6)

So the audience have probably laughed at his audacity, and anticipate with lively interest how far he can succeed in his pretence of romance.

⁇ *Now read 1.2., looking closely at:*

- Anne's opening speech
- the fury of her opening exchanges with Richard
- the ways in which Richard destroys her arguments

Anne's opening speech is formal and elaborate, full of rhetorical devices which enact the ritual nature of her mourning. She speaks with authority in commanding the coffin-bearers to 'set down, set down your honourable load.' Her language is **performative**: first in effecting the mourning rites (obsequies); then in her curses. She uses **apostrophe** – 'O cursed be the hand'; **anaphora** and **antanaclasis** ('Cursed be the heart that had the heart to do it'). Equally, her opening lines echo with alliteration ('key-cold ... King') and funereal vocabulary, 'obsequiously lament ... Pale ashes'.

When Richard appears, she immediately and vigorously attacks Richard. She continues to assume authority over her attendants – 'What, do you tremble? Are you all afraid?' and forcefully expresses her hatred of Richard and his deeds: 'Blush, blush, thou lump of foul deformity'. She is far from being the conventional picture of meek and silent womanhood, nor is she intimidated by Richard himself.

Their exchanges from 'Villain, thou knowest no law of God nor man. (70) to the point where she spits at him reveal Richard's brilliance. Once she has descended to this physical gesture, she has lost the verbal and emotional battle. He undermines her first by blandly agreeing with her: 'Didst thou not kill this king? / I grant thee'. Anne confronts him with the enormity of regicide and he simply shrugs and agrees. Richard's conventional praises – 'divine perfection of a woman' – leave her unmoved; she turns these back against him. The fact that she attacks him with accusations that he simply accepts is disorientating, however. The first dramatic climax occurs with Richard's shocking and unexpected 'Your bed-chamber' (114). The half-line **stichomythia** signifies Richard's bullying coercion. It is immediately apparent that she is at a loss to reply and from this point it is Richard who dominates. His next disorientating technique is to lay the blame upon Anne herself with his rhetorical question, 'Is not the causer .../As blameful as the executioner?' Using the anaphora characteristic of her earlier exchanges, he makes her responsible: 'Your beauty was the cause .../Your beauty that did haunt me.' Richard has successfully led her into his trap and makes himself the centre of the scene: 'Name him ... Where is he?' she asks and with his single word 'Here', she spits.

Richard follows this with his own tale of past histories; his father's death and the murder of his brother, young Rutland. He too uses **hyperbole** ('trees bedashed with rain'). He reminds her of her father, Warwick, weeping 'like a child'. This displaces Anne in her role of mourner and unites them as victims of the civil wars.

Richard completes his railroading with the physical action of offering her his sword – naked steel and bared breast. Can she kill him in cold blood? Of course not. But he has trapped her with two unacceptable alternatives: 'Take up the sword again, or take up me.' It is a consummate piece of emotional blackmail. The final exchanges of half-line stichomythia demonstrate how completely Anne has been defeated. She is left with helpless generalizations, 'To take is not to give.' And he places the ring on her finger, signifying their formal betrothal, and her total defeat.

The balance of power within the scene shifts from Anne to Richard: Anne is wholly confrontational at the beginning; her speeches are longer and full of the absolute certainty of moral accusation. Yet Richard succeeds in shocking and bewildering her and he then becomes the dominant voice. The audience knows, as she does not, that Richard is acting. Critical judgement is divided: 'Anne is a victim ... in part a willing one' (C. Moseley, *Richard III*, 1989, 63). To Jan Kott, she is totally isolated in her hatred and despair:

Lady Anne does not give herself to Richard out of fear. She will follow him to reach rock-bottom – to prove to herself

that all the world's laws have ceased to exist ... Lady Anne
goes into Richard's bed to be destroyed.

(Shakespeare Our Contemporary, 37)

Richard III as the fascist 1930s: Loncraine's film (1995)

Richard Eyre's National Theatre production, 1990, was
adapted into the 1995 film with Shakespeare's text heavily
cut and altered by McKellen. The staged version suggested
totalitarianism through lighting and costume; the film not
only takes this over but emphasizes and cements the play in a
1930s proto-fascist setting where familiar London landmarks
create the unsettling effect of an English Nazism. McKellen
argues the greater clarity of the twentieth-century context:

It is impossibly confusing to try and distinguish between a
multitude of characters who are all done up in floppy hats
and wrinkled tights. *Richard III* has a long complex cast
list but it is not a pageant. It analyses a sophisticated group
of powerful and would-be powerful players.

(Shakespeare's Richard III, 1996, 12)

The film opens with the implied end of the Battle of Tewkesbury;
a few words establish the identity of the besieged Henry VI
and his son just before, with dramatic effect, a Soviet T54
tank bursts through the wall and the Lancastrians are brutally
slaughtered. Richard eliminates Prince Edward before seeking
out the saintly King and shooting him as he kneels in prayer.
In an extraordinary juxtaposition, the next shot reveals
Richard casually smoking in the back of the car taking him
over Westminster Bridge to the Yorkist's Victory Ball. The
extended victory sequence which follows establishes the new
'royal family'; a wheezing and decadent King Edward, his

glamorous young wife and young sons; the matriarch Duchess (Maggie Smith). The Glenn Miller-style band, though, are playing a version of Christopher Marlowe's 'Come live with me and be my love' – a neat ironic twist. The impression is of a complacent upper-class world, happy to endorse the new ruling elite, although they are snobbishly dismissive of the King's American relatives in a way which resembles British prejudice against Wallis Simpson. Soldiers on guard outside the glittering gathering create a more ominous impression of martial law. Richard's opening soliloquy intrudes into the celebrations: he takes over the microphone, pays a gracious compliment to Edward, and the remainder of the speech is addressed to his reflection in the lavatory mirror. 'Plots have I laid' is spoken directly to the camera, inviting the viewer's complicity in his schemes.

The wooing of Anne (Kristin Scott Thomas) in a mortuary is profoundly shocking; a compelling way of externalizing the aberrance of Richard's proposal. Anne moves as though sleep-walking through hospital corridors full of the maimed and injured. She is seeking the body of her murdered husband (rather than father-in-law) and this is no stately funeral procession but a cold and clinical mortuary displaying the gruesome instruments of the trade. Richard's 'wooing' thus takes place over the body itself and effectively conveys the impression of her as totally traumatized. Richard's deformity is highlighted when he removes the ring from his finger with his teeth and transfers it to her from his mouth. The scene is in every respect disturbing: the silent mortuary; the presence of the dead prince; Richard's sexual power over Anne, all followed by jaunty music and Richard dancing up the stairs, crudely boasting his prowess.

The total defeat of Anne is later confirmed when she is seen injecting herself, presumably with heroin, as she travels to the coronation. In a highly effective metafilmic moment, the coronation seems to be experienced through Anne's drugged perspective and the camera moves from the solemn religious ritual to the black-and-white televised playback which Richard is watching with Anne, still totally expressionless, beside him. It is evident that Richard has already decided that she impedes his plans: 'Rumour it abroad that Anne, my wife, is sick and like to die' (4.2.57). The final shot of her still face, unmoved as a spider walks across it, is strangely disturbing. Richard's ruthlessness is never in doubt but the film hints, darkly, at aberrant pleasures and a profoundly disturbed psyche. After Hastings has been summarily hanged, Richard clearly enjoys studying the photographic evidence, humming along to a jazz record as he does so. Before the final battle, Buckingham is savagely dispatched in the back of a jeep, a twitching curtain suggesting Richard's watching presence.

Significant changes to Shakespeare's text occur with the women; most notably the absence of Queen Margaret, some of whose lines are transferred to Elizabeth and the Duchess. Yet powerful moments of the women's anguish break into the politics and warfare of the action. The film is faithful to the structure of the text so that Act 3 concludes with a fascist celebration of Richard's triumph accompanied by martial drums and *fortissimo* chords in a disturbing minor key. The effect is strongly reminiscent of filmed Third Reich rallies. Act 4 opens with a group of the play's royal women visiting the Tower and the two young princes imprisoned within. Elizabeth's anguished 'I am their mother. Who shall bar me from them?' (4.1.21) is an effective contrast to the preceding power-politics. Later, we see her evident courage in searching for Richard through the chaos of an army in order to scream 'where are my children?' (4.4.144) Here, too, his mother's emphatic curse is one moment that clearly unsettles him completely.

The politics of the play translates persuasively enough: secret meetings and discussions such as Catesby (Tim McInnerny) sounding out Hastings in the car would be a good example, as would the naked ambition of Tyrrel (although even he appears subdued by the murder of the children). The medieval religious world transfers less successfully to this context, however, and the appearance of a corpulent Archbishop of Canterbury seems incongruous. Richard's final fall into the flames of Hell appears surreally inappropriate after the strenuous efforts to make the battle scene contextually consistent. The concluding frames cite James Cagney in the 1949 film *White Heat* where Cagney is a gangster who dies in an explosion of fire, yelling 'Made it, ma! Top of the world!' A bizarre end for the last of the Plantagenets.

Further thinking

➢ How far do you think that plays such as *Henry V* have been used to reinforce particular views of English culture and history? Does the language of the text itself invite such interpretation?

➢ After analysing Richard's wooing of Anne, look at the later scene where Richard, desiring to marry the young Elizabeth, addresses his proposal to her mother (4.4.199–431). She brings the scene to a close when Richard threatens 'Death, desolation, ruin and decay' and Richard believes he has conquered her – but have his persuasive techniques failed him here?

➢ Thinking about Loncraine's film, how dramatically stimulating do you find such historical mixing of periods? Compare Loncraine with other examples, such as Branagh's *Hamlet*?

Afterlives …

Al Pacino's *Looking for Richard* (1996) is an intriguing and original venture: a documentary about filming *Richard III* in which the American cast argue, query, and drink copious amounts of coffee in their search for the play's vital meaning. The costumed extracts are performed with intense energy and conviction. Judge for yourself whether the play emerges successfully.

12

Cymbeline: 'An experimental romance'?

Defined as an 'experimental romance' by the Arden 2 editor, J. M. Nosworthy, *Cymbeline*'s multiple disguises, indefinite temporality, unlikely happenings and tangled plotting have often proved puzzling to playgoers and readers alike. Of all the plays considered in this volume, it is arguably the least well known, appearing relatively rarely in theatre repertoires and prescribed study lists. Over the past two decades or so, developments in genre theory, feminist and psychoanalytic criticism, theatre history and, most recently, British Studies have afforded the romance greater scholarly attention. At the same time, postmodern sensibilities have encouraged stage companies and their audiences to embrace its offbeat qualities.

This chapter

- looks at how new light has been shed on the play's representation of British identity
- examines the possible influence on Shakespeare's late plays of the opening of the indoor Blackfriars theatre
- analyzes some of the structural elements at work in what has sometimes been considered an 'off-centre' drama
- considers the Kneehigh Theatre Company's radical adaptation of Shakespeare's text

British Studies and the 'Welsh play'

'British Studies' is a relatively new literary critical approach, making its mark on Shakespeare studies only in the past dozen or so years. It takes its lead from the revisionist scholarship of what is known as the 'British history': a radical reappraisal of major events in the history of Britain from a non-Anglocentric perspective. Writing in *Nation, State and Empire in English Renaissance Literature: Shakespeare to Milton* (2003), Willy Maley declares:

> I want to stake a claim for the space of 'Britain' in the time of Shakespeare as an exemplary postcolonial site. Drawing on the new British history, I shall maintain that this revisionist scholarship on the 1640s can be instructively read back into the early part of the seventeenth century, a time when England was moving from postcolonial nation to empire state.

> (31)

Critics such as Maley concentrate their attention on the geopolitical complexities of Shakespeare's day: wars with Ireland, the accession of a Scottish king intent on a unified Britain, and the beginnings of colonial expansion. In so doing, they bring the discourse of postcolonial theory closer to Shakespeare's own world, exploring how the Irish, the Scots and the Welsh have been perceived and positioned as peripheral and Other.

While in its practices British Studies has some links to new historicism, its engagement with postcolonial perspectives and its tendency to draw connections between modern-day British politics and those of the early modern period, makes it temperamentally amenable to presentist approaches to the literary text. In the past half-century, separatist rhetoric and action have featured large in British politics, as Ireland, Scotland and Wales have fought with varying degrees of nationalist support and vigour for independence. British Studies investigates how the present moment can be illuminated through examining representations of national identity and origins in early modern drama and poetry. One important consequence of such an approach is to refocus some of Shakespeare's major works, so that the historical elements of plays such as *Macbeth*, *King Lear*, *Cymbeline* and *The Tempest* are foregrounded and placed in the context of Jacobean politics and culture.

Cymbeline's anachronistic mix of locales, accommodated to some extent by its generic multifariousness, sets up important questions about English cultural and political identity. Willy Maley sees the play as:

> clearly preoccupied with the implications of empire and its aftermath. England, former Roman colony, is – in Shakespeare's time – part of an emerging British empire, its own colonies consisting of the very Celtic nations that comprised ancient Britain. *Cymbeline* is thus a touchstone text for critics concerned with how Britain is written.

> ('*Cymbeline*, the Font of History, and the Matter of Britain:
> From Times New Roman to Italic Type', *Alternative
> Shakespeares 3*, ed. Diana E. Henderson, 2008, 120)

British identity in *Cymbeline* is explored primarily through Britain's relationship with Rome and through the play's representation of Wales (though critics have also suggested analogies with both Scottish and Irish affairs). Until the latter part of the twentieth century, the critical consensus was to view the play's Welsh location as no more than symbolic, a form of the pastoral commonly found in Renaissance tragicomedy. British Studies has challenged such a consensus through historicizing the play's setting and producing some pioneering studies of its presentation of Anglo-Welsh relations.

Of the Celtic nations ruled by England, the Welsh were probably the most familiar to Shakespeare's audience and, as

Philip Schwyzer and Willy Maley point out in their editorial introduction to *Shakespeare and Wales* (2010), 'Welsh characters and locales feature even more frequently in the plays than does contemporary Italy'(2). However, the Welsh elements of *Cymbeline* are markedly different from those of other plays. There are no 'stage Welsh' voices such as that of Sir Hugh Evans in *The Merry Wives of Windsor*, whose accent is captured phonetically in consonantal shifts (his 'very good' is written as 'ferry goot', for example); nor are there any figures from Welsh history, such as the exuberant rebel leader Owen Glendower (*1 Henry IV*) who, in associating himself with Celtic legend and claiming to be able to 'command the devil' (3.1.53), evokes a strong sense of Wales as a place of mysticism, poetry and ancient secrets. In fact there are no indigenous Welsh characters at all, unless we count the two beggars mentioned in passing by Imogen as she makes her first entrance dressed as a boy (3.6.8–9). A sense of place is indicated primarily by the naming of Milford Haven, the largest port in Wales and a site signifying the victory of the first Tudor king, Henry VII. Yet, while the name is spoken several times by characters intent on making their way there, the place itself is never actually reached in the action of the play: Imogen fails to find it, as does Cloten. Indeed, chosen as it is for the venue for Imogen's killing, the birthplace of the Tudor dynasty takes on an ambiguous status, perhaps mirroring the kind of Stuart anxieties highlighted by Garrett A. Sullivan: 'Sixteenth-and seventeenth-century government officials thought about Milford Haven less as the site of Henry Tudor's historic arrival than as a potential point of penetration into England by Spanish invaders' (*The Drama of Landscape: Land, Property, and Social Relations on the Early Modern Stage*, 1998, 136).

As critics such as Philip Schwyzer have pointed out, the geography of Wales posed numerous challenges to cartographers and, when Cloten draws attention to the possibility that Pisanio's directions to Milford Haven may not be 'mapp'd … truly' (4.1.2), he may well be voicing a contemporary reality.

The Welsh landscape in *Cymbeline* is non-specific, presented largely in terms of the cave and the mountains: a form of savage pastoral, where exiles can take refuge before being received back into the more distinct region of 'Lud's town' (5.5.482). The relationship between Cymbeline's Britain and Wales is as ambiguous as its geography. Posthumus writes to Imogen that he is '*in Cambria* [the ancient Latin for Wales] *at Milford-Haven*' (3.2.43) and Cymbeline insists that Lucius should be escorted 'Till he have cross'd the Severn' (3.5.17), both examples indicating that Wales is a separate jurisdiction, and perhaps reflecting the fact that, despite the union of England and Wales under Henry VIII, Welsh nationalist impulses persisted.

Recent studies of *Cymbeline* have argued for its being seen as a dramatizing of competing versions of British origins, an exploration of contemporary historiographical questions. Holinshed's *Chronicles of England, Scotland and Ireland* (1587) provided Shakespeare with his main historical source for the play (one he used with a good deal of imaginative licence). A fusion of fact and myth, Holinshed's account of the history of Britain drew on the writings of Geoffrey of Monmouth, a twelfth-century Welsh monk, whose *Historia Regum Britanniae* purported to provide a complete narrative of the kings of England over a period of 1,900 years. Sometimes referred to as the 'Galfridian' tradition, Geoffrey's history told the story of the British Isles from its founding by Brute (great-grandson of the Trojan Aeneas) to the seventh-century Cadwallader. His account was the first to recall the days of King Arthur in any detail and his writings did much to popularize the legendary figure and his court. It also positioned the inhabitants of Wales as the 'true' Britons, driven west by invading forces; indeed, Geoffrey claimed to have drawn on a 'most ancient book in the British tongue', thought to be a Welsh chronicle. Geoffrey's highly romantic account of British history, though deeply embedded in the consciousness of Shakespeare's contemporaries, was nonetheless considered to be factually dubious. A thoroughgoing revision of the

Galfridian version had been undertaken by Polydore Vergil in his *Anglica Historia* (1534), and by William Camden, whose encyclopaedic *Britannia* (1586) dismissed Geoffrey's work entirely, drawing instead on Roman historians such as Suetonius. Banishing the romantic Galfridian image of the ancient Britons, Camden presented them as barbarians, very much in need of the civilizing influence of the Roman invaders.

Cymbeline can be seen to take in various elements of both the Galfridian story and later revisionist writings. Immediately noticeable is that the character most set on figuring the ancient past as a time of noble independence and heroic resistance is the Queen. In a speech frequently compared to the 'sceptred isle' rhetoric of John of Gaunt (*RII*, 2.1.31–68), she echoes Geoffrey of Monmouth's antipathy towards Julius Caesar in dismissing the invader's shipping as 'Poor ignorant baubles!'(3.1.28), and celebrating Britain's 'natural bravery' (3.1.19). In associating the villain of the piece with the earlier historical tradition, Shakespeare seems to reject not only the kind of narrow-minded nationalism espoused by the Queen, but also the idealization of pre-Roman Britain. At the same time, the play's Welsh locale invites the audience to see in the stolen princes a bygone world of ancient valour, a valour which turns out to be crucial to Cymbeline's success in battle. Yet, as British Studies makes clear, such an image is constantly undercut. Guiderius' appearance clutching Cloten's head might demonstrate his physical prowess and courage (viewed by Belarius as an innate royal quality), but it is also a moment of barbarism, making him appear more the Wild Man than king-in-waiting. As the play progresses, both princes naturally incline towards the world of Roman civilization, a progress which moves them away from Geoffrey's idealized depiction of the ancient Welsh and recalls Belarius's observation: 'I' th' cave wherein they bow, their thoughts do hit/The roofs of palaces' (3.3.83–4).

Yet if *Cymbeline* can be seen as a play about the ancient past, it can also be read as a commentary on the present. Some critics have made connections between Shakespeare's

Welsh play and the investiture of Henry Frederick as Prince of Wales in 1610 (the year before *Cymbeline* is known to have been performed), seeing in the portrayal of the lion-hearted Guiderius a dramatized image of the sport-loving son of King James. Critical attention has also been directed to the contemporary significance of the *rapprochement* between the British and the Romans at the play's end. Puzzling though it might seem in the immediate world of the drama, the peace accord between Augustus and Cymbeline has been seen as a playing out of James's own self-image as a *Rex Pacifus*, as well as an acknowledgement of the importance of Roman influence in the shaping of the British nation. The image of the Roman and British flags waving 'Friendly together' (5.5.482) is not one of recapitulation but of mutuality, one that anticipates a time of British imperialism. As several commentators have pointed out, the drama eschews a narrow patriotism, seeming instead to espouse a more international outlook, captured in Imogen's plucky question to Pisario: 'Hath Britain all the sun that shines?' (3.4.136).

The advent of the Blackfriars theatre

Shakespeare and the Globe Theatre are inextricably linked in the popular imagination. After all, the vast majority of the plays were written for and performed at the Southwark venue and critics have found numerous allusions to it in the letter of the texts, the 'wooden O' mentioned in the Prologue to *Henry V* chief among them. The naming of the modern reconstruction of the theatre in London reinforces the marriage of playwright and performance space: it is not just 'the Globe', or even the 'New Globe', but 'Shakespeare's Globe'. Yet from about 1610, Shakespeare's company, the King's Men, also played at the Blackfriars theatre and this new indoor venue is thought by some Shakespearean scholars to have had a substantial influence on the writing of the late plays.

What is, strictly speaking, the *second* Blackfriars Theatre first came into being in 1608 and was managed by Richard Burbage, one of the King's Men. A decade or so earlier, his father James Burbage had fitted out the theatre, but was prevented from mounting performances there by the Privy Council who had taken on board residents' objections to the noise and disruption likely to be caused by actors and spectators. The second Blackfriars was the first purpose-built theatre in England. At the forefront of London cultural life, it was a great commercial success, as well as providing a model for Restoration theatres. As with the Globe, there is no existing internal or external image of the Blackfriars, though a set of drawings, until recently considered to be by the architect, Inigo Jones, though now thought to be by his protégé John Webb, are generally regarded as the best surviving evidence of what it might have looked like. Its first season was probably in 1610, from which time, the King's Men were able to perform all-year round: at the 'private' Blackfriars for the winter period and at the 'public' Globe during the summer months (the labelling of the theatres as 'private' and 'public' was one of the ways the social distinction between the audiences was indicated). Shakespeare is thought to have held a similar proportion of shares in the indoor and outdoor theatres and it is presumed that he was equally committed to them both.

So what differences would those playgoers with experience of both venues have noticed most? Immediately striking would have been the intimacy of the space. In the hall playhouse, the viewing area was much more restricted, allowing for an audience total of around 600 (though scholarly estimates vary) compared to a staggering 3,000 at the Globe. The stage, too, would have been much smaller, with no supporting posts impeding the view across it and with no spectators standing around it. All playgoers at the Blackfriars were seated: on benches in the pit, around the tiered galleries or, if they could afford two whole shillings, on stools placed along the flanks of the stage. Not only did this individual seating set the pattern for modern auditoria, it also engineered a narrower demographic than that found at the Globe. Just the entry price (sixpence) was twice that charged at the public theatre, where it would have been enough to purchase the 'lord's room', today's equivalent of the royal box. In short, the Blackfriars was a much more elite theatre and one that somewhat complicates the image of Shakespeare as a man of the people which tends to be fostered by the Bankside Globe. However, that is not to say that the wealthy set that made up the Blackfriars had any finer literary sensibilities than their poorer counterparts out in the open. It is well known that wealth is no guarantee of aesthetic sensibility and there was no doubt a fair number of Clotens who sat in the expensive seats of the indoor venue.

Once seated, the Blackfriars audience could enjoy a sensory experience in most respects more pleasurable than that at the Globe. Being protected from the elements by a roof and four walls, meant that lightweight clothing could be worn and the display of fine materials such as silk, satin and taffeta would doubtless have gratified the eye. Music would have featured before the performance and in between acts when there were brief intervals to allow for the trimming of candles; the ears, then, would have been would have been treated to the sound of highly trained musicians, inherited from the company of boy players formally in occupation. Less enticing, perhaps, would have been the smell of tobacco smoke which would have grown increasingly pungent as the performance went on (usually between two and six o'clock in the afternoon).

So, what impact did this new theatrical venue have on the actual composition of Shakespeare's plays? One leading expert on Shakespeare's theatre, Tiffany Stern, argues that 'from the moment of acquiring use of the richer and grander theatre in 1608/9 plays were constructed with the indoor playhouse primarily in mind' ('Taking Part: Actors and Audience on the Stage at Blackfriars', *Inside Shakespeare*, ed. Paul Menzer, 2006, 41) and that, even if there is no record of them actually being played there during Shakespeare's lifetime (there is an account of a 1611 performance of *Cymbeline* written by the astrologer, Simon Forman, but with no mention of venue), the texts alone provide compelling evidence. Stern cites the appearance in *Cymbeline* of Jupiter sitting upon an eagle as an example of the prominence of winged creatures in the romances, a trend which may have developed thanks to the proximity of the many feather sellers who traded in the Blackfriars district. Another fusing of environment and fiction which Stern proposes is the haze of audience tobacco smoke being incorporated into the narrative of the drama. When, for example, Imogen loses her way to Milford Haven, the smoke wafting across the stage might well have evoked the moment in physical terms.

Stern also argues that the romances invite more 'close up' moments than the earlier plays and that these would have been best suited to the intimacy of an indoor theatre. Certainly, Act 2 Scene 2 of *Cymbeline* seems ideally suited for an enclosed candle-lit space. Imogen asks for a taper to be left burning (perhaps a metatheatrical reference to the candles illuminating the Blackfriars stage) and Iachimo gets close enough to the sleeper to smell the perfume of her breath and view the distinctive mole beneath her breast. At the same time, there are other scenes, such as the army skirmishes, which seem to require the more expansive public stage. It is, of course, entirely possible, if not likely, that Shakespeare wrote the drama with *both* venues in view.

Tiffany Stern's writing on the Blackfriars is often highly evocative, encouraging readers to enter the consciousness of a Jacobean audience. Ultimately, though, her theories are founded more on the intuition of a subject expert than on any verifiable facts. Theatre scholar, Andrew Gurr, is rather more cautious in his thinking about the relationship between the Blackfriars and Shakespeare's late plays, believing *The Tempest* to be the only romance that can be regarded as specifically written for the indoor theatre. Gurr points out that, more than any play in the canon, the final romance incorporates musical performance into its stage action, taking full advantage of the superior music facilities which were available at the Blackfriars.

He also points out that it offers conclusive evidence of being written with the five-act structure of the candle-lit performance in mind, as the fourth act ends with Prospero and Ariel exiting the stage and the following act begins with them both entering it. And there are some critics, such as Steven Mullaney, who view the idea of Shakespeare's later writing being directed towards Blackfriars performances as a 'critical fiction ... an exaggeration not only of the differences between audiences attending plays within and without the city but also of their power to shape or determine a dramatic repertory' ('"All That Monarchs Do": The Obscured Stages of Authority in *Pericles*' in *Shakespeare: The Last Plays*, ed. Kiernan Ryan, 1999, 90).

Given the varying opinions of experts regarding the part the Blackfriars played in Shakespeare's life and art, it is likely that research in this area will continue to expand and thrive. The construction of a replica theatre on the site of Shakespeare's Globe, due for completion in late 2013, looks set to play an important role in ensuring that it does.

Cymbeline's dramatic structure

Unlike novelists and poets, whose works are likely to be read incrementally over a period of time, playwrights have the privilege of commanding the attention of an audience in one uninterrupted session (give or take an interval or two). The structural elements of a drama perform a vital role not only in shaping meaning, but also in maintaining audience attention. Playgoers might be 'captured' by the physical constraints of the auditorium, but only the dramatist's art can guarantee they are also 'captive'. A seated audience might not be as aware of structural devices as it is of, say, the dynamics of stage dialogue, though that is not to say that such devices have less impact. Appreciating the subtleties at work in the crafting of a play's complete shape, and the interconnections within it, requires a close reading which, among other things, is alert to:

- the sequencing and juxtaposition of scenes
- the placing of key episodes
- the management of separate plot strands
- aural and visual repetitions
- parallel events
- patterns created through groupings of characters
- the ending of the play and its relationship to the whole

Printed editions of the works of Shakespeare and his contemporaries follow the basic five-act structure generally thought to originate with classical literature, especially the plays of the Roman writer and philosopher, Seneca, whose works were available in translation in the sixteenth century. Yet there is no evidence that Shakespeare ever marked out the five acts of his plays. Quarto versions bear no act or scene divisions (digital copies of these can be viewed on the British Library website) and those provided in the First Folio were most likely inserted by the editors. The relatively open theatre space of theatres like the Globe was made for fluid performance and the natural breaks and pauses clearly discernible in the texts, along with the rhyming couplets used to stamp the end of scenes or acts, clearly sufficed as structural indicators. Audiences might not have recognized five distinct acts but they would doubtless have internalized a strong sense of a play's momentum and shape: the crisis of the tragedy; the point at which the confusions of the comedies begin to be untangled; the wonder of recovery which characterizes the romances.

⑦ *Map a basic outline of* Cymbeline *taking note of:*

- the location of each scene
- the number of lines in each scene
- the point at which Imogen dresses as Fidele

It is immediately noticeable that the play moves at its mid-point out of the confines of indoor places (Cymbeline's court, Imogen's chamber) to the wide open expanses of Wales. With the exception of Cymbeline and the Queen, all of the play's major characters are brought together into this wilderness to undergo mental (and in Cloten's case physical) changes in readiness for the final reconciliation scene. Two scenes stand out as especially lengthy: the second scene of Act 4 (4.2) and the concluding scene (5.5). The first of these pulls together all three main plot strands, connecting characters from court and country. Events are structured in such a way that audiences are required to oscillate from the tragic to the comic mood. They witness the appalling sight of Cloten's severed head, listen to the lyrical beauty of the funeral song, and after barely a pause, see Imogen embrace the headless trunk which she assumes to be Posthumus, an embrace so grotesque it would seem to preclude any recovery of hope or spirit. Yet one of the features of Shakespeare's romances is that they allow for even the deepest wounds to be healed (if not forgotten) and Imogen is able to resist despair and choose instead to live. Indeed, this extended scene in the wilds of Wales has been interpreted as a pastoral interlude in which the evils of misogyny, brutality and court corruption are purged away through the killing of Cloten – described by Roger Warren in the Introduction to the Oxford Shakespeare as the play's 'scapegoat' (51).

Imogen takes on the identity of Fidele almost exactly half-way through the play. In some respects her disguise resembles that of Viola in *Twelfth Night*: it enables her to assume a different class and gender at a moment of deep unhappiness in her life and it remains in place for the duration of the play. Imogen's cross-dressing, though, also changes her nationality and her appearance in Roman attire at the close of the play not only places her visually on the same side as Posthumus (whose dizzying costume changes conclude with him dressed as a Roman), but also seems in keeping with the play's spirit of internationalism. However, some feminist critics resist such a harmonious reading, seeing Imogen's male garb as a sign of her loss of self-determination. Janet Adelman, in her influential reading of the play, argues that:

> As she takes on the disguise, she gives up command with a vengeance ... From this point on, she will no longer generate the action through her own will; that role increasingly passes from her to Posthumus, as his repentance, his vision, and his heroism become the focus and motivator of the action.

> (*Suffocating Mothers*, 1992, 210)

According to Adelman, then, the structural centre of the play is also the point at which Imogen loses her selfhood; cross-dressing may have empowered her comic counterparts, but it serves only to strip her of the sexuality so feared by her husband and to present her as a mere servant, whose claims to the kingdom have passed to the newly discovered male heir.

In the absence of a 'master text', Shakespeare's editors have sometimes disagreed over the placing of act and scene divisions. For example, the Folio text of *Cymbeline* marks the Gentlemen's exit as the end of the first scene, while some recent editions extend the scene to the exit of Imogen, the Queen and Pisanio at line 181. While such variations might have a minor impact in certain performance spaces, they are unlikely to alter meaning significantly. However, if the actual sequencing of scenes were in question, the case would be quite different. Some of *Cymbeline*'s scenes could be reversed or reordered without changing the chronological sequence of events, but not without significantly altering dramatic mood and meaning.

Read 2.2 and 2.3 and consider the dramatic impact of the juxtaposition:

Placing the scenes alongside each other underlines some interesting similarities between the Roman Iachimo and the Briton

Cloten – a balance very much in tune with the play's refusal to side with any one nationality. Both episodes present a flagrant violation of Imogen's privacy. The would-be lovers imagine penetrating her body, both drawing on high culture to express sexual desire: Iachimo likens himself to Tarquin, the legendary Roman rapist of classical literature, while Cloten talks in double entendres of 'penetrating' the object of his desire with a poetic **aubade**. But there are also some crucial differences. The first scene is one of intense **scopophilia**, in which the sleeper becomes the unwitting object of the male **gaze**; the second is very much a public scene, with Cloten noisily exhibiting the courtship urged on by his scheming mother by knocking on the chamber door. As one scene follows the other, so the dramatic tone changes from one of sinister threat and violation to one of loutish, though ultimately harmless, display. It is the enemy within who will do most to damage Imogen's happiness.

George Bernard Shaw believed that the final act of *Cymbeline* was tedious, sentimental and prolonged to the point of absurdity (he even published his own rewriting of the ending in 1936). On the other hand, his contemporary, the Shakespearean critic Edward Dowden, saw the resolution of the drama as both ethically and spiritually satisfying.

ⓘ *Read the last act in its entirety and comment on how it functions in terms of the play's dramatic structure:*

One of the most striking aspects of the play's closing scene is its bringing together of the three major plot strands, each of which has moved from disruption and fracture to redemption and reconciliation: the erring parent has his children (and foster child) restored; the jealous husband is reunited with his wife; the warring nations are back on amicable terms. After a state of turmoil that endures longer than in any of the other romances (in stage-time at least), the audience is invited to 'suspend disbelief' and marvel at a sequence of revelations and disclosures too numerous to count on the fingers of two, let alone one, hand. Objects such as Posthumus' ring and Imogen's bracelet, which have provided a form of visual structure throughout the drama, appear again as symbols of love restored, returned to their rightful owners by the scheming Iachimo. And images woven through the play's language also reach a kind of completion here. The family tree so rudely disrupted by the removal of the princes is restored to life, its *'lopp'd branches'* successfully rejoined to the *'stately cedar'* (5.5.439); the reunited lovers, too, articulate their love in terms of being joined like hanging fruit is to a tree, where once Cymbeline's 'tyrannous breathing of the north' threatened to prevent the 'buds' (1.4.36–7) of their relationship from growing.

The defining feature of this final act is its bringing together of characters who have previously been divided or exiled. This shift from the individual to the collective is underscored by the absence of soliloquy. In the first four acts, the play's unusually high count of soliloquies serve as a major structuring agent, opening and closing scenes, providing vital plot details (and reminders) to the audience, and underlining the emotional or physical isolation of individuals. *Cymbeline*'s finale renews bonds and promises and, though it by no means erases past hurts and traumas, it does restore the kind of direct and open communication that will allow them to be spoken about, arguably a form of healing in itself.

'Not an evening for purists': Kneehigh Theatre's *Cymbeline* (2006/7)

When Paul Taylor warned readers of the *Independent* that Kneehigh's adaptation of *Cymbeline* was not for 'purists', he could have been accused of understatement. The small Cornish company presented a world inhabited by drug-taking royals and a parka-clad under-class, who moved to the strains of a live – and very loud – rock band. Yet the production's radical edge lay not so much in its visual or aural shocks, but in its abandoning of all but a few of the play's original lines.

A theatre company that started life as a series of amateur workshops, Kneehigh has gone on to establish itself as one of the most experimental and exciting of Britain's non state-funded companies. Commissioned as part of the Royal Shakespeare Company's *Complete Works* festival, its *Cymbeline* played at Stratford's Swan Theatre in September 2006 and the Lyric Hammersmith in early 2007. Inevitably, perhaps, director Emma Rice's unrelentingly modern take on the play, combined with Paul Grose's complete overhaul of the text, met with some critical animosity; however, it was also lauded by some members of the scholarly community. Valerie Wayne, the Arden 3 editor of *Cymbeline*, felt that the production 'conveyed not the letter of the text, but its spirit' (*SQ*, 58, 2007, 231), a sentiment which was articulated by a number of newspaper reviewers, including one of its most vehement critics, Charles Spencer, who, despite disliking almost every detail of the show, had to concede that it achieved 'a genuinely Shakespearean glow' (*Daily Telegraph*).

Some of today's Shakespeare experts might take issue with the idea of a play having a 'spirit' that can withstand even the most thoroughgoing of rewritings and might regard the company's remodelling of a seventeenth-century drama to suit the preoccupations and cultural index of a twenty-first century audience as capturing the spirit of its *own* age, rather than some mysterious essence of Shakespeare's. Yet whatever the academic rights and wrongs of making Shakespeare 'relevant' for new audiences, Kneehigh managed to pull off a modernization of the text which not only proved highly entertaining, but which also raised some vital questions about the way we live now.

Rice wrote that her production was 'about families, as we know them, damaged, secretive, surprising and frustrating' (*Cymbeline*, Adapted by Emma Rice. Written by Carl Grose,

2007, 5) and her foregrounding of the family tilted the play towards a more sympathetic Cymbeline. Rice's king was much more obviously affected by the loss of his children than is Shakespeare's, deadening his pain through the injections of heroin and lines of cocaine supplied by his wife. He tore down the flowers and soft toys that had been hung on his castle walls to form a makeshift shrine to the missing princes (recalling a cultural practice which grew out of the flowers left at the gates of Kensington Palace following the death of Diana, Princess of Wales in 1997) and immured himself in his castle of metal scaffolding, dressed in tatty string vest. Like Cymbeline, Cloten could not function without the Queen; he wandered round the stage like an overgrown baby, at one point giving his mother 'a long, slow kiss' (Grose, 34) in exchange for her supplying him with Rohypnol, the 'date-rape' drug that he uses to sedate Imogen. And it was not only the central family which was shown to be dysfunctional. Iachimo (played as the stereotypical 'Italian stallion') has a father who 'Sold his body down by the docks/To oil-skinned women desperate for cock' (Grose, 52). Yet the momentum of the production was always towards resolving familial rupture. Jupiter deposited not a tablet, but a box of family photographs, allowing siblings to renew the memories that bind them together in time for the play's closing scene. Finally, Cymbeline could be the good father, tucking up in bed all four of his children (Posthumus now counted among them) and singing them a lullaby – a resolution very much in keeping with the company's own roots as a family-based enterprise.

As a consequence of Rice's finding the play's heart in the family, the political elements of Shakespeare's play were only sketchily, if nonetheless vividly, drawn. The Romans were represented by two huge photographs of Caesar (one smiling, one frowning), with surges of operatic music marking particularly bellicose moments. At one stage, Cymbeline stood in front of an enormous map and moved toy soldiers around as if playing chess. If masculinity is defined partly though militarism in *Cymbeline*, in Rice's production it was shown to reside in rather less glorious pursuits. Dressed in a beanie hat and Parka to disguise her true gender, Imogen (renamed Ian) is told that to be a man:

> You must linger around bus shelters
> You must light fires in wooden sheds
> When drunk, you must wear a traffic cone on your head
>
> (Grose, 44)

The pernicious misogyny which is shown to be so much part of the male condition in Shakespeare's play was tempered in Rice's production; men appeared more emotionally vulnerable and less disposed to see women as Other. That is not to say that men were let off the hook entirely. While Posthumus was relieved of the antifeminist rant of the original, he was nonetheless shown to be in need of 'male bonding', retreating into a close relationship with Iachimo that hinted at homoerotic dependency. The woman as object of the male gaze was also less in evidence. Imogen's body is not marked by a mole but by a tattoo:

> our little secret
> Scratched on chaste and hidden skin
> With blood-red ink and rusty pin
>
> (Grose, 37)

An indelible mark of the love between two first-time lovers, the tattoo of Grose's playscript stands for a quasi-sexual act of union – though a cynic might see it as just another form of male penetration.

Rice describes her first encounter with the language of the play in terms that might strike a chord with school students:

> The language is tough, dense and archaic. My modern, sluggish brain struggled with the complexity of the plot and the long descriptions of emotion. No one talks about

how hard Shakespeare can be, what an alien form his work
has become.

(Grose, 5)

It was a view that infuriated the *Daily Telegraph*'s Charles
Spencer, who regarded Rice's decision to work with a
completely modernized script as 'characteristic of everything
that is lazy and second rate about our culture'. Yet the majority
of newspaper critics were unperturbed by the absence of
Shakespearean text, perhaps because *Cymbeline* is a relatively
unfamiliar work, with far fewer cherished lines than, say,
Hamlet. Reading Grose's script alongside its foundation text
reveals that a substantial number of speeches (especially
Imogen's) are, in fact, faithfully reproduced. Lines such as
Posthumus' plea to Imogen 'Hang there like fruit, my soul,
/ Till the tree die' (5.5.263–4) are retained as much for their
piercing beauty as for their accessibility to modern ears. And
the much reworked dirge sung by the princes over Fidele's body
is also retained more or less intact, though 'chimney-sweepers'
(4.2.263) becomes 'dandelions', a replacement based on the
theory that in the Warwickshire vernacular, a dandelion is a
'golden lad' when in flower and a 'chimney-sweeper' when
gone to seed. Some of the play's key verbal images were woven
into performance by means of stage properties. Cymbeline was
made to tend an ailing Bonsai tree, an activity which gestured
towards the withering of his own family tree, as well as the
urban dwellers' alienation from nature and the outdoors. It
also connected with Jupiter's riddle wherein Cymbeline is '*a
stately cedar*', whose '*lopp'd branches*' will eventually revive
and flourish.

Cymbeline is one of the most generically hybrid of
Shakespeare's plays. Nowadays classified as a romance, it
nonetheless continues to exercise genre critics who see in it
features typical of tragedy, tragicomedy, comedy, the Roman
plays and the histories. Rice embraced this uncertainty from
the outset, describing the play as one 'that breaks the rules,

that doesn't seem to care what it is', and pronouncing it 'Perfect Kneehigh material!' (Grose, 5) Judging by the critical consensus, what resulted from the meeting of one of Britain's most radical theatre companies and one of Shakespeare's quirkiest plays was, if not quite 'perfect', highly entertaining, thought-provoking and not without its moments of sweet lyricism .

Further thinking

➤ One of the aims of British Studies is to examine the geopolitics of Shakespeare's day. How is the relationship between England and Ireland presented in *Richard II*?

➤ Select a striking structural change made by the director of any one of the Shakespeare films discussed in the performance sections. Does it affect the play's meaning in any significant way?

➤ Has the proliferation of online reviews and social-networking sites diminished the power of theatre critics? Do you think radical productions of Shakespeare's plays are more or less likely to thrive in a climate where 'Joe Public' has a voice?

Afterlives ...

The opening two lines to the dirge in *Cymbeline* provide a major structuring device for Virginia Woolf's 1925 novel *Mrs Dalloway*. Numerous critics have explored the complexities of Woolf's appropriation of Shakespeare's text, none better than Diana E. Henderson in her illuminating study: *Collaborations with the Past: Reshaping Shakespeare across Time and Media* (Ithaca, 2006).

13

The Winter's Tale: Tyranny, trials, time

In *The Winter's Tale* a darkly tragic opening is succeeded by pastoral idyll and youthful love, the dramatic climax being an entirely unexpected and seemingly miraculous resurrection. Early critics struggled to appreciate its radicalism and reconcile the two distinct aspects of the play; now there is an interest in seeing the play as an experiment in tragic writing – a new reality for the survivors of the catastrophe. Feminist approaches have emphasized the power of Hermione's desire to preserve life for the sake of her daughter.

This chapter

- examines feminist approaches to literary texts
- considers early modern attitudes to madness and melancholy
- looks at the significance of time and place in the text
- discusses the role of the BBC's productions of Shakespeare and Jane Howell's *The Winter's Tale*

Feminism/s

All the feminist is asserting, then, is her own equivalent right to liberate new and perhaps different significances from these same texts; and, at the same time, her right to choose which features of a text she takes as relevant because she is, after all, asking new and different questions of it.

(Kolodny, 'Dancing Through the Minefield', 1980)

Feminism is, first, women's rights: the international political movement activating for political, economic and sexual rights for women. In Britain a coherent women's movement can be identified from the end of the nineteenth century, in the fight for women's representation in Parliament. From the mid-twentieth century, the right to equal pay became a central concern and the 1960s saw legislation to legalize abortion and enable access to contraception. Feminism in terms of literary study can also be associated with the 1960s and 1970s, when the male dominance of the literary canon began to be challenged. Reclaiming neglected female authors was inevitably the next step. At the same time, feminist critics engaged with textual evidence from the past to analyze and interrogate the representation of gender and, in particular, identify gender stereotyping. The first generation of feminist critics was actively campaigning; theirs was a political and ideological struggle for women's writing and women's perspectives. Anti-essentialism was a crucial first premise and, concomitantly, liberal neutrality was rejected as a conservative adherence to the (male) status quo. Textual study meant political engagement:

A radical critique of literature, feminist in its impulse, would take the work first of all as a clue to how we live, how we have been living, how we have been led to imagine ourselves, how our language has trapped as well as liberated us; and how we can begin to see – and therefore live afresh.

(Adrienne Rich, 'When We Dead Awaken: Writing as Re-Vision', 1971)

Feminist criticism is pluralist: it embraces a wide range of critical perspectives and methodologies. There are connections with Queer theory and gender studies; Marxist feminists study the structures of economic power and production; psychoanalytic critics reinterpret Freudian ideas of the unconscious from a feminist viewpoint. Feminist critiques should not be seen simply as taking over existing models of textual study, however: for Elaine Showalter, deconstructionist theory is 'the sterile narcissism of male scholarship' ('Feminist Criticism in the Wilderness', 1981). Showalter calls for a critical practice that investigates not just stereotypes of women in literature but also omissions and misconceptions. In terms of Renaissance writing, Catherine Belsey also characterizes the feminist critic in pursuit of new directions, previously ignored: 'Feminism attends to the power relations inscribed in the areas patriarchal history treats as incidental: sexuality, private life and personal relations' (General Editor's Preface in Traub, *Desire and Anxiety*, 1992, ix).

In *A Room of One's Own* (1928),Virginia Woolf invents 'Judith Shakespeare', a 'wonderfully gifted' sister for the playwright, damned inevitably to failure, suicide, a pauper's burial and eternal obscurity. Brusquely turned away from the library of an Oxbridge college, Woolf does not find the situation for scholarly women much improved. Yet, outside academe, women had, for over a century, made a major contribution to Shakespeare scholarship even if, in the case of Mary Lamb and Henrietta Bowdler, their brothers took the credit. It is perhaps ironical to single out Henrietta Bowdler: a profoundly religious woman, she was responsible for vigorously pruning the texts of any blasphemies or obscenities. Not a notably feminist stance, but she made Shakespeare available to succeeding generations of female readers and is the first female appropriator of the plays. Bowdler enabled the writing of Anna Jameson for whom Shakespeare's heroines were a means of attacking the misogyny of nineteenth-century society (*Shakespeare's Heroines*, 1832). The first female editor of the texts was Mary Cowden-Clarke

(1809–98); a prolific writer, responsible for producing a series of annotated editions (1863–8) as well as compiling the first Concordance of Shakespeare's writing (1844–5). She, too, typified Shakespeare's heroines as inspirational models for female readers (*The Girlhood of Shakespeare's Heroines*, 1850–2).

The feminist critic of Shakespeare now

Feminist critics were initially dismissed as narrowly thematic – reductively forcing the plays into paradigms of patriarchy and resistance. Now, it should be acknowledged that feminist criticism operates across a wide spectrum of analytical and pedagogic perspectives, engaging with editorial procedures; performance history, and social and artistic Renaissance contexts. Forty years of critical thinking has inevitably produced widely divergent interpretations; some favourable to the plays, others distinctly hostile. Juliet Dusinberre's landmark work, *Shakespeare and the Nature of Women* (1975), is resoundingly positive, finding proto-feminist possibilities in Renaissance drama:

The ideology, the literature, the social reform, the activism, and the increased awareness necessary to all of them dominated the society for which Shakespeare and his contemporaries wrote their plays.

(1)

For Kathleen McLuskie, on the other hand, the plays operate in a male-dominated environment and enact the oppressive conventions of that society. In her discussion of the 'Patriarchal Bard' and *King Lear*, she argues that tragedy is an inherently patriarchal genre and *Lear* a representation of misogyny (in Dollimore and Sinfield, *Political Shakespeare*). Lisa Jardine's early work acknowledges the 'strong interest in women' in

Elizabethan and Jacobean drama but interprets this as a sign of 'the patriarchy's unexpressed worry about the great social changes which characterise the period' (*Still Harping on Daughters*, 6).

Textual and source studies have feminist implications too, as Ann Thompson has shown. Questioning why there have always been plenty of female readers of the texts but few editors, Thompson suggests that feminist editors might pursue new principles of editorial practice, finding fresh implications and emphases in the plays where male predecessors have 'neglected, distorted, and trivialised topics that are of interest to women' ('Feminist Theory and the Editing of Shakespeare' in *The Margins of the Text*, ed. Greetham, 1997, 91). She finds '[the] typical rhetorical stance of the male editor is aloof, patronizing and overtly or covertly misogynistic' (93). Feminist criticism has also made new discoveries in theatre history: Irene Dash in *Wooing, Wedding and Power* (1981) shows how female roles were altered and abridged in a male-dominated theatrical tradition. Her examination of promptbooks from the eighteenth to the twentieth century reveals how frequently female roles were cut. Garrick's 1750 text of *Romeo and Juliet*, for example, reduces Juliet's status, denying her independence and emotional strength. Such attitudes survived well into the twentieth century: Harley Granville-Barker (1877–1946), actor and producer, seems quite unable to attribute adult sexuality to Cleopatra: 'a child's desires and a child's fears ... balance of judgement none' (*Prefaces to Shakespeare*, 1930, III, 91).

Feminist readings of *The Winter's Tale*

In *Suffocating Mothers* (1992), Janet Adelman argues that Hermione's visible pregnancy 'disrupts the idealized male pastoral' (221). Hermione acts as a painful reminder to Leontes that he and Polixenes enjoyed perfect pastoral innocence until sexual knowledge destroyed their Eden. Adelman connects

Leontes with Hamlet in her argument that both protagonists suffer 'the anguish of a masculinity ... that can read in the full maternal body only the signs of its own loss' (222). Because his own identity is threatened, Leontes creates the fantasy of Hermione's infidelity: 'better the "something" of cuckoldry than ... nothingness':

> Naming himself a cuckold ... he finds in the culturally familiar fiction of female betrayal in marriage [an] acceptable narrative for his sense of primal loss.
>
> (224)

Leontes descends to the tragic depths of seeking the violent destruction of all his familial female bonds: repeatedly insisting that his newly-born daughter be 'instantly consumed with fire' (2.3.132) and proclaiming his right over the life of Hermione: 'say that she were gone, / Given to the fire, a moiety of my rest/ Might come to me again' (2.3.7–9). But once he has lost wife and daughter, he knows only 'barren mountain, and still winter/ In storm perpetual' (3.2.209–10). Redemption is then achieved through Perdita herself, 'free'd and enfranchis'd' from the womb. Throughout the second part of the play 'great creating nature' will be the 'presiding deity of recuperation' (228), as the language of the play adopts female imagery. Perdita herself symbolizes both goddess and Proserpina, lost daughter, as she performs her queenly tasks and bestows the gifts of nature upon her pastoral guests. The heart of Adelman's thesis is the 'otherness' of the female pastoral world that Leontes has denied himself. Wife and daughter will be restored – to each other and to him – through two female agencies, Nature herself and Paulina, 'the archetypally unruly woman'. Adelman finds particular significance in the moment that Hermione 'turns away' from Leontes, to bless and embrace her daughter:

> Shakespeare marks and validates Hermione's separateness as the source of her value ... [and] simultaneously opens up

a space for the female narrative – specifically the mother-daughter narrative – his work has thus far suppressed.

(234)

Adelman observes that restoration takes place within a patriarchal framework yet – unlike *Cymbeline* – the future of Leontes' state is wholly dependent upon the return of his female heir. This is a feminist reading which draws upon psychoanalytical analysis of Leontes' delusions, shows how the text exposes the misogyny of sexual anxiety, and pursues a radical movement away from tragedy and towards regeneration.

The mythic tale of Ceres and Proserpina is reinterpreted by Shakespeare to empower rather than victimize the lost daughter. Perdita identifies herself with Proserpina and, similarly, her return to her mother signifies the return of spring and fertility. Hermione, similarly, is Ceres-like in her devoted maternal dedication to her daughter's survival:

> I,
> Knowing by Paulina that the oracle
> Gave hope thou wast in being, have preserved
> Myself to see the issue.

(5.3.126–8)

Through all the years of loss, Hermione has chosen to remain concealed until the injustice of her daughter's fate has been atoned for, and her child restored to her. She is closer to the world of classical myth than the teaching of Christian forgiveness and reconciliation. Perdita, though, has a freedom that her mythic sister, Proserpina, lacks; she is joyously confident in her sexual love for Florizel. Paulina's authority merits discussion too: she prevails with Leontes at the beginning of Act 5 when his courtiers beg him to re-marry: 'My true Paulina/We shall not marry till thou bidd'st us.' (5.1.82–3) Equally, her control over the statue scene is absolute – 'the stone is mine'. The central importance of Paulina, Hermione and Perdita in the final scene of music and the marvellous, is the corrective to Leontes' false and solipsistic rituals.

Madness and melancholy

> Of all passions ... love is most violent, and of those bitter potions which this love-melancholy affords, this bastard jealousy is the greatest, as appears by those prodigious symptoms which it hath, and that it produceth ... 'Tis a more vehement passion, a more furious perturbation, a bitter pain, a fire, a pernicious curiosity, a gall corrupting the honey of our life, madness, vertigo, plague, hell.

> (Richard Burton, *The Anatomy of Melancholy,* 1621)

Early modern attitudes towards extreme mental states were, in some respects, more accepting and tolerant than modern attitudes – perhaps surprisingly so. The assumption that 'lunaticks' were only to be laughed at (as, say, in Middleton and Rowley's *The Changeling*, 1622) is only part of the story. Of course intense emotion would derange the balance of the mind – Camillo describes Leontes as 'in rebellion with himself' – but that derangement could be temporary and curable. In *King Lear*, when Cordelia enquires, 'What can man's wisdom/In the restoring his bereaved sense' (4.4.8–9) the attendant Gentleman assures her 'There is means, madam ... many simples operative, whose power/Will close the eye of anguish.' The concept of 'insanity' as an incurable mental affliction simply does not appear in the early modern period. Carol Thomas Neely establishes in *Distracted Subjects* (Neely, 2004) that '[The] familiar terms "madness" and "melancholy" are in the period used diffusely and imprecisely. Both terms ... signify conditions either figurative or literal and ranging from mild to severe' (3). For the most part, 'melancholy' is the preferred term for states of mental distress and this is a condition that received extensive discussion in the early modern period. Shakespeare would have been familiar with Timothy Bright's *Treatise of Melancholie* (1586); Burton's magisterial treatment of the subject, *The Anatomy of Melancholy* is a post-Shakespearean work (first published 1621) but reflects the ideas and attitudes of the time. Both texts derive their thinking about the relationship between mind and body from the Hippocratic tradition, originally Greek and disseminated through Europe by medieval writers. The implication of this is the theory of the four humours governing the human body: blood (hot and moist), phlegm (cold and moist), yellow bile (hot and dry) and black bile (cold and dry) all of which must be perfectly balanced for the individual to be in mental and physical harmony. An imbalance would lead to various types of 'distemper'.

To the modern reader it seems extraordinary that this ancient theory should survive long into the Renaissance period, indeed much later texts such as Alexander Pope's 'Cave of Spleen' (in *The Rape of the Lock*, 1714) draw on precisely the same pseudo-medical thinking. As a governing thesis, it offers a semblance of empiricism: diagnosis is always made in terms of the individual person's symptoms, and 'remedies' are then specifically devised. Causality, together with the possibility of a cure, translates well into the more scientifically questioning seventeenth century. As Neely observes, Renaissance humoral medicine is not 'mere matter for arcane footnotes' but a 'supple conceptual framework that generates powerful diagnoses and practices – and promotes change' (Neely, 1).

Shakespeare's theatre often portrays extreme mental states: the four major tragedies, in particular, dramatize characters whose pain and suffering drive them beyond the bounds of reason to states of distracted despair. Intriguingly, though, Shakespeare may well have been influenced by comic writing in his depiction of Leontes' jealous suffering. His fellow-playwright Ben Jonson produced two 'humours' plays, the first of which, *Every Man in his Humour*, was first performed

(in 1598) by the Chamberlain's Men and featured Shakespeare
in the cast. In Jonson's play (and the later *Every Man out of
his Humour,* 1599) the man of 'humours' is satirized as both
a fool and dangerously selfish. Although the earlier play
is a comedy, it features the jealous merchant, Kitely, who
torments himself with delusions of his wife's infidelity – an
obvious connection with *The Winter's Tale.* Shakespeare's
audience would certainly be aware of the many references
to mental sickness in *The Winter's Tale,* indeed everyone
around Leontes uses the same range of vocabulary to describe
his deranged state: Camillo when he first hears Leontes'
hysterical 'nothings' (1.2.290–4) attributes these opinions to
sickness:

> Good my lord, be cured
> Of this diseased opinion, and betimes,
> For 'tis most dangerous.
>
> (1.2.294–6)

He uses precisely the same terms when he warns Polixenes
that his life is in danger:

> There is a sickness
> Which puts some of us in distemper, but
> I cannot name the disease, and it is caught
> Of you that yet are well.
>
> (1.2.380–3)

Both men clearly understand that there is nothing to be gained
from remonstrating with Leontes, and assuring him of the
truth; in his 'humour' of jealousy, his judgement is totally
clouded. Paulina fears the danger of his madness – 'These
dangerous, unsafe lunes i' th' king, beshrew them!' (2.2.29)
but she believes that she comes as 'physician' (2.3.53) and
that the sight of his innocent new-born child will effect the
necessary cure:

I
Do come with words as medicinal as true,
Honest as either, to purge him of that humour
That presses him from sleep.

(2.3.35–8)

Leontes' own language, though, reveals precisely what type of madness Shakespeare intends. Othello, and Posthumus in *Cymbeline,* might be seen to be analogous in terms of jealous rage over a loved and trusted wife, but there is no Iago or Iachimo here to undermine and persuade. In *The Winter's Tale* Leontes' jealousy is entirely self-generated; it is the sole cause of the tragedy. In Shakespeare's source material, Greene's *Pandosto* (1588), the protagonist's jealousy is totally destructive, causing the death of wife and son and ending with the suicide of Pandosto himself, in a 'melancholy fit'. The prose tale begins with the defining of jealousy in the characteristic language of Bright and Burton:

> Among all the passions wherewith human minds are perplexed, there is none that so galleth with restless despite as the infectious sore of jealousy ... Yea, whoso is pained with this restless torment doubteth all, distrusteth himself, is always frozen with fear, and fired with suspicion.
>
> (quoted Arden 3, 406)

When Leontes first speaks of 'th' infection of my brains' (1.2.145) it would be clear to his original audience that he is deluded; both language and his chaotic syntax betray his lack of reason:

> Affection? – Thy intention stabs the centre,
> Thou dost make possible things not so held,
> Communicat'st with dreams – how can this be? –
> With what's unreal thou coactive art,
> And fellow'st nothing. Then 'tis very credent

Thou may'st co-join with something, and thou dost,
And that beyond commission, and I find it,
And that to the infection of my brains
And hard'ning of my brows.

(1.2.138–46)

'Affection' here is far from the modern usage of warm and
friendly emotion; the OED definition II.7 is the relevant
meaning: 'abnormal bodily state; a disease; a medical complaint
or condition.' As Arden editor John Pitcher observes, tracing
the source of 'Affection' back to Latin *affectio* clarifies
Leontes' meaning:

> In Tudor reference books, *affectio* was used of deranged
> minds ... It was a kind of severe mental sickness, a seizure
> with recognisable physical symptoms: agitation followed
> by palpitations, feverish sleeplessness and exhaustion, all
> of which Leontes experiences.
>
> (41)

Leontes' moral and emotional breakdown is overwhelming
because he himself believes that it gives him inescapable but
intolerable insights in which reality itself is threatened with
annihilation:

Is this nothing?
Why then the world and all that's in't is nothing,
The covering sky is nothing, Bohemia nothing,
My wife is nothing, nor nothing have these nothings,
If this be nothing.

(1.2.290–4)

This is the only play to turn on the imaginings of one
individual, and the tragic effects are far-reaching. The opening
moments of the play offer a vision of the happy marriage,
adored son, and life-long friendship which Leontes might

enjoy. He loses all those affective and familial relations together with the respect of his courtiers, the future of his state, political alliances with Bohemia, and ultimately his own self-respect and honour. Shakespeare's audience would recognize the intemperate and solipsistic language of a tyrant once Leontes speaks of treachery, and threatens both wife and daughter with fire – the punishment for witchcraft.

The motif of sickness and melancholy also forms part of the play's resolution. When Leontes looks upon the 'statue' of Hermione, he feels that he is experiencing a new delusion:

> No settled sense of the world can match
> The pleasure of that madness.
>
> (5.3.72–3)

And when Paulina offers to 'afflict' him further, he pursues her metaphor of illness, but this time identifies the image of Hermione as his cure:

> For this affliction has a taste as sweet
> As any cordial comfort.
>
> (5.3.76–7)

In Greene's *Pandosto*, by contrast, the effects of jealousy are wholly destructive; the years of sorrow and repentance bring only 'dolorous passions' to the king. The tale is driven by the depiction of jealousy at its most extreme:

> a hell to the mind, and a horror to the conscience, suppressing reason and inciting rage: a worse passion than frenzy, *a greater plague than madness*.
>
> (Arden 3, 420, my italics)

Time and place

'The Triumph of Time' is the sub-title of Greene's prose romance *Pandosto* and Time is the subject of his prefatory epigraph:

> [Although] by the means of sinister Fortune Truth may be concealed, yet by Time in spite of Fortune it is most manifestly revealed ... *Temporis filia veritas*. [Truth is the daughter of Time]
>
> (Arden 3, 406)

Time, then, is far more than a structuring device: it is a significant thematic concern with moral and spiritual implications. It certainly seems striking that Shakespeare should introduce on stage an abstract **personification,** speaking in stilted couplets and breaking entirely the urgent dark tone of the first part of the play. The audience of the time would be accustomed to such **emblematic** representations, whether iconographically or dramatically. Old Father Time, with sickle and hour-glass, always symbolizes the transience of mortality and the inevitability of death; he would be seen at masques and pageants, as well as in morality plays. Such a figure is, however, unexpected in the middle of a play that appears to be firmly in the tradition of Shakespearean tragedy. Early writing on *The Winter's Tale* is generally dismissive of Shakespeare's boldly unambiguous **trope:** Dryden (1672) found '[plots] made up of some ridiculous incoherent story ... either grounded on impossibilities, [or] ... meanly written'. Editors Quiller-Couch and Dover Wilson concluded that Shakespeare was failing in dramatic judgement:

> having to skip sixteen years after Act 3, he desperately drags in Father Time with an hour-glass ... Shakespeare simply did not know how to do it.
>
> (Cambridge text, 1931, xi)

Modern audiences are perhaps less troubled: if a film cuts away from the action to declare 'Sixteen years later', the statement is simply accepted as part of the artifice of the genre. *The Winter's Tale* spans, in its imagined and emotional time, far more than the sixteen years announced by the figure of Time: Camillo, in the opening scene, looks backward to the childhoods of Leontes and Polixenes and their happy affection 'which cannot choose but branch now' (1.1.24). He also conjures a hypothetical futurity: that the elderly long to survive in order to see Mamillius grow to manhood. The nine months of Polixenes' visit and Hermione's pregnancy is specific time that has fostered Leontes' fears; a nightmare that will destroy time entirely for Mamillius and Hermione. Leontes enacts the sonnets' rapacity: 'this bloody tyrant, Time' (sonnet 18); 'Devouring Time' (sonnet 19) is a trope that appears frequently in the sonnets' reflections upon mutability. In the play, though, it is not 'Time's injurious hand' (sonnet 63) that destroys the hope represented by Mamillius, but Leontes himself. In the speed that follows his accusations and revenges, Truth itself is denied; both in his insistence on his version of reality – 'All's true that is mistrusted' (2.1.48) – and then, disastrously, when he denies the oracle: 'There is no truth at all i' th' oracle' (3.2.136). For Paulina, time cannot bring atonement for Leontes:

> A thousand knees,
> Ten thousand years together, naked, fasting,
> Upon a barren mountain, and still winter
> In storm perpetual, could not move the gods ...
>
> (3.2.207–10)

And he concurs: 'shame perpetual ... and tears .../Shall be my recreation' (3.2.235–7). Time is frozen in Sicilia until Paulina, welcoming Perdita, can also 'resurrect' Hermione:

> 'Tis time; descend; be stone no more; approach.
> [..]

Dear life redeems you.

(5.3.99,103)

Life can begin again and the characters move beyond the time of the play to tell the story of 'this wide gap of time since first/ We were dissevered' (5.3.154–5).

Place

From the sea-coast of Bohemia

Before the audience encounter the stylized figure of Time, the final scene of Act 3 brings violent transition: Perdita's arrival on the sea-coast of Bohemia, accompanied by storm and the death of Antigonus, Leontes' final victim. Nature appears to offer the babe no kindly protection; like the birth of Marina in *Pericles* who has 'as chiding a nativity/As fire, air, water, earth, and heaven can make' (*Per* 3.1.32–3). In common with the opening of *The Tempest* or *Twelfth Night*, the storm is symbolic, ushering in radical change. Antigonus' final speech, describing the 'ghost' of Hermione, validates Paulina's announcement, thereby making the final scene even more remarkable and unexpected. The famous bear is the hinge: both tragic and (invariably) comic. Thereafter, there is discovery: fairy gold, a changeling child and 'things newborn'. To the shepherd ''Tis a lucky day ... and we'll do good deeds on't' (3.3.135–6).

To pastures new

The sheep-shearing festival (4.4.) is one of Shakespeare's longest scenes and its amplification and leisurely pace makes an important point. Stage time is needed to create a sense of distance from Leontes; equally, Shakespeare clearly intends to emphasize the pastoral in all its joyous plenitude. He would have known the failure of John Fletcher's first experiment in tragicomedy, *The Faithful Shepherdess* (1608) where the audience apparently felt cheated by Fletcher's omission of certain conventions and 'missing Whitsun-ales, cream, wassail, and morris dances, began to be angry' (Fletcher's Preface). Shakespeare was running no risk of disappointing his public who would obviously be delighted with first, a dance of shepherds and shepherdesses followed by Autolycus' songs and ballads and finally twelve 'Rustic Dancers' dressed as satyrs who perform a dance to music. In the classical pastoral tradition, idealized shepherds and shepherdesses tend their flocks in an idyllic landscape, uncorrupted by worldly knowledge. This literary world is re-invented in the sixteenth-century writing of Spenser (*The Shepheards Calendar*, 1579), Sidney's *Arcadia* (1590) and the lyric verses of Marlowe in 'The Passionate Shepherd to his Love' (ca 1588). In *As You Like It*, Shakespeare sets up Arcadian expectations – 'Sermons in stones and good in everything' (2.1.17) but also undermines it, not simply with physical discomforts such as the 'winter wind', but also in the inhabitants of Arden who can be less than utopian: 'My master is of a churlish disposition/ And little recks to find the way to heaven/By doing deeds of hospitality' (2.4.78–80). Shakespeare's pastoral, then, includes the carnivalesque revelry of the seasons' festivities with a colder dose of Elizabethan reality. In *The Winter's Tale*, he maintains the English inheritance of pastoral tradition while adding layers of reference; essentially this is an Ovidian world where love and transformation are possible. Florizel alludes to Ovid's *Metamorphoses* while also distancing himself from the masculine lawlessness implied:

> The gods themselves,
> Humbling their deities to love, have taken
> The shapes of beasts upon them. Jupiter
> Became a bull and bellowed; the green Neptune
> A ram and bleated; and the fire-robed god,
> Golden Apollo, a poor humble swain,
> As I seem now. Their transformations

Were never for a piece of beauty rarer,
Nor in a way so chaste, since my desires
Run not before mine honour, nor my lusts
Burn hotter than my faith.

(4.4.25–35)

Meanwhile, Perdita identifies herself with Proserpina, thereby complicating the transformation imagery by drawing attention to the complex levels of identity accruing around her. She is both the lost daughter of the legend and a royal princess (although wholly unaware of both); appearing as a shepherdess, but disguised for the festivities as Flora, goddess of spring and flowers.

The presiding spirit of this rural world is Autolycus; his first song introduces the flowers and song-birds of spring and the delights of 'tumbling in the hay' (4.3.12). Introducing himself as a thief, his own personal code lies in his particular brand of dishonesty:

If I thought it were a piece of honesty to acquaint the king withal, I would not do't. I hold it the more knavery to conceal it, and therein am I constant to my profession.

(4.4.683–6)

Yet his crimes appear to leave no ill-effects; he steals from the Clown but brazenly turns up at the sheep-shearing where he expects to 'fleece' more victims. His ballads are a scandalous joke – 'how a usurer's wife was brought to bed of twenty money-bags' – but, as they are in print, 'we are sure they are true' (4.4.261).

The only threat to the pastoral is the court; Polixenes, discovering the truth of his son's affections, expresses his rage and authority in language troublingly similar to Leontes': the old Shepherd is threatened with hanging and Perdita denounced as 'fresh piece/Of excellent witchcraft' (4.4.427–8) thus suggesting, as her father had at her birth, that she will be burnt. It seems darkly ironical that both Hermione and Perdita are accused of wanton sexuality in profoundly different circumstances:

> if ever henceforth thou
> These rural latches to his entrance open,
> Or hoop his body more with thy embraces,
> I will devise a death as cruel for thee
> As thou art tender to't.

(4.4.442–6)

Yet Perdita is 'not much afeard', secure in her knowledge that the 'selfsame sun' looks alike on court and cottage.

Polixenes' attitudes contrast with the benign acceptance of human sexuality expressed by the Shepherd when he first discovers Perdita. He assumes wrong-doing because of the way the child has been abandoned yet will 'take it up for pity' (3.3.74–5) and makes a joke of the 'backstairs work' of the conception. Shakespeare is constant to the world of comedy here: the savageries and jealousies of the court will be righted in the green world beyond, whether Arden, Bohemia or a forest outside Athens. Just as Time has a symbolic function, so also does Perdita's pastoral world: it is where Truth can flourish and identity be discovered:

> I cannot be
> Mine own, nor anything to any, if
> I be not thine. To this I am most constant.

(4.4.43–5)

BBC Shakespeare and Jane Howell's *The Winter's Tale* (1981)

The BBC's Shakespeare project was an ambitious attempt to screen all 37 plays of the then accepted canon across a period of some seven years (December 1978–April 1985); a vast enterprise initially suggested by the series' first producer, Cedric Messina (succeeded by Jonathan Miller in 1980). A commitment to textual fidelity and Elizabethan/Jacobean or historically appropriate costume was inherent from the beginning, driven, in part, by commercial considerations. Funding came from the American company Time-Life and financial backing was dependent upon traditional production style. Two areas of consideration might be introduced here: the role of the BBC in British cultural life, and the individual's experience of watching a play on small screen. In 'Bard on the Box' Graham Holderness draws an intriguing parallel between Elizabethan theatre and the role of public broadcasting:

> In the space of some thirty years at the end of the sixteenth century, a varied, heterogeneous and pluralistic medium became a virtual ... state monopoly. When the BBC was granted its first Royal Charter in 1927 and 'public service broadcasting' was born, a relatively new technological medium with enormous and hugely varied possibilities ... was shaped into a national institution.
>
> (*Visual Shakespeare*, 2002, 4)

Certainly, the BBC's commitment to the Shakespeare project exemplified the cultural seriousness of Lord Reith's original vision. Academics advised on the series and each performance received scholarly as well as mainstream reviews. For film writer Michael Brook (see BFI website) this meant that the entire series had a 'notoriously conservative approach', raising the question of whether Shakespeare as cultural icon is a potentially stultifying notion. As Holderness expresses it, BBC Shakespeare is either 'classical monument of national culture or an oppressive agency of cultural hegemony' (*Visual Shakespeare*, 23). Critics of televised Shakespeare have often proposed that the television medium is an inherently social experience, inviting shared responses and simultaneous comment, unlike modern theatre, where silence is the norm (performances at London's Globe theatre are perhaps the exception in this respect). The relationship between the medium and the viewer needs radical re-thinking now that viewing can be the solitary experience of small screen private technology. Television viewing was once an experience of shared domestic space plus national involvement (because the programme could only be watched at the scheduled time). Modern devices now enable entirely individual viewing choices. It could be argued that seeing the play in this way is closer to the private reading experience, it is certainly a world away from Shakespeare's theatre.

Jane Howell had a major role in the BBC Shakespeare series, directing the first tetralogy of history plays plus *Titus Andronicus* and *The Winter's Tale*. The latter production broke decisively from the more cluttered style of the earlier plays, with minimalist, abstract sets and symbolic lighting effects. Howell's choice of a permanent set surrounding the acting space creates an effect close to the spatial world of the theatrical stage, emphasizing the intensity of the first part of the play. Here, the bare simplicity of the white blocks and grey patterned floor evoke the wintry world of Sicilia, further emphasized by the formidable fur hat and cloak of Leontes (Jeremy Kemp). The atmosphere is sombre and Leontes' jealousy implied from the outset. His asides are spoken directly to the camera and his brooding face physically fills the screen so that for the viewer, as well as his court, there is no escape from his fantasies and delusions. The presence of his counsellors, troubled by his illogic, together with the brutal physicality of his language, also works effectively in the plain space. The male courtiers are uniformly dressed in black gowns of a somewhat Puritanical style; clearly, this is a dignified and sober world, not given to the frivolous pleasures of the Renaissance court. Camillo's initial rejection of Leontes' suspicion is matched by the indignant disbelief of his fellows; they cluster around Leontes to protest their belief in Hermione's innocence. Indeed, the scenes in this first, tragic, part of the play are designed to emphasize Leontes' isolation and paranoia: although he believes he is the object of gossip ('Sicilia is a so-forth') his revelations astonish all hearers. The men gather around him again when Paulina appears with the newly-born Perdita, again distancing themselves from his views and pleading for the child. There is humanity in their trust that he is 'in rebellion with himself', implying the possibility of cure, and also in their hope that the oracle will restore order. The women form an effective contrast in their neutral but lighter garments and affectionate teasing of Mamillius. Hermione (Anna Calder-Marshall) appears vulnerable in her innocent trust that justice will prevail and Leontes will regret his error. Mamillius is a key presence – innocently running after his ball when he first appears and subject to his father's first suspicious mutterings. 'Go play, boy, play' disturbs the child who runs from his father and then slowly returns as Leontes is speaking his most repellent lines: 'sluiced in's absence/And his pond fished by his next neighbour' (1.2.193–4). Declan Donnellan's production at the Crucible, Sheffield (1999) included a ghostly Mamillius in the last scene, as husband and wife are reunited; a reminder that sorrow cannot wholly be dispelled and a bleak comment on what has been lost as well as found.

Howell demonstrates her fidelity to the text with the difficult decision to retain the figure of Time – screen can, perhaps exploit the advantages of surreal effects to convey abstractions. Here, the aged, wintry figure of Time appears in a white background, as if speaking from a cloudy obscurity. He ushers in the pastoral scenes where the acting space is transformed into a resemblance of English meadows with a token tree centre-stage. Lighting and the brighter colours of the patterned fields create a symbolically rejuvenating effect in which the youthful Perdita and Florizel appear particularly idealized. The magic of the final scene, though, is the greatest challenge: how to achieve the miraculous while maintaining emotional credibility. Lighting and costume are key effects: Paulina has gathered the courtiers into a dark room in which they can view the statue; light then is focused on Hermione, dressed entirely in white, and in an alcove surrounded with gauzy white curtains. Perdita, similarly, is in white clothing and is positioned in front of her mother. The camera dwells on Leontes' tears, Perdita's evident emotion and the tense faces of the courtiers gathered around. Howell seems to emphasize Youth and Age in her conclusion: Paulina and Camillo lead the court out of the darkened room and the company follow, disappearing into a luminous brightness together.

Further thinking

> ➢ Consider Adelman's proposition that 'the female narrative' is 'suppressed' in Shakespeare's drama. How far would you agree in terms of other romance plays OR in comparison with plays of other genres?
> ➢ Compare Shakespeare's dramatic treatment of madness in male and female characterization. Do you find a significant difference?
> ➢ Think about the implications of watching Shakespeare via different media. Can a large-scale production (such as Branagh's *Hamlet*) survive small-screen viewing?

Afterlives ...

Charles and Mary Lamb's *Tales from Shakespeare* (1807) provided the most accessible and available form of some twenty of the plays for nineteenth-century readers. The inferences, omissions and re-writings can suggest different emphases and altered perspectives. The 'happy-ever-after' ending to *The Winter's Tale* outdoes Shakespeare's.

14

The Tempest: Where 'Thought is free'

The Tempest was one of the first plays to be revived when London's theatres re-opened in the 1660s and has remained ever-popular but ever-changing, to suit different audiences. Once a theatre experience of magic, music and dance; more recently a grim allegory of western imperialism, it is a play which invites new and creative readings.

This chapter

- examines genre theory as a means of discussing the text
- discusses the traditions of Jacobean masque
- explores the concept of 'tone'
- discusses Thomas Adès's 2004 opera, *The Tempest*

Genre theory

As a subject of artistic discourse, genre is one of the oldest areas of discussion in western literature, with roots in classical writing and theorizing. The debate continues, but with considerably more genres to consider as academic study subdivides text into ever more specific generic units. Gothic novel, revenge tragedy, *film noir* are analyzed in terms of specific stylistic conventions and parameters. Perhaps the most telling question, in terms of the reception of a given literary or film text, is how far response is guided or controlled by genre expectation. The audience of a Jacobean revenge tragedy, for example, will expect some spectacularly bloodthirsty action, but will also be conditioned to expect a certain type of resolution. Wrong-doers will be called to account and punished, even if unlawfully. Readers of murder mysteries such as, say, Agatha Christie's, can similarly anticipate a certain type of narrative closure. Secrets from the past will come to light; apparently random and insignificant details will turn out to have striking importance and, to the surprise of all, the identity of the guilty party will be revealed. The genre creates enjoyable suspense rather than anxiety. For some theoreticians, though, genre has significance beyond the classification of artistic forms; it shapes individual understanding of the world:

> [Genre] is central to human meaning-making and to the social struggle over meanings. No speaking or writing or any other symbolically organised action takes place other than through the shaping of generic codes.
>
> (John Frow, *Genre*, 2005, 10)

This touches on linguistics; how language is used to comprehend, formulate and communicate understanding. In its widest application, it is a philosophical question: whether, as human beings, all our activities operate within determined generic codes.

Renaissance writers were strongly attached to the discipline of genre – hence disapproving of Shakespeare who flouted the rules. Sir Philip Sidney famously objected to dramatic action which leaped from one country to another, or spanned an entire generation in two hours:

> But, besides these gross absurdities ... [the] plays be neither right tragedies nor right comedies, mingling kings and

clowns ... with neither decency nor discretion; so as neither the admiration and commiseration, nor the right sportfulness is by their mongrel tragi-comedy obtained.

(*The Defence of Poesie*, 1583)

Shakespeare shows his awareness of genre debate in *Hamlet*, when Polonius pompously develops extreme versions of theatrical modes: 'tragical-comical-historical-pastoral'. And in *A Midsummer Night's Dream,* Peter Quince's play is advertised as 'the most lamentable comedy' offering 'very tragical mirth'.

The Tempest has accrued an impressive range of generic definition: is it an allegory of colonial exploitation, a wedding masque, or the playwright's 'farewell to the stage'? Is it, perhaps, Shakespeare's final version of a revenge drama? The organization of the First Folio perplexes rather than enlightens: there are three categories – Comedy, History, and Tragedy. The volume opens with *The Tempest* (no question of 'lateness' there) with *The Winter's Tale* placed at the end of the Comedies. *Cymbeline* appears at the end of the tragedies, in the concluding position. *Pericles* is not included in the First Folio so there is no concept of four last romances as a unit. William Warburton, editor of the plays in 1747, drew his own conclusion from the chronology of the First Folio:

These two first plays, the *Tempest*, and a *Midsummer-night's Dream* are the noblest efforts of that sublime and amazing Imagination, peculiar to Shakespear [*sic*] which soars above the Bounds of Nature without forsaking sense.

(*The Works of Shakespeare*, I, 3)

The tendency to sub-divide is essentially twentieth century: Roman plays, city comedies, problem plays, the 'late plays' are all terms which suggest a modern desire to discuss the plays within certain constraints.

The Tempest as tragicomedy or romance

Shakespeare's contemporary playwright John Fletcher usefully defined tragicomedy in his address 'To the Reader' appended to the first edition of his pastoral drama, *The Faithful Shepherdess* (1608). The play had puzzled its first audience to the extent that Fletcher felt the need to 'justify my poem and make you understand it':

> A tragi-comedy is not so called in respect of mirth and killing, but in respect it wants deaths, which is enough to make it no tragedy, yet brings some near it, which is enough to make it no comedy.

This does not offer the clearest definition in terms of Shakespeare's final plays: in *The Winter's Tale* the deaths of Mamillius and Antigonus are felt as tragic even in the final moments of the play's resolution. The death of Cloten in *Cymbeline* is brutal and grotesque. The action of *The Tempest* is so closely conceived and controlled by Prospero that the prospect of sudden tragic death seems improbable. The mixing of 'clowns and kings' that Sidney objects to is central to *The Tempest*, but also important to *A Midsummer Night's Dream* or *Hamlet*. Perhaps the ending of *The Tempest* could be seen as tragicomic: the resolution brings rediscovery and joy, but the lack of remorse in Sebastian and Antonio is problematic. Fletcher's ideas of tragicomedy derive from the Italian writer Guarini who defends the genre as possessing its own integrity: the interweaving of elements of both tragedy and comedy creates 'a third thing that will be perfect of its kind.'

Romance, as Helen Cooper observes 'was the major genre of secular fiction for ... five hundred years' (*The English Romance in Time*, 2008, 2). Coleridge was probably the first writer to perceive a definable difference in *The Winter's Tale* and *The Tempest* and describes them as 'a different genus ... romantic drama, or dramatic romances.' The term identifies key areas of structuring; theatrical spectacle, and the nature of resolution. Significant motifs tend to include:

- sea-journeys, quests and shipwrecks (where the sea itself symbolizes change or mutability)
- idyllic pastoral settings/Utopias
- music/masque; heightened artifice/magic
- confusions of identity/disguise/princes and princesses in exile
- the loss or seeming death of wife and/or children, sometimes following the trial or suspicion of the central female character
- a final reunion involving apparent resurrection, forgiveness and restoration; the workings of a merciful Providence/benign gods/the transcendent
- new generations/young love/the promise of futurity

The Victorian writer Dowden brought the term romance into critical play; he was the first to distinguish *Pericles*, *Cymbeline*, *The Winter's Tale* and *The Tempest* as a discrete group, cementing them firmly in the canon as late plays celebrating regeneration through spirituality and love – a reading which prevailed until the mid-twentieth century:

> The dissonances are resolved into a harmony; the spirit of the plays is one of large benignity; they tell of the blessedness of forgiveness ... each play closes with a victory of love.
>
> (*Introduction to Shakespeare*, 1893, 82)

Shakespeare's sophisticated engagement with romance as a genre is perhaps at its strongest in *The Winter's Tale* with the repeated insistence upon the impossibility of events – 'so like an old tale' – and revelations that defy belief:

They looked as they had heard of a world ransomed, or one destroyed. A notable passion of wonder appeared in them.

(5.2.14–6)

Helen Cooper suggests that it is the motif of travel itself that dominates *The Tempest*: the exile and return of Prospero and Miranda; the voyage to Tunis for the marriage of Claribel and subsequent homeward journey:

> A summary of the journeys that result in the action of *The Tempest* is also a summary of its colonialist, psychological, and ethical concerns; and finally of its religious concerns, too. No romance quest outside *Sir Thopas* is there merely for the story. The word 'quest' itself means seeking, not finding.

(*The English Romance in Time*, 67)

The central significance of the quest is always its inner meaning so, for the courtly characters of Naples and Milan, the return to their real world is not simply a going-back but 'a return on which they will take with them something of the changed perception of the ordinary' (Cooper, 66). This is the revelation articulated by Gonzalo in the final scene:

> O, rejoice
> Beyond a common joy, and set it down
> With gold on lasting pillars: in one voyage
> Did Claribel her husband find at Tunis;
> And Ferdinand, her brother, found a wife
> Where he himself was lost; Prospero his dukedom
> In a poor isle; and all of us ourselves,
> When no man was his own.

(5.1.206–13)

Romance idealism is difficult to reconcile with postcolonial readings: Prospero's island could never seem the same after

Simon Russell Beale's Ariel spat in Prospero's face as he is given his freedom (RSC, 1993). Kiernan Ryan suggests that romance as a genre can possess liberating and radical possibilities: '[inviting] us to recognise and play experimentally with imaginable alternatives, which strengthen our conviction that a different kind of world could actually be realized' (*Shakespeare*, 2002, 107).

The Tempest and the myth of lateness

Romance does not inhere simply in the content of *The Tempest* and related plays; it is also attached to a narrative of Shakespeare's life whereby Prospero's farewell to his art becomes the playwright's farewell to the stage before retirement in Stratford. '*The Tempest* is ... a record of Shakespeare's spiritual progress and a statement of the vision to which that progress has brought him' (Wilson Knight, *The Crown of Life*, 1965, 27). This assumes that the chronological position of the play can determine its interpretation. Textual critics now challenge the notion of 'last play' for three essential reasons: either *Winter's Tale* or *Cymbeline* could be later than *The Tempest*; Shakespeare went on to co-author *Henry VIII, Two Noble Kinsmen* and the lost *Cardenio*; he may well have been revising his text of *King Lear* for publication in 1608. All of these factors complicate easy assumptions of creativity and 'lateness'. *Henry VIII* would seem to be a play returning to the interests of the English History plays; *Two Noble Kinsmen* is a tragicomic story of young lovers. If Shakespeare was revising earlier texts such as *Lear*, a different perspective on the oeuvre also emerges. Cultural expectations of 'lateness' tend to emphasize maturity and summation, the artist at the peak of his powers – but perhaps contemplating creative finality and his own death. Greenblatt finds in the late plays an 'autumnal retrospective tone' and ascribes this to Shakespeare's fear of a 'loss of power and the threat of dependency posed by age' (*Will in the World*, 2004, 369). Clearly, the question here is whether there is a desire to find in the plays a reading that fits the governing myth of 'the Bard'. It could be argued that Shakespeare is choosing to return to leading motifs and sources from the drama of the 1590s. Both *Comedy of Errors* and *Twelfth Night* can be seen in the confused identities, sea-journeys and familial reunions of the final scenes. In terms of identifying Shakespeare as Prospero, it might also be borne in mind that Prospero is a complex figure; irascible, vengeful and possessive, not simply the serene Mage and overlord.

The notion of lateness introduces some fascinating and contradictory approaches: few critics would endorse Lytton Strachey's view that Shakespeare had simply become 'bored with people, bored with real life, bored with drama.' Equally, there is no universal agreement over a valedictory quality in the chosen four final plays. Michael O'Connell, indeed, sees in this period of Shakespeare's writing '[the] most experimental ... and most daring theatrical ventures' ('The experiment of romance' in *The Cambridge Companion to Shakespearean Comedy*, 2001, 215).

The masque

The court masques of the Stuart kings evolved into a consistent generic form of spectacle and display after the accession of James I, and the creative partnership between playwright Ben Jonson and the great architect Inigo Jones. The Tudors were no strangers to theatrical ritual: Henry VIII was famously ostentatious and Elizabeth presided over masques in her honour, but for James and his Queen, Anne of Denmark, elaborate show was a declaration of royal power. Later, Charles I used masque to develop his own royal iconography whereby the perfection of the monarchs, and their idealized love, ensured the continuing well-being of the nation. These highly elaborate entertainments were all occasional: their ostensible purpose was to celebrate a notable courtly event (the betrothal of the royal princes, for example) so their magnificence and display was all directed towards a single momentous production. Unlike theatre, where text is central and its performance can be repeated, Jacobean masques united extremes of the ephemeral and the extravagant. Characteristically, masques involved music, dance, verse and exotic stage spectacle. Fabulous costume would be typical of the deities within the masque and the courtiers who were both audience and, often, participants in the final dance. Spectacular sets and extraordinary dramatic effects were designed and engineered by Inigo Jones. Indeed, his inventions came to dominate productions to such an extent that Jonson, author of the playscripts, argued bitterly and publicly with him over the pre-eminence of spectacle over text. The subject of the short drama would invariably be allegorical, often drawing on classical myth and featuring a wide array of gods, mythical beasts, and allegorical figures. The masque, then, might appear to be a refined theatrical development, pursuing the arts of illusion to new heights; in fact, its artistry was all intended to be an act of homage in praise of the monarch. The lavish spectacle was designed to impress the king's court and visiting dignitaries: politics rather than aesthetics could be seen as the driving force. The Venetian ambassador's comment on Jonson's *Masque of Beauty* establishes the effect on the visitor:

> The apparatus and the cunning of the stage machinery was a miracle, the abundance and beauty of the lights immense, the music and dance most sumptuous. But what beggared all else ... was the wealth of pearls and jewels that adorned the Queen and her ladies, so abundant and splendid ... no other court could have displayed such pomp.
>
> (cited David Lindley, *The Court Masque*, 1984, 10)

These heights of frivolity and expense were controversial, provoking early seventeenth-century Puritan outrage which intensified once the Queen's active involvement came to light.

Shakespeare's company was licenced as the King's Men within months of James's accession. As such the actors would often be required to perform the spoken roles of the masque. The ordered sequence of the form would thus be familiar to Shakespeare: usually, poetic induction/antimasque/masque/ revels and epilogue. Jonson's *Masque of Queens* (1609) supplies an excellent example of antimasque: a coven of witches emerge from Hell, enumerating diabolic ingredients which suggest the influence of *Macbeth* (as well as the King's interest in demonology). Their purpose is chaos but they are vanquished by the forces of good; Hell disappears and Heroic Virtue announces a roll-call of historic queens, the greatest of whom must be 'Bel-Anna', who, alone, exemplifies all virtues. Thus the governing fiction becomes the 'reality' of the Queen and the grandeur and dignity of the court is elevated to Olympian heights. In this respect, the masque can be seen as furthering the Stuart myth of monarchical divinity: disorder is defeated by the majesty of the Queen. Jonson, as author of the majority of the Jacobean masques, was at pains to argue the intellectual seriousness of his work; his Preface to *Hymenaei* (1606) is an attempt to establish that 'the glory of its solemnities' was not designed to perish 'like a blaze [in] the beholders' eyes' but would satisfy the desire for learning and truth. Princes, he argues, are

[Not] only studious of riches and magnificence in the outward celebration or show ... but curious after the most high and hearty inventions to furnish the inward parts, and those grounded upon antiquity and solid learnings.

(*Court Masques: Jacobean and Caroline Entertainments 1605–1640*, ed. D. Lindley, 1995, 10)

Hymenaei was designed to celebrate the wedding of the young Earl of Essex to the daughter of the Earl of Suffolk (both were, in fact, little more than children) and typifies the genre at its most intricate and ambitious. Performed at Whitehall, the masque takes the form of a Roman wedding ceremony and bride and groom appear accompanied by Hymen, the symbol of sexual love and fertility. Together with musicians, they approach the altar of Juno who will bless the marriage. However, the greater deity is seen to be James himself: 'The King and priest of Peace!' The threatening antimasque is a dance of the Humours and Affections restrained by the figure of Reason. The masque proper is then a celebration of micro and macrocosmic unions, from the two betrothed teenagers to James's political union between England and Scotland, and beyond to harmony between heaven and earth.

'Some vanity of mine Art': Masque in *The Tempest*

Prospero, too, conjures a Jonsonian masque by way of **epithalamium** for Miranda and Ferdinand. The antimasque here is the notion of unchastity: Miranda has already been threatened by Caliban's desire to '[people] ... This isle with Calibans' (1.2.352). Furthermore, Stephano and Trinculo have united with Caliban to murder Prospero and possess Miranda. The protection of her 'virgin-knot' is sternly reinforced by Prospero who warns Ferdinand that if he anticipates the 'full and holy rite', curses rather than blessings will befall them:

> barren hate,
> Sour-eyed disdain and discord shall bestrew
> The union of your bed with weeds so loathly
> That you shall hate it both.

(4.1.19–22)

Prospero demands silence, then music announces the mythological figures of the masque itself which opens with an invocation from Iris, messenger of the gods, as well as biblical symbol of hope after tempest. The stylized verse typifies the artifice of the form: Iris's fifteen lines pursue a single sentence of imperative to summon Ceres. Whereas in *The Winter's Tale* Ceres evokes the darker connotations of the loss of Proserpina, she appears here as the symbol of fecundity and abundance:

> Spring come to you at the farthest,
> In the very end of harvest.

(4.1.114–5)

The disharmony of the gods is also emphasized: like the immortals in *A Midsummer Night's Dream,* the gods' rivalry and discord is significant. Ceres has 'forsworn' the company of Venus after the ravishing of her daughter. But the potential threat of erotic love has been banished by the restraint of the lovers who can thus receive Juno's blessing:

> Honour, riches, marriage-blessing,
> Long continuance and increasing,
> Hourly joys be still upon you;
> Juno sings her blessings on you.

(4.1.106–9)

The dance, central to masque as a symbol of harmony, is performed by 'temperate nymphs' and harvest reapers, a symbolic linking of earth and water. But where the dance would traditionally conclude with the involvement of the betrothed couple, Shakespeare breaks up the entertainment when he recalls Caliban's conspiracy. The illusion dissolves into the genuine anger of Prospero – passion such as Miranda has never witnessed. Thus, the climax of the spectacle is undermined and its joyous and affirmative quality disrupted.

The masque-like elements of *The Tempest* extend beyond the formal ritual commanded by Prospero to impress his future son-in-law. As Anne Righter suggests, the play 'is charged with meaning of an essentially non-verbal kind'

(New Penguin text, 1968, 17). A full discussion of the role of illusion and artifice in the play needs to consider:

- the storm and shipwreck – which leave the courtiers' garments 'fresher than before'
- Ferdinand performing the symbolic task of carrying logs
- the mysterious banquet, accompanied by music and 'strange shapes' who dance 'with gentle actions of salutation'
- Ariel appearing like a harpy to banish the banquet and accuse the 'three men of sin'
- the exhibition of finery that distracts Stephano and Trinculo
- the noise of hunting hounds that pursues Caliban and his fellow conspirators
- Ferdinand and Miranda revealed playing chess
- the songs and instrumental music throughout

In terms of masque, *The Tempest* lacks the resolution and closure conventional to the genre. *Hymenaei*, for example, ends decisively and moralistically: 'Vivite concordes, et nostrum discite munus!' (Live in harmony, and learn to perform our duty). As Stephen Orgel observes in his Introduction to the play, 'The sense of unfinished business is finally the life of the play. Prospero's is a story for which Shakespeare provides no ending' (Oxford World's Classics, 1994, 56).

Tone

Tone is an elusive quality to identify and define. The mood or atmosphere of a poetic extract or a scene from a play evoke subtly shifting nuances which reader or audience respond to but do not necessarily pause to analyze. As part of the aesthetic experience of a work, tone is both localized (perhaps an individual speech in a scene) as well as contributing to the distinctive character of the whole. The language of *The Tempest* is invariably described as unusually intense and powerful; where, previously, Shakespeare used extended metaphor or **hendiadys**, he invents compound nouns such as 'sea-sorrow, 'sea-change', 'cloud-capped'. These curious figures of speech yoke two discrete ideas together in a way that defies simple exegesis. As Anne Righter reflects:

> They have simply been hurled together and left to work out their complex and unstable union within the reader's mind … These paired and evenly weighted words expand almost indefinitely in the consciousness, in widening circles of meaning.
>
> (*New Penguin* edition, 1968, 14)

The repetition (in a very short script) of sea, sleep, dream, transformation, creates an unusually mysterious, sometimes hallucinatory effect, particularly when the action moves in every act between illusion and realism. The play is inherently enigmatic, leaving some questions unresolved at the end, but something of its differences of tone can be explored.

The enchantment and mysteriousness of the island derives, in part, from its music:

> Sitting on a bank,
> Weeping again the King my father's wreck,
> This music crept by me upon the waters,
> Allaying both their fury and my passion
> With its sweet air.
>
> (1.2.390–4)

The combination of syntax and participles ('sitting', 'weeping') makes the sentence complex and compressed. Ferdinand omits 'I' so that 'This music' seems to be the subject of the sentence, with the stress falling on 'music'. The unstressed syllables at the ends of lines ('waters', 'passion') create the 'dying fall' that Orsino refers to in the opening speech of *Twelfth Night* and the **alliteration** and **assonance** that echo across the lines intensify the impression of emotion: 'weeping ... waters', 'father ... fury', 'weeping ... sweet'. The otherworldliness is emphasized in the one finite verb, 'crept', strangely animating the music as if it might be tangible, but also implying in the preposition, 'upon' that the music emanates from the sea itself. The song that has drawn him appears to commemorate Alonso's death and offer consolation, 'Full fathom five thy father lies/Of his bones are coral made'. Ferdinand's impression is that the musical lament 'is no mortal business' yet the audience know from Prospero that the shipwreck has not harmed 'any creature in the vessel'. So, Ferdinand believes he hears inexplicable and supernatural music, while the audience question Prospero's motives in perpetuating his conviction of his father's death.

However, the most significant statement about the magical nature of the island comes from Caliban, and the earlier speech could be seen as a form of prologue to this more developed panegyric:

> The isle is full of noises,
> Sounds and sweet airs that give delight and hurt not.
> Sometimes a thousand twangling instruments
> Will hum about mine ears; and sometimes voices,
> That if I then had waked after long sleep,
> Will make me sleep again; and then in dreaming,
> The clouds, methought, would open and show riches
> Ready to drop upon me, that when I waked
> I cried to dream again.

> (3.2.135–43)

The poetry of the speech is created through its intricate patterns of **sibilance**, repetition and assonance, in particular through the key words 'sleep' and 'dream'.

⟨?⟩ *Look closely at:*

- the complexity of the syntax and in particular Caliban's use of tenses
- the correspondence between **phonemes** and the 'sweet airs' described; the 'd' and 't' sounds of the second and third lines; the 'm' sounds following 'hum'
- the long vowel sounds in 'clouds', 'open, 'show'
- enjambement (especially 'riches/Ready')
- the hard 'k' sound that links 'clouds', 'waked', 'cried'
- metre and the emphases of stressed syllables (for example, the **onomatopoeic** 'twangling')
- the structuring assonance (beginning and ending the speech): 'afeard', 'sweet', 'ears', 'sleep', 'sleep', 'dreaming', 'methought', 'Ready', 'dream'; how far does this create an irregular internal rhyme?

Caliban's affective sensibility is the most important aspect of the speech, of course: the capacity for ecstatic enjoyment of music; the dream of transcendence and the yearning to rediscover the lost vision. Above all, perhaps, the poignant sadness that he weeps to dream again. It is not surprising that the Romantic poets responded to Shakespeare's radical vision here: Coleridge saw Caliban as a 'noble being'; Wilson Knight, later, found an 'innocence and pathos' and, in his 'masses of poetry' something 'beautiful'. What Shakespeare suggests through language and tone is a capacity in Caliban that links him with Ferdinand, the refined courtier and, beyond, with Prospero's language:

> We are such stuff
> As dreams are made on, and our little life
> Is rounded with a sleep.

(4.1.156–8)

Tone, here, is both poetic colour and, beyond, radical utopianism.

The tone of the courtiers' scenes repays investigation for the ways in which Shakespeare can suggest their cynicism and worldliness. The opening prose establishes a significant levelling: 'What cares these roarers for the name of king? To cabin! Silence! Trouble us not' (1.1.16–8). Authority within the ship lies only with the Master and Boatswain; the repeated shouts of 'We split, we split!' symbolize the complete breakdown of rank and hierarchy. Even in the few opening exchanges, the churlish nature of Sebastian emerges clearly: 'A pox o' your throat, you bawling, blasphemous, incharitable dog.' And Antonio also seems unlikely to be turning to prayer in extremis: 'Hang cur! Hang, you whoreson, insolent noise-maker!' This succinct characterization is firmly established in 2.1. where the courtiers attempt to console Alonso for the loss of his son, or, in Sebastian's case, taunt him for his double loss: '' Twas a sweet marriage and we prosper well in our return.' The contrariness of Antonio and Sebastian creates a perpetually grudging undertone:

> ADRIAN: The air breathes upon us here most sweetly.
> SEBASTIAN: As if it had lungs, and rotten ones.
> ANTONIO: Or, as 'twere perfumed by a fen.
> GONZALO: Here is everything advantageous to life.
> ANTONIO: True, save means to live.

> (2.1.49–53)

Antonio and Sebastian are trapped in venal and corrupt ways of thinking: in proposing the murder of Alonso and Gonzalo, every image of Antonio's speech is reductive – murder means nothing to him:

> SEBASTIAN: But for your conscience?
> ANTONIO: Ay, sir, where lies that? If 'twere a kibe
> 'Twould put me to my slipper [...]

Here lies your brother,
No better than the earth he lies upon.

(2.1.276–8, 281–2)

How far do Antonio and Sebastian experience the 'heart's sorrow/And a clear life ensuing' that Prospero intends? When Alonso thinks that the winds and the thunder have spoken of his crimes, Antonio and Sebastian merely attempt to fight, and, in the final scene, Antonio cannot express penitence or, indeed, address Prospero at all. His only contribution to the reconciliations of the scene is a sardonic aside to Sebastian that Caliban could be a saleable as a curiosity. Tone in this scene is complicated by such obdurate refusal: doubt and stubborn refusal co-exist with Gonzalo's euphoria.

Shakespeare and opera: Thomas Adès's *The Tempest* (2004)

In terms of the richly fascinating appropriations of Shakespeare's plays, music offers one of the most enduring legacies. This is, in part, because songs and instrumental music are an important part of many of the plays; every performance of *The Tempest* requires musical accompaniment, thus necessitating new composition or adaptation. Music was also central to the earliest theatrical revivals: Davenant and Dryden's Restoration re-working, *The Tempest, or The Enchanted Island* (1667) altered the plot considerably, adding new female characters (sisters for Miranda and Caliban), and transforming the structure of the play with considerably more music and dance, as well as an antimasque of devils. Such changes reflected new theatrical tastes and the appearance on stage of actresses rather than the young boys of Shakespeare's time. Shadwell's revised version (1674) effectively made the play into an opera with music by a consortium of composers.

Pepys greatly admired the work and it was sufficiently popular to be re-shaped yet again with additions by Purcell (authorship has been questioned, but the work still tends to be described as Purcell's *Tempest*). The play as masque and spectacle – with 'Flyings and Musicke' – survived in this form until Macready's production of the original text in 1838.

If *The Tempest* in its Restoration form might, justifiably, be seen as the first operatic treatment of Shakespeare, *The Oxford Companion to Shakespeare* (Michael Dobson and Stanley Wells (eds), 2005) now cites nearly three hundred Shakespearean operas to date, although many of these have lapsed into obscurity. Interestingly, *The Tempest* has been set most frequently, followed by *A Midsummer Night's Dream*, *Hamlet*, *Twelfth Night*, *Romeo and Juliet*. To the opera-lover, Verdi's *Otello* would doubtless top the Shakespeare league, with Prokoviev's *Romeo and Juliet* the most favoured ballet. The key point, as with the various symphonic tone poems, is the attempt to give musical expression to the essence of the work, rather than attempt to 'translate' it into music. Stanley Wells makes the useful distinction that, while there are highly successful settings of Shakespeare's songs, only rarely is Shakespeare's dramatic dialogue set to music:

> In operas, librettists working usually at a distance from the original texts have stimulated their composers to create independent masterpieces that provide new perspectives on Shakespeare's works, complementing his art, perhaps even transcending it, but never merely providing a musical accompaniment to that which is self-contained in itself.
>
> ('Shakespeare: Words and Music', The Royal Opera House programme to Adès, *The Tempest*, 2007, 39)

The Tempest has inspired large-scale symphonic works by Tchaikowsky, Sibelius and Frank Martin, as well as opera by Tippett (*The Knot-Garden*, 1970) and Luciano Berio (*Un re in ascolto*, 1984). Adès's ambitious proposal for the Royal

Opera House's commission was to convey the play in its entirety – not as an approximation of the original play but as a challenging new work of art. The result has been described as 'a world of huge emotional and musical range'. One of the surprises of the work is that scenes which appealed to earlier audiences, with a taste for masque and lyric song, do not appear in Adès's opera. There is no betrothal masque, just a haunting love-duet between Miranda and Ferdinand; Ariel's final song, 'Where the bee sucks, there suck I' (one of Shakespeare's most frequently set pieces) is also absent. The libretto, produced by playwright Meredith Oakes, compresses the work into three acts, written in rhyming couplets with occasional reference to Shakespeare's language. As well as seeming verbally concentrated, the emotions of the play also appear in starker colours: the opening is coloured by the shipwreck where, rather than the ship's men and courtiers, there is only an offstage chorus singing, 'Hell is empty/All the devils here.' The orchestral overture builds up from a *pianissimo* (very quiet) opening to a forceful and dissonant climax, and the repeated 'Hell is empty' slowly emerges as a refrain against the dense orchestration. Prospero's vengeful resentment is immediately apparent in his possessive identification with Milan; the old world of power-politics still consumes him:

> Milan the fair
> Milan the artful
> Milan the rare
> Milan the skilful
> Milan my library
> Milan my liberty

The concept of Providence delivering Prospero his opportunity for forgiveness and reconciliation is replaced by a colder 'Fate has brought my enemies to this shore/They must suffer as I did before.' Miranda's innocence and apartness is emphasized as she distances herself from her father's tale:

What you have told me
Means nothing to me
Words full of fury
Distant and strange.

Ariel's first entrance is one of the most striking scenes of
the opera: Adès scored the role for Cyndia Sieden and the
range is unnaturally high, even for colouratura soprano (the
operatic virtuoso of the highest female range). Repeated top
Es and long passages at the upper end of the range result
in a strangely inhuman sound, reinforced, in Tom Cairns's
Opera House production, by costume and painted face. Ariel
appeared green and blue, as though a creature of the sea itself.
Adès's Ariel, though, is far from remote from the intense
emotions articulated by Prospero: she appears as a blaze of
fury crying 'Fear to the sinner/Fire to the impure/Storm to the
villain/Harm to the wrongdoer'. Indeed, Prospero rebukes
her with 'Ariel, that's enough ... They must not be harmed' at
which point the same melody turns into 'Aid to the victims/
Help to the stricken ...' as though it matters little to Ariel
whether to destroy or rescue. Adès and Oakes maintain the
structure of Shakespeare's opening Act so that Prospero's
treatment of Ariel and Caliban is juxtaposed, demonstrating
his dominance over both: 'Abhorrent slave/Go to your cave'.
The interpretation of Caliban is likewise telling: he appeared
in a costume of elaborate shreds and patches imparting a
strange grandeur and contrasting with Ariel's non-human
appearance. The choice of vocal range is also significant:
traditionally monsters and savages would be allocated a
low bass range whereas Ian Bostridge, who first performed
the role, is a high lyrical tenor, just the same as the romantic
lead, Ferdinand. Caliban's opening words are 'Sorcerer, die'
and he goes on to rebuke Prospero for his ingratitude and
scorn, 'When I first found you/You were weak/Crouched
by a rock/your child in your cloak'. The remaining scene in
Act 1 echoes Shakespeare's verse most closely with Ariel's
song ('Five fathoms deep/Your father lies')and interweaves

phrases of the original with subtly different nuance. The epiphanic meeting between Miranda and Ferdinand leaves Ariel unmoved, and her mocking comment is reminiscent of Puck:

> These mortals and their woe, bow-wow
> When will they let me go bow-wow.

Ariel remains detached to the end of the opera: there is no touching 'Do you love me master?', only an anguished appeal for freedom:

> Twelve years your slave
> Soon to be free
> I only thrive
> In liberty

The guiding comment to Prospero that even Ariel would pity the sufferings of the courtiers, 'were I human', is thus all the more effective as Ariel has consistently seemed other than human. And their farewell is only emotional on Prospero's part; Ariel's final words are 'This task/Is the last' whereas Prospero, breaking his stave, sings:

> Ariel
> Stay with me
> Ariel
> Save me
> Ariel
> Farewell

Adès's Prospero is oppressive but far from all-powerful: the raised platform dominating the Opera House stage meant that Prospero could always view events from above but his heavy descending phrases suggest his troubled fallibility. Watching the lovers sing their lyrical duet, he admits his powerlessness over Miranda:

Miranda
I've lost her
I cannot rule their minds
My child has conquered me
A stronger power than mine
Has set the young man free.

The depiction of the courtiers is satiric and emphasizes their Machiavellian corruption and the futility of their political ambition. Equally, their instinctive exploitation of Caliban links Adès with postcolonial interpretations of the text. The final scenes maintain the distinction between the King's remorse and the joyousness of the lovers in comparison with Antonio's unrepentant loathing: 'You'll forgive at no cost/ You've won I've lost'.

Perhaps the most striking effect comes at the very end of the opera where only Caliban and Ariel remain. Ariel now sings a series of long, drawn-out vowel sounds –A-i-e – at the characteristically high pitch, as though human language is no longer appropriate nor desirable. Caliban concludes that he has been dreaming – recalling the music of his earlier song, 'the island's full of noises'. He can now rejoice in himself and his possession of the island:

In the gleam of the sand
Caliban
In the hiss of the spray
In the deep of the bay
Caliban

He places a crown on his head; Ariel's unearthly sound fades away and the curtain falls on the smiling Caliban.

Further thinking

➢ Masque is highly-stylized theatrical display: how far do you consider that film, with all its resources, changes the way that masque is performed and perceived? Take a look at a filmed or televised version of the play with this in mind.

➢ Look closely at the language of Prospero's narrative to Miranda (1.2). How does Shakespeare vary Prospero's syntax, imagery and metre to give a sense of his emotion?

➢ The 'Clown' scene in *Antony and Cleopatra* (5.2.240–77) has subtle tonal effects: analyze Shakespeare's language and think about how a distinctive tone is achieved.

Afterlives ...

The Tempest has inspired new and original creations in every genre. Aimé Césaire's play *Une Tempête* (1969) is a postcolonial re-writing where the oppression of Ariel and Caliban is the central subject. The ending of Césaire's drama is particularly compelling.

GLOSSARY OF CRITICAL TERMS USED IN THIS BOOK

Alexandrine verse line of twelve syllables

Alliteration repeated consonants especially at the beginnings of words

Anaphora patterned repetition of a word or group of words

Antanaclasis the repetition of a word with a changed meaning; e.g. Othello's 'Put out the light, and then put out the light'

Antimetabole words in an initial clause repeated in reverse grammatical order in a succeeding clause

Antithesis words or ideas set up in contrast to each other, usually in balanced constructions

Aposiopesis a rhetorical device in which speech is left uncompleted

Apostrophe an exclamatory address, usually to an object, abstract idea or a person who is absent or dead

Assonance repetition of similar vowel sounds

Aubade literally 'dawn song'; usually lovers' farewell

Blank verse unrhymed iambic pentameter

Caesura (e) a break or pause in a poetic line; medial caesura is where this occurs exactly in the middle of the line

CGI Computer Generated Image

Diegetic sound in film terms, the sound, music or voice effects that form part of the screen world

Dimeter verse line with two strong stresses

Emblem pictorial depiction of symbols/ personifications, often for the purpose of moral instruction

End-stopped where the metric end to the line coincides with the conclusion of the meaning

Enjambement running on of one line of verse to the next with no punctuation break

Epithalamium wedding song

Epizeuxis repetition of a word within a verse line, usually without
intervening words

Establishing shots usually a distant shot which establishes
character(s) in a particular setting

Euphuism highly wrought rhetorical language

Film noir literally, 'dark film', usually referring to thriller or
detective films with low-key lighting

Folio printed work (literally 'leaf' where the printer's sheet is folded
once to create four pages).

Formalist literary interpretation where the formal devices of a text
are all-important; author and context are disregarded

The Gaze usually used of male voyeuristic scrutiny of women

Hendiadys a rhetorical figure where two nouns stand for the same
idea, usually linked by 'and'; e.g. Macbeth's 'sound and fury'

High-angle shot camera shot taken from above, sometimes to
convey a sense of power

Homophonic a word which sounds the same as another, but is
spelt differently; e.g. foul/fowl

Hyperbole conscious use of verbal exaggeration

Iambic pentameter the basic metre of Shakespeare's verse: five
iambic feet (five stresses per line)

Image system in film, the use of patterns of colour or sound for effect

In medias res literally, 'in the middle of things'; often used for
openings of plays or scenes where characters seem to be involved
in discussion

Low-angle shot camera shot taken from below

Medium/long shots refers to the relative size of an object filling
the screen; 'long-shot' frames a human figure within the screen;
'medium-long shot' frames most, but not all, of an adult figure

Metaphor comparative figure of speech where one thing is
described in terms of another

Metonymic poetic figure where an attribute is used to denote a
concept; e.g. Hollywood to suggest the entire US film industry

Non-diegetic in film, non-diegetic sound is background music or
any sound not represented on screen

Onomatopoeia the notion that the sound of a word can represent
its meaning, e.g. 'crackle'

Oxymoron figure of speech where two opposing words are side by
side, e.g. 'fair devil' (*Othello*)

Pentameter five strong stresses in a verse line

Performative language speech acts which 'perform' a specific function; e.g. swearing an oath, exchanging marriage vows

Personification attributing human qualities to inanimate objects

Phonemes a basic sound unit; e.g. 't' and 'd' are separate sounds; 'c' and 'k' may be the same (as in cork)

Ploce the repetition of a word in the same clause or line

Plosive in phonetics, a consonant which creates a 'stop' in the sound; e.g. 'mob'

Polyphony term used by Bakhtin to denote plurality of voices within a text

Polyptoton the repetition of a word with the same root in a different form; e.g. 'love is not love / Which alters when it alteration finds' (Sonnet 116)

Proleptic language which suggests a future event

Quarto printed text where printer's sheets are folded twice to make eight pages

Quatrain a stanza or section of four lines, rhymed or unrhymed

Scopophilia connected with the 'gaze'; a form of voyeurism

Sibilance repeated 's' sounds in a verse line

Simile comparison introduced by 'like' or 'as'

Spondee metrical foot of two stressed syllables

Stichomythia dialogue of alternate single lines, often a kind of verbal parrying

Synecdoche a figure of speech in which the part stands for the whole; e.g. 'hands' to represent workers

Tetrameter four strong stresses in a verse line

Transferred epithet figure of speech where the epithet (usually an adjective) modifies a noun to which it cannot be literally attached; e.g. 'incestuous sheets' (Hamlet)

Trimeter three strong stresses in a line of verse

Trochaic metrical foot which is the reverse of iambic; i.e. a stressed, followed by an unstressed syllable

Trope figurative language including metaphor, simile and personification

Unstressed ending line of verse which concludes with an unstressed syllable

ABBREVIATIONS

ELR	English Literary Renaissance
SQ	Shakespeare Quarterly
SS	Shakespeare Survey
AC	Antony and Cleopatra
AW	All's Well That Ends Well
AYL	As You Like It
CE	The Comedy of Errors
Cor	Coriolanus
Cym	Cymbeline
E3	King Edward III
Ham	Hamlet
1H4	King Henry IV, Part 1
2H4	King Henry IV, Part 2
H5	King Henry V
1H6	King Henry VI, Part 1
2H6	King Henry VI, Part 2
3H6	King Henry VI, Part 3
H8	King Henry VIII
JC	Julius Caesar
KJ	King John
KL	King Lear
LC	A Lover's Complaint

LLL	Love's Labour's Lost
Luc	The Rape of Lucrece
MA	Much Ado about Nothing
Mac	Macbeth
MM	Measure for Measure
MND	A Midsummer Night's Dream
MV	The Merchant of Venice
MW	The Merry Wives of Windsor
Oth	Othello
Per	Pericles
PP	The Passionate Pilgrim
PT	The Phoenix and Turtle
R2	King Richard II
R3	King Richard III
RJ	Romeo and Juliet
Son	Sonnets
STM	Sir Thomas More
TC	Troilus and Cressida
Tem	The Tempest
TGV	The Two Gentlemen of Verona
Tim	Timon of Athens
Tit	Titus Andronicus
TN	Twelfth Night
TNK	The Two Noble Kinsmen
TS	The Taming of the Shrew
VA	Venus and Adonis
WT	The Winter's Tale

REFERENCES

Adelman, Janet, *Suffocating Mothers: Fantasies of Maternal Origin in Shakespeare's Plays, Hamlet to The Tempest* (New York, 1992)

Almereyda, Michael, *William Shakespeare's Hamlet: A Screenplay Adaptation* (London, 2000)

Bakhtin, Mikhail, *Rabelais and His World* (Bloomington, IN, 1984)

—*Speech Genres and Other Late Essays*, (eds) Caryl Emerson and Michael Holquist (Austin, 1986)

Barber, C. L., *Shakespeare's Festive Comedy: A Study of Dramatic Form and Its Relation to Social Custom* (New York, 1963)

Barker, Harley Granville, *Prefaces to Shakespeare* (London, 1930)

Belsey, Catherine, 'Disrupting Sexual Difference: Meaning and Gender in the Comedies' in *Alternative Shakespeares*, ed. J. Drakakis (London 1985)

—*Why Shakespeare?* (London, 2007)

—*Shakespeare in Theory and Practice* (Edinburgh, 2008)

Bevington, David, *Murder Most Foul: Hamlet Through the Ages* (Oxford, 2011)

Billington, Michael, *Directors' Shakespeare: Approaches to Twelfth Night* (London, 1990)

Bloom, Harold, *Shakespeare: The Invention of the Human* (London, 1999)

Boas, F. S., *Shakspere and his Predecessors* (London, 1896)

Boose, Lynda E., 'Othello's Handkerchief: "The Recognizance and Pledge of Love"' *English Literary Renaissance* 5 (1975), 360–74

Bradley, A. C., *Shakespearean Tragedy* (London, 1904)

Branagh, Kenneth, *Beginning* (London, 1989)

Bray, Alan, *Homosexuality in Renaissance England* (London, 1995)

Bristol, Michael D., *Big-time Shakespeare* (London and New York, 1996)

Brook, Peter, 'Shakespeare on Three Screens', *Sight and Sound* 34 (1965), 66–70

—*The Shifting Point: Forty Years of Theatrical Exploration,*
   1946–1987 (London, 1987)

Brown, Carolyn E., 'Erotic Religious Flagellation and Shakespeare's
   Measure for Measure', *English Literary Renaissance* 16 (1986),
   139–65

Bullough, Geoffrey, *Narrative and Dramatic Sources of*
   Shakespeare, 8 vols (London and New York, 1957–75)

Cameron, Deborah, 'Gender and Language Ideologies' in *Language*
   and Gender: A Reader, (eds) Jennifer Coates and Pia Pichler, 2nd
   edn (Oxford, 2011)

Clemen, Wolfgang, *Shakespeare's Soliloquies* (London, 1987)

Cook, Carol, '"The Sign and Semblance of Her Honor": Reading
   Gender Difference in *Much Ado About Nothing*' in *Shakespeare*
   and Gender: A History, (eds) Deborah E. Barker and Ivo Kamps
   (London, 1995)

Cooper, Helen, *The English Romance in Time: Transforming*
   Motifs from Geoffrey of Monmouth to the Death of Shakespeare
   (Oxford, 2008)

Creaser, John, 'Forms of confusion' in *The Cambridge Companion*
   to Shakespearean Comedy, ed. A. Leggatt (Cambridge, 2001)

Daileader, Celia R., *Racism, Misogyny, and the Othello Myth:*
   Inter-racial Couples from Shakespeare to Spike Lee (Cambridge,
   2005)

Dash, Irene, *Wooing, Wedding and Power: Women in Shakespeare's*
   Plays (New York, 1981)

Dollimore, Jonathan and Alan Sinfield, (eds) *Political Shakespeare:*
   New Essays in Cultural Materialism (Manchester, 1985)

Dowden, E., *Introduction to Shakespeare* (London, 1893)

—*Shakespeare as a Comic Dramatist* in *Representative English*
   Comedies, ed. C. M. Gayley (London, 1903)

Du Bois, W. E. B., *The Souls of Black Folk*, (eds) Henry Louis
   Gates and Terri Hume Oliver (New York, 1999)

Dusinberre, Juliet, *Shakespeare and the Nature of Women* (London,
   1979)

Dutton, Richard and Richard Wilson, *New Historicism and*
   Renaissance Drama (London, 1992)

Eagleton, Terry, *Literary Theory: An Introduction* (Oxford, 1983)

—*William Shakespeare* (Oxford, 1986)

Empson, William, *The Structure of Complex Words* (London,
   1951)

Foster, Verna, *The Name and Nature of Tragicomedy* (Aldershot, 2004)

Foucault, Michel, *The Will to Knowledge* (Harmondsworth, 1990)

Fowler, Roger, *The Languages of Literature: Some Linguistic Contributions to Criticism* (London, 1971)

—*Linguistic Criticism* (Oxford, 1986)

French, Marilyn, *Shakespeare's Division of Experience* (London, 1983)

Freud, Sigmund, The Pelican Freud Library, 15 vols (Harmondsworth, 1974)

Frow, John, *Genre* (London, 2005)

Gajowski, Evelyn, ed. *Presentism, Gender, and Sexuality in Shakespeare* (Basingstoke, 2009)

Gibson, Joy Leslie, *Squeaking Cleopatras: The Elizabethan Boy Player* (Stroud, 2000)

Grady, Hugh, 'Shakespeare Studies, 2005: A Situated Overview', *Shakespeare* 1 (2005), 102–20

Grady, Hugh and Terence Hawkes, (eds) *Presentist Shakespeares* (London, 2007)

Greenblatt, Stephen, *Shakespearean Negotiations* (Berkeley, CA, 1988)

—*Learning to Curse: Essays in Early Modern Culture* (London, 1990)

—*Hamlet in Purgatory* (Princeton, 2001)

—*Will in the World: How Shakespeare Became Shakespeare* (London, 2004)

Grose, Carl, *Cymbeline*, adapted by Emma Rice; written by Carl Grose (London, 2007)

Gurr, Andrew, *The Shakespearean Stage 1574–1642*, 4th edn (Cambridge, 2009)

Halio, Jay L., *A Midsummer Night's Dream: Shakespeare in Performance* (Manchester, 2003)

Hall, Kim F., *Things of Darkness: Economies of Race and Gender in Early Modern England* (Ithaca, NY, 1995)

Hawkes, Terence, *Shakespeare in the Present* (London, 2002)

Hindle, Maurice, *Studying Shakespeare on Film* (Basingstoke, 2007)

Hirsh, James, *Shakespeare and the History of Soliloquies* (Madison, 2003)

Holbo, John, 'Shakespeare Now: The Function of Presentism at the Critical Time', *Literature Compass* 5 (2008), 1097–110

Holderness, Graham, *Shakespeare: The Histories* (London, 2000)

—*Visual Shakespeare: Essays in Film and Television* (Hatfield, 2002)

Holland, Norman N., *Psychoanalysis and Shakespeare* (New York, 1964)

Holland, Peter, 'Shakespeare Performances in England 1994–1995', *Shakespeare Survey* 49 (1996), 235–67

Hope, Jonathan, *Shakespeare and Language: Reason, Eloquence and Artifice in the Renaissance* (London, 2010)

Hopkins, Lisa, 'Marriage as Comic Closure' in *Shakespeare's Comedies*, ed. Emma Smith (Oxford, 2004)

Howard, Jean E., *The Stage and Social Struggle in Early Modern England* (London, 1994)

Howard, Jean E. and Marion F. O'Connor, (eds) *Shakespeare Reproduced: The Text in History and Ideology* (London, 1987)

James, VI and I, *Political Writings*, ed. J. P. Somerville (Cambridge, 1994)

Jardine, Lisa, *Still Harping on Daughters: Women and Drama in the Age of Shakespeare* (Sussex, 1983)

Jones, Ann Rosalind and Peter Stallybrass, *Renaissance Clothing and the Materials of Memory* (Cambridge, 2000)

Jorgens, Jack J., *Shakespeare on Film* (Bloomington, 1977)

Kahn, Coppélia, *Man's Estate: Masculine Identity in Shakespeare* (Berkeley, CA, 1981)

Kamps, Ivo, 'The Writing of History in Shakespeare's England', *A Companion to Shakespeare's Works: Shakespeare's Histories*, (eds) R. Dutton and J. E. Howard (Oxford, 2005)

Kelly, Henry Ansgar, *Divine Providence in the England of Shakespeare's Histories* (Cambridge, MA, 1970)

Kermode, Frank, Introduction to *Macbeth* in *The Riverside Shakespeare*, 1st edn, (eds) Harold T. Miller and G. Blakemore Evans (Boston, 1974)

—*Forms of Attention* (Chicago, 1985)

—*Shakespeare's Language* (New York, 2000)

Keyser, Dorothy, 'Cross-sexual Casting in Baroque Opera: Musical and Theatrical Conventions' in *Queering the Pitch: The New Gay and Lesbian Musicology*, (eds) P. Brett, E. Wood, G. Thomas (London, 1994)

Klett, Elizabeth *Cross-Gender Shakespeare and English National Identity: Wearing the Codpiece* (Basingstoke, 2009)

Knight, Wilson G., *The Wheel of Fire: Interpretations of Shakespearian Tragedy* (London, 1960)

—*The Crown of Life: Essays in Interpretation of Shakespeare's Final Plays* (London, 1963)

Knights, L. C., *Some Shakespearean Themes* (London, 1960)

Kott, Jan, *Shakespeare Our Contemporary* (London, 1983)

Kozintsev, Grigori, *Shakespeare: Time and Conscience* (London, 1967)

—*King Lear: The Space of Tragedy: the Diary of a Film Director* (London, 1977)

Laroque, François, *Shakespeare's Festive World* (Cambridge, 1991)

Leavis, F. R., 'The Greatness of *Measure for Measure*', *Scrutiny* 10 (1942), 234–46

Leggatt, Alexander, *Shakespeare's Comedy of Love* (London, 1974)

Levenson, Jill, 'Comedy' in *The Cambridge Companion to English Renaissance Drama,* (eds) A. R. Braunmuller and Michael Hattaway (Cambridge, 1994)

Lindley, David,*The Court Masque* (Manchester, 1984)

—*Court Masques: Jacobean and Caroline Entertainments, 1605–1640* (Oxford, 1995)

—*Shakespeare and Music* (London, 2006)

Loomba, Ania, *Shakespeare, Race, and Colonialism* (Oxford, 2002)

MacGregor, Neil, *Shakespeare's Restless World* (London, 2012)

Mac Liammóir, Micheál, *Put Money in thy Purse* (London, 1952)

Maley, Willy, *Nation, State and Empire in English Renaissance Literature: Shakespeare to Milton* (Basingstoke, 2003)

—'*Cymbeline*, the Font of History, and the Matter of Britain: From Times New Roman to Italic Type' in *Alternative Shakespeares 3*, ed. Diana E. Henderson (London, 2008)

Maley, Willy and Philip Schwyzer, (eds) *Shakespeare and Wales: From the Marches to the Assembly* (Farnham, 2010)

Mapstone, Sally, 'Shakespeare and Scottish Kingship: A Case History' in *The Rose and the Thistle: Essays on the Culture of Late Medieval and Renaissance Scotland* (East Linton, 1988)

McDonald, Russ, *Shakespeare's Late Style* (Cambridge, 2006)

McKellen, Ian, *Shakespeare's Richard III* (London, 1996)

McLuskie, Kathleen, 'The Patriarchal Bard: Feminist Criticism and Shakespeare: *King Lear* and *Measure for Measure*' in *Political Shakespeare: Essays in Cultural Materialism*, (eds) J. Dollimore and A. Sinfield (Manchester, 1985)

Meredith, George, *An Essay on Comedy and the Uses of the Comic Spirit* (London, 1897)

Moseley, C. W. R. D., *Richard III* Penguin Critical Studies (London, 1989)

Mullaney, Steven, '"All That Monarchs Do": The Obscured Stages of Authority in *Pericles*' in *Shakespeare: The Last Plays*, ed. Kiernan Ryan (London, 1999)

Neely, Carol Thomas, *Distracted Subjects: Madness and Gender in Shakespeare and Early Modern Culture* (Ithaca, NY, 2004)

Newman, Karen, '"And wash the Ethiop white": Femininity and the Monstrous in *Othello*' in *Shakespeare Reproduced: The Text in History and Ideology*, (eds) Jean E. Howard and Marion F. O'Connor (London, 1987)

Normand, Lawrence and G. Roberts, *Witchcraft in Early Modern Scotland: James VI's Demonology and the North Berwick Witches* (Exeter, 2000)

O'Connell, Michael, 'The Experiment of Romance' in *The Cambridge Companion to Shakespearean Comedy*, ed. Alexander Leggatt (Cambridge, 2001)

Olivier, Laurence, *On Acting* (London, 1986)

Orgel, Stephen, *The Tempest* The Oxford Shakespeare (Oxford: 1994)

—'Shakespeare, Sexuality and Gender' in *The New Cambridge Companion to Shakespeare*, (eds) Margreta de Grazia and Stanley Wells (Cambridge, 2010)

Ovid, *Metamorphoses*, translated Arthur Golding, ed. Madeleine Forey (London, 2002)

Pater, Walter, *Walter Pater: Three Major Texts*, ed. William E. Buckler (New York, 1986)

Patterson, Annabel, *Shakespeare and the Popular Voice* (Oxford, 1989)

Pequigney, J., 'The Two Antonios and same-sex love in *Twelfth Night* and *The Merchant of Venice*' in *English Literary Renaissance* 22, 201–22 (1992)

Polanski, Roman, *Roman* (London, 1984)

Prosser, Eleanor, *Hamlet and Revenge* (London, 1967)

Purkiss, Diane, *At the Bottom of the Garden: A Dark History of Fairies, Hobgoblins and Other Troublesome Things* (New York, 2000)

Rackin, Phyllis, *Stages of History: Shakespeare's English Chronicles* (Ithaca, NY, 1990)

Righter, Anne, ed. *The Tempest* New Penguin Shakespeare (Harmondsworth, 1969)

Rivkin, Julie and Michael Ryan, (eds) *Literary Theory: An Anthology* (Oxford, 1998)

Rothwell, Kenneth, *A History of Shakespeare on Screen: A Century of Film and Television*, 2nd edn (Cambridge, 2004)

Rutter, Carol [Chillington], *Clamorous Voices: Shakespeare's Women Today*, ed. Faith Evans (London, 1988)

—'Fiona Shaw's *Richard II*: The Girl as Player-King as Comic', *Shakespeare Quarterly* 48 (1997), 314–24

Ryan, Kiernan, *New Historicism and Cultural Materialism* (London, 1996)

—*Enter the Body: Women and Representation on Shakespeare's Stage* (London, 2001)

—*Shakespeare*, 3rd edn (Basingstoke, 2002)

—*King Lear* Penguin Shakespeare series (London, 2005)

—'*Troilus and Cressida*: The Perils of Presentism' in *Presentist Shakespeares*, (eds) Hugh Grady and Terence Hawkes (London, 2007)

—*Shakespeare's Comedies* (London, 2009)

Rylance, Mark, *Play: A Recollection in Pictures and Words of the First Five Years of Play at Shakespeare's Globe Theatre* (London, 2003)

Said, Edward W., *Orientalism* (London, 1978)

Shaheen, Naseeb, *Biblical References in Shakespeare's Comedies* (Newark, 1993)

Shapiro, Michael, *Gender in Play on the Shakespearean Stage: Boy Heroines and Female Pages* (Ann Arbor, 1994)

Shaughnessy, Robert, *The Routledge Guide to William Shakespeare* (London, 2011)

Siemon, James, '"The Power of Hope?" An Early Modern Reader of *Richard III*' in *A Companion to Shakespeare's History Plays*, (eds) R. Dutton and J. E. Howard (Oxford, 2003)

Sinfield, Alan, '*Macbeth*: History, Ideology and Intellectuals' in *Macbeth: New Casebook* ed. Sinfield (Basingstoke, 1992) 121–35

Smith, Bruce, *Twelfth Night: Texts and Contexts* (Boston, 2001)

Smith, Emma, *Othello* (Horndon, 2005)

Speaight, Robert, Review of *Shakespeare – Time and Conscience* by Grigori Kozintsev, *Shakespeare Quarterly* 19 (1968), 90–1

Spurgeon, Caroline, *Shakespeare's Imagery and What It Tells Us* (Cambridge, 1935)

Stern, Tiffany, 'Taking Part: Actors and Audience on the Stage at Blackfriars' in *Inside Shakespeare: Essays on the Blackfriars Stage*, ed. Paul Menzer (Selingsgrove, 2006)

Stone, Lawrence, *The Family, Sex and Marriage in England 1500–1982* (London, 1982)

Sullivan, Garrett A., *The Drama of Landscape: Land, Property, and Social Relations on the Early Modern Stage* (Stanford, 1998)

Tennenhouse, Leonard, *Power on Display: The Politics of Shakespeare's Genres* (London, 1986)

Thompson, Ann, 'Feminist Theory and the Editing of Shakespeare: *The Taming of the Shrew* Revisited' in *The Margins of the Text*, ed. D. C. Greetham (Ann Arbor, 1997)

Tiffany, Grace, 'How Revolutionary *Is* Cross-cast Shakespeare? A Look at Five Contemporary Productions', *Shakespeare: Text and Theatre. Essays in Honor of Jay L. Halio*, (eds) Lois Potter and Arthur F. Kinney (Newark, 1999)

Tillyard, E. M. W., *Shakespeare's History Plays* (London, 1969)

Traub, Valerie, *Desire and Anxiety: Circulations of Sexuality in Shakespearean Drama* (London, 1992)

Troncale, Joseph, 'The War and Kozintsev's Films: *Hamlet* and *King Lear*' in *The Red Screen: Politics, Society, Art in Soviet Cinema*, ed. Anna Lawton (London, 1992)

Veeser, H. Aram, ed. *The New Historicism* (London, 1989)

Vickers, Brian, *Appropriating Shakespeare: Contemporary Critical Quarrels* (New Haven, 1993)

Walsh, Brian, 'The Dramaturgy of Discomfort in *Richard II*' in *Richard II: New Critical Essays*, ed. Jeremy Lopez (London, 2012)

Warren, Roger, *A Midsummer Night's Dream* Text and Performance (London, 1983)

—*Cymbeline* The Oxford Shakespeare (Oxford, 1998)

Wayne, Valerie, 'Kneehigh's Dream of *Cymbeline*', *Shakespeare Quarterly* 58 (2007), 228–37

Wells, Robin Headlam, *Shakespeare on Masculinity* (Cambridge, 2000)

Wilde, Oscar, *The Complete Letters of Oscar Wilde* (London, 2000)

Williams, Raymond, *Culture and Materialism* (London, 2005)

Woodbridge, Linda, *Women and the English Renaissance: Literature and the Nature of Womankind 1540–1620* (Brighton, 1964)

Wright, George T., *Shakespeare's Metrical Art* (Berkeley, 1988)

Yeats, W. B., *Selected Criticism*, ed. A. Norman Jeffares (London, 1976)

Zimmerman, Susan, *Erotic Politics: Desire on the Renaissance Stage* (London, 1992)

INDEX

Page references in **bold** indicate whole sections of text